REDEEMING A PRISON SOCIETY

REDEEMING A PRISON SOCIETY

A LITURGICAL AND SACRAMENTAL RESPONSE TO MASS INCARCERATION

AMY LEVAD

Fortress Press
Minneapolis

REDEEMING A PRISON SOCIETY

A Liturgical and Sacramental Response to Mass Incarceration

Cover image: © Rick Vink Photography

Cover design: Laurie Ingram

Library of Congress Cataloging-in-Publication Data

Levad, Amy, 1979-

Redeeming a prison society : a liturgical and sacramental response to mass incarceration / Amy Levad.

pages cm. Includes bibliographical references.

ISBN 978-0-8006-9991-8 (pbk. : alk. paper) — ISBN 978-1-4514-6512-9 (ebook)

1. Imprisonment–Religious aspects–Christianity. 2. Criminal justice, Administration of–United States. I. Title.

HV8687.L485 2014

261.8'336–dc23   2013034854

The paper used in this publication meets the minimum requirements of American National Standard for Information Sciences — Permanence of Paper for Printed Library Materials, ANSI Z329.48-1984.

Manufactured in the U.S.A.

This book was produced using PressBooks.com, and PDF rendering was done by PrinceXML.

For Katy

CONTENTS

Acknowledgements ix

Introduction 1

1. Our Crisis of Justice 11

2. Catholic Responses to Our Criminal Justice Crisis 45

3. A Liturgical and Sacramental Approach to Justice 79

4. A Model for Criminal Justice Reform 111

5. A Movement for Justice 149

Epilogue 197

Bibliography 201

Index 225

Acknowledgements

This book has come about after several years of reflection and research, culminating in a couple of years of intense writing. It would not be complete without acknowledging the numerous people who contributed to it.

Colleagues have helped me deepen and hone the argument of this book. Through conversation, the occasional forwarded article or recommended book, and friendly encouragement, they helped me to carry this project forward. I am especially grateful to Cara Anthony, Jennifer Ayres, Matthew Bersagel-Braley, Claire Bischoff, Stacia Brown, Brad Burroughs, Letitia Campbell, Corrine Carvalho, Wylin Dassie, Massimo Faggioli, Michael Hollerich, Sherry Jordon, Anne King, Anne-Marie Mingo, Terry Nichols, Barb Sain, Gerald Schlabach, John Senior, Katy Shrout, Anjulet Tucker, Kelly Wilson, Paul Wojda, and Nikki Young. Several people also read early drafts of parts of the book. I appreciate the additional time and insights of Liz Bounds, Bernard Brady, Tom Bushlack, Karen Guth, Jennifer McBride, Mark McInroy, and Kathryn Getek Soltis. My research assistant, Matthew Selby, helped me put the finishing touches on the manuscript. The editorial staff at Fortress Press has been exceptionally professional, helpful, and supportive of this project. Michael Gibson, David Cottingham, Lisa Gruenisen, Kate Crouse, and Marissa Wold deserve deep gratitude for their work in improving the book. Without the guidance, care, support, and wisdom of all of these people, this book would not have come to be.

I am indebted to the University of St. Thomas in St. Paul, Minnesota for research support, including a Faculty Development Grant that gave me time and resources to jumpstart this project. Faculty Writers' Retreats led by Susan Callaway provided space, time, and collegiality during the writing process. I cannot name the numerous writers who joined me in these retreats, but I nevertheless appreciate the ways they both commiserated and celebrated with me as I completed the book. Funding for a research assistant came from the Dean's Office of the Saint Paul Seminary School of Divinity. I greatly appreciate the assistance that various offices and centers at St. Thomas provide for faculty research.

People in prison revealed to me much of what I came to see and know about the issues discussed in this book. For their privacy, their names will remain confidential. However, I would like to express particular gratitude to the women who participated in the Certificate in Theological Studies Program at Metro State Prison in Atlanta, GA (the program has moved to Lee Arrendale State Prison for Women). I had the honor of working with them as I helped to establish the program, which is funded by the Atlanta Theological Association through Columbia Theological Seminary, McAfee School of Theology at Mercer University, Candler School of Theology at Emory University, and the Interdenominational Theological Center. The women at Metro taught me about the possibilities of reconciliation and communion among the most excluded members of our society. I will always treasure memories of the commitment of one woman who helped me build a theological library, even though she would be released any day, but who desperately wanted to make sure that she left something good behind for the women who would remain after she left; of the care and kindness these women provided for a fellow prisoner who was severely developmentally delayed and for their only fellow prisoner on death row; of the value these women placed in being able to own a book and to discuss it with friends; of the joy and pride they found in training service dogs for people with disabilities whom they would never meet. These experiences would not have been possible without the vision and tenacity of Susan Bishop and Liz Bounds, who brought me into this project. I am also grateful to my fellow teachers, especially Marian Broida, Anika Jones, Dave Garber, Lerone Martin, and Jenny McBride.

I owe more thanks than I can fully express to my family for their love and unfailing support. Although many others deserve acknowledgement, four family members merit more attention here. My sister, Katy, inspired my interest in the topic of this book in the first place. She is a tough woman; she is also astonishingly kind and generous. She exemplifies inclusive table fellowship every day with the people she serves at Waffle House—bringing flowers to the elderly widower at one table on the anniversary of his wife's death; learning American Sign Language to take orders for scattered, smothered, and covered hash browns for hearing impaired customers at another table; on the other side of the restaurant, welcoming a regular customer with Down's Syndrome with open arms. I am grateful for the example Katy provides of how to love one's neighbors, especially those who are typically marginalized in our society. This book is dedicated to her.

My parents, Richard and Karen, created a household in which the liturgical and sacramental life were valued and celebrated. When I was a child, they regularly hosted communion services in our living room with close friends (and their guitars, of course). They fostered my interest in theology; they awoke my imagination to the beauty and complexity of God's grace disclosed in the world.

Their formation is the starting point of my recognition that the liturgy and sacraments are the roots of our hope for the world, especially in the work for justice. To them, infinite thanks.

Finally, when I started writing this book, I was pregnant with my daughter, Iris. As the book goes to press, she is two years old. Needless to say, I could not have written this book or reared this child alone, even if Iris is a pretty easy kid. I am blessed by the support of my husband, Mark DelCogliano, who carved out time from his own research and writing schedule to ensure that I could complete my work and that our daughter would always have the care of one parent or another. He is a fine intellectual, a genuine partner, and a kind father. I am glad we get to do all of this together.

Introduction

Caring about people in prison is difficult. We can easily picture incarcerated people as dangerous and dirty, as despicable, as animals in cages. People behind bars are there for good reason—to protect us law-abiding, tax-paying, upstanding citizens from them. We are better off without these people. Good riddance. I have spoken with many people in my family, classroom, and church who have asked me why I care about people in prison. They seem baffled that anyone would care. Some people even suggest to me that it is wrong to care for people in prison. To them, it seems that extending care to incarcerated people somehow denies the seriousness of their crimes and undermines the rule of law.

I do not know whether I would have ever come to care about people in prison had not someone I already cared about ended up being one of them. While my relationship with my incarcerated loved one had been strained by a long series of disappointments, mostly rooted in her drug use, I could not look at her as dangerous or dirty; I could not despise her. I could not see how the prison protected anyone else from her—her crime was a nonviolent drug offense and the person she harmed most was herself. I knew that her family was not better off without her, as I saw her children struggle in poverty and wrestle with the stigmatization and isolation of having a mother in prison. And I saw no way that the prison would better enable her to reenter society and to do well as a mother, employee, or citizen. My recognition that prison offered nothing in terms of rehabilitation or reintegration into society proved true, as years after my loved one's release, she reestablished herself and stopped using drugs—not because of any assistance or guidance from our criminal justice systems, but because of her grit and perseverance alone. Even still, she continues to struggle in poverty, existing always on the edge of survival for herself and her family. Prison did not improve my loved one, her family, her community, or her society.

When I came to care about one person in prison, it was difficult for me to remain indifferent to the plight of anyone in prison. In the United States, caring about people in prison entails the acknowledgment, first, that they are indeed people, human persons; that we now hold more people in prison than any other nation and more people than we ever have incarcerated in our history; that our practices of incarceration equate to throwing these people away; that relatively few people in prison need to be there to ensure public safety; and that the reasons we throw so many people away is tied up with social injustice. My loved one is white, female, and from a middle-class background. Young, black men who grow up impoverished socioeconomically are much more likely to be incarcerated, especially in comparison with their representation in the general population. Caring about people in prison in our context requires recognizing that our criminal justice systems uphold what civil rights attorney Michelle Alexander calls "the New Jim Crow," what director of The Sentencing Project Marc Mauer calls "mass incarceration," and what social theorist Loïc Wacquant calls "the first genuine prison society."[1]

[Our criminal justice systems are in crisis, and this crisis both _reflects_ and _helps sustain_ a broader crisis of social justice.] Since the early 1970s, our criminal justice systems have grown at an unprecedented rate. To explain this growth, many people assume that the cause is an unprecedented rise in crime rates. Our prison populations, however, have consistently become larger while our crime rates have periodically fluctuated. Growing crime rates cannot explain the creation of the first genuine prison society. In fact, while prison populations have continued to grow, crime rates have at times dropped significantly. [Instead several social, cultural, economic, and political factors rooted in social injustice have led to the advent of mass incarceration in the United States, independently of crime rates.] In turn, locking up ever more people in our country exacerbates social injustice. While mass incarceration has contributed only a small amount to falling crime rates since the late 1990s, [it has worsened conditions in neighborhoods that see many of their residents cycle in and out of prison.] [Prisoners, their families, and their communities experience greater levels of poverty, political exclusion, and social isolation, as well as potentially even higher rates of crime as a result of our society's punitive turn.] The ways in which our criminal justice crisis is fundamentally intertwined with a crisis of social justice are the topic of chapter 1 of this book. From this discussion, it becomes clear that any adequate response to mass incarceration must not only provide resources for addressing crime and individual wrongdoing. It must also attend to the connections between criminal and social justice. If we are to care about people in prison, we must begin by examining the factors rooted in social injustice that fostered mass incarceration and, in turn, the consequences to social justice caused by mass incarceration.

1. Michelle Alexander, *The New Jim Crow: Mass Incarceration in the Age of Colorblindness* (New York: The New Press, 2012). Marc Mauer, *Race to Incarceration*, revised edition (New York: The New Press, 2006). Loïc Wacquant, "Deadly Symbiosis: When Ghetto and Prison Meet and Mesh," in *Mass Imprisonment: Social Causes and Consequences*, ed. David Garland (Thousand Oaks, CA: Sage, 2001), 82–120.

My understanding of social justice in this text draws upon Catholic social teaching, built upon the conviction that every human person bears the image of God. This conviction has social, cultural, economic, and political implications as it demands that we treat all members of our society as fully human persons. We are required to take care that each person has the resources necessary to participate in the "dignity, unity, and equality of all people."[2] Any systems, institutions, or structures that contribute to the marginalization, disempowerment, or endangerment of any human person must be dismantled. We are called to serve the common good, which can only be realized by assuring that each individual can reach her full potential as a human person. [HUMAN DIGNITY] Human dignity is both inviolable and inalienable. One consequence of this conviction is that we must ensure that even people who violate the law and harm others are not tossed away; we must uphold even their full human personhood. If people are incarcerated not simply because of individual wrongdoing, but also because we have come to rely on prisons as a way of discarding people on whom we as a society have given up, then we must also respond to the conditions of social injustice linked to mass incarceration. The image of God borne by each person calls us to care about everyone, even if we must enter prisons to do so.

Despite our heritage of Catholic social teaching, Catholic leaders and theologians have paid little attention to our intertwining crises of justice. Among those authors who have addressed these issues, a consensus has arisen that upholds the human dignity of all persons, including people who are in prison. Acknowledging the inviolability and inalienability of human dignity places limitations on punishment, which must aim toward the internal reform and social reintegration of offenders. Punishment ought never to be justified for the sake of punishment itself, for retribution, or for utilitarian reasons. People, as moral agents, must be held responsible for their actions, but the purpose of any response to a wrongdoer must be to provide the resources for him to change [CHANGE] his life for his own good and for the common good. Punishment ought to be "medicinal" in the sense that it can succor people who have done wrong so that they may rejoin the community.

Notwithstanding this consensus, few Catholic leaders or theologians offer responses that could adequately address our crises of criminal and social justice. Some strategies, such as that of Peter Karl Koritansky in his *Thomas Aquinas and the Philosophy of Punishment*, remain aloof from the practical realities of our criminal justice systems.[3] While offering practical guidance, the U.S.

2. Pontifical Council for Justice and Peace, *Compendium of the Social Doctrine of the Church* (Washington, DC: United States Conference of Catholic Bishops, 2004), ¶164. See also ¶164–170, 201.

Conference of Catholic Bishops (USCCB) focuses too narrowly on criminal justice reform and does not account sufficiently for the ways in which our criminal justice crisis both reflects and helps sustain social injustices.[4] As a result, the bishops are less prophetic than they ought to be. A third approach, Andrew Skotnicki's in his *Criminal Justice and the Catholic Church*, fails practically, theologically, and morally.[5] Skotnicki calls for a return to the model of monastic and ecclesiastical prisons as the "normative means of punishment" in Catholic tradition. However, even the best prisons cannot achieve what he hopes for them, he misidentifies monastic and ecclesiastical prisons as central to Catholic tradition, and his recommendation of these prisons as a model for our criminal justice systems is out of touch with the realities of mass incarceration in the United States. Given these flaws in Catholic strategies thus far, it seems that Catholics need to generate a new response to our crises of criminal and social justice. Chapter 2 analyzes each of these approaches.

An adequate response to our criminal and social justice crises must satisfy several criteria. It must begin with an accurate reading of the "signs of the times" with respect to the nature of these crises. While offering resources for responding to crime and individual wrongdoing, it will move beyond concerns with reducing reoffending, reintegrating offenders into society, maintaining public safety, and attending to victims. These concerns cannot be ignored; it is necessary to address them in any functioning criminal justice system. However, it is not sufficient to stop at criminal justice reform. Alone, achieving these goals in responding to crime and individual wrongdoing will not answer the social injustices connected to mass incarceration. An adequate response, therefore, must also address the social, cultural, economic, and political factors that led to the creation of the first genuine prison society in the United States, as well as attend to the ways in which mass incarceration exacerbates the social injustices

---

3. Peter Karl Koritansky, *Thomas Aquinas and the Philosophy of Punishment* (Washington, DC: Catholic University of America Press, 2012). Kathryn Getek Soltis, in her 2010 dissertation from Boston College, "Just Punishment? A Virtue Ethics Approach to Prison Reform in the United States," offers a Thomistic approach to a Catholic interpretation of criminal justice, but offers more grounded, practical recommendations for how to apply this theoretical framework to our circumstances with mass incarceration.

4. United States Conference of Catholic Bishops, *Responsibility, Rehabilitation, and Restoration: A Catholic Perspective on Crime and Criminal Justice* (Washington, DC: United States Conference of Catholic Bishops, 2000). Available online at http://www.nccbuscc.org/sdwp/criminal.shtml.

5. Andrew Skotnicki, *Criminal Justice and the Catholic Church* (Lanham, MD: Rowman & Littlefield, 2008). See especially chapter 4, "Prison as the Normative Means of Punishment," 73–114. Also, "Foundations Once Destroyed: The Catholic Church and Criminal Justice," *Theological Studies* 65 (2004): 792–816.

underlying these factors. It will draw us away from questions only about guilt and desert, about costs and benefits of particular criminal justice strategies, about profits and losses in our society, about deterrence, retribution, or incapacitation as justifications for punishment. [An adequate response will require us to ask *What kind of society* ourselves what kind of society we ought to become if we are no longer to be the first genuine prison society.] Our answers to this question will provide a basis for addressing the social injustices tied to mass incarceration. In addition to satisfying these criteria, for a response to be called Catholic, it must also concur with the consensus among Catholic theologians and leaders described above while drawing upon the heart of Catholic moral and theological tradition.

In chapter 3, I argue that the sacramental and liturgical life lies at the heart of Catholicism and provides a moral and theological foundation for a new Catholic response to our criminal and social justice crises. Some challenges make an appeal to liturgical and sacramental ethics complicated, including the difficulties of the privatization and politicization of worship; pluralism both within and beyond the church; injustice within church practices and institutions; and issues concerning whether and how participation in sacrament and liturgy can be morally formative. To overcome these challenges, I argue for an expansive view of liturgy and sacraments as the public service of the church in making the grace of God perceptible to us, thus consecrating our lives in the world. Rather than otherworldly, apolitical, or privatized religious practices, the liturgy of the sacraments draws us more deeply into the world in anticipation of the ultimate mystery of God's reign in which life, freedom, justice, love, and peace fully take hold in our existence. Through our worship, we are called to emulate Jesus Christ, the Son of God, through the Holy Spirit, by serving God and neighbors, particularly our neighbors who have been victims of injustice. This more expansive understanding of liturgy and sacraments, while rooted in Catholicism, should be accessible to other Christian traditions as well.

The central insight here is that our ritual lives in church communities ought to shape Christians toward the justice disclosed in the vision of God's reign conveyed in worship. Liturgical theologian Don Saliers argues that liturgy shapes the quality of our consciousness by guiding us through this vision and presenting to us a "world-picture" that stands in contrast with our worldly perspectives.[6] We are asked in liturgy and sacraments to adopt a world-picture from God's perspective, and with this perspective, we are led to appreciate the needs of others in light of God's outpouring of grace. This vision alters us as God's will for the world becomes our own will. Our consciousness is

6. Don E. Saliers, "Liturgy and Ethics: Some New Beginnings," *Journal of Religious Ethics* 7, no. 2 (1979): 180.

transformed as we continually reenter the world-picture rehearsed in liturgy and sacraments. The task of liturgical and sacramental ethics is to discern the world-picture revealed in our ritual lives and to examine how this vision shapes Christians to see the world according to the hidden reality of salvation and to work for justice in accordance with God's reign. The sacramentality of liturgy calls us to seek this vision in all of our experiences, including our experiences outside of worship practices.

The particular sacraments of Eucharist and of Penance and Reconciliation uphold norms and values for Christians that are relevant for how we enact justice in the world.[7] An examination of the biblical roots of each of these sacraments and their development in Catholic tradition uncovers what they may indicate for responses to our criminal and social justice crises. On one hand, based on the openness of Jesus Christ's table fellowship, the Eucharist conveys a vision of covenantal relationships in which all people are included and the needs of everyone—especially the poor and oppressed—are fulfilled.[8] This sacrament provides a foretaste of God's reign in which death, violence, hatred, indifference, and sin are ultimately overcome. As we participate in its liturgy, we recall Jesus Christ's death as a convicted criminal, which is emblematic of his ministry to the most despised and degraded in his midst. The Eucharist also awakens our "eschatological imaginations" by exposing the ways in which we continue to fall short of the world-picture of God's reign and by offering hope that God will ultimately triumph over the principalities and powers that contribute to the marginalization, disempowerment, and endangerment of our neighbors.[9] As we are invited into the body of Christ in the Eucharist, we must

---

7. Throughout the text, I will occasionally use "Penance" and "Reconciliation" interchangeably to refer to the sacrament of "Penance and Reconciliation." Using "Penance and Reconciliation" every time is stylistically awkward, but choosing only "Penance" or "Reconciliation" alone fails to capture the full scope of this sacrament. The *Catechism of the Catholic Church* refers to the sacrament as "Penance and Reconciliation," and each of these terms describes different aspects of the sacrament that neither term fully encompasses alone. If we speak only of Penance, the end of reconciling relationships can often be lost. If we speak only of Reconciliation, the work that must be done by the penitent toward rebuilding relationships can often be lost. It is also important to note that the words one uses to designate this sacrament can often lead readers to make unfounded assumptions about the author's leanings: liberals use "Reconciliation" while conservatives use "Penance." I find that pegging an author in this way can be a distraction from what the author is trying to communicate; I am not making a political statement by using either "Penance" or "Reconciliation" at any particular point. Where readers see "Penance," they should think also "Reconciliation," and vice versa.

8. I recognize that non-Catholic readers may bristle at the claim of a Catholic author for the inclusiveness of the Eucharist, given their exclusion from full participation in the mass. However, I hope that throughout this book I can point toward the ideal of Jesus Christ's table fellowship while acknowledging the ways in which all churches, including the Catholic Church, fall short of this ideal.

examine our individual consciences and communal relationships so that sin and injustice cannot break that body. In this sacrament, we are reoriented toward justice in God's reign as we confront ongoing injustices in our world.

On the other hand, our practices of Penance and Reconciliation flow from the vision of ultimate justice found in the Eucharist. These practices offer alternative norms and values to retribution and punitiveness for responding to individual wrongdoing. While we need discipline and judgment within our communities, this sacrament guides us to uphold the possibility of forgiveness and to work toward the reincorporation in community of people who have harmed others and done wrong. Underlying the emphasis on eventual forgiveness in Penance is an understanding that individual wrongdoing (or sin, in theological terms) is primarily a wounding of relationships and not only a violation of law. Where discipline and judgment are necessary, the end of any penitential actions is not to cause pain to an offender for the sake of punishment or to exact retribution, but to bring about circumstances in which a wrongdoer could be restored to full relationship. Discipline and judgment must always occur in a communal context in which all community members take responsibility for the social reintegration and internal reform of wrongdoers by offering guidance and support. Practices of Reconciliation maintain the human dignity of sinners for the image of God within each person is inviolable and inalienable.

Although the emphasis within the sacrament of Penance and Reconciliation has typically fallen on responsibility for individual sins, this sacrament also offers guidance for addressing broken communal relationships. Penance reminds us that we are all sinners in need of forgiveness from God and our neighbors. In particular, everyone is complicit in social sin that creates the broader context of individual wrongdoing and that fosters the injustices that undergird poverty, marginalization, and oppression. Because we must seek redemption from social sin as well as personal sin, we may find in Penance and Reconciliation resources for responding not only to individual wrongdoing, but also to our participation in and responsibility for social injustice.

The response of liturgical and sacramental ethics to crime and individual wrongdoing is the topic of chapter 4. Standing alone, the argument of this chapter does not meet the criteria of an adequate response to our criminal and social justice crises because it focuses only on criminal justice reform. Readers should not read chapter 4 separately from the preceding or following chapters. Nevertheless, while insufficient for addressing mass incarceration,

9. Andrea Bieler and Luise Schottroff, *The Eucharist: Bodies, Bread, and Resurrection* (Minneapolis: Fortress Press, 2007).

criminal justice reform is necessary in order to present alternatives to prisons. Too often people assume that the only alternative to prisons is to let criminals go without any consequences for their actions, leaving victims without justice and communities vulnerable to more crime. Our options seem to be either prison or nothing. But they are not our only options; we have access to a range of alternatives to incarceration that are more effective than prisons at reducing reoffending, reintegrating offenders into society, maintaining public safety, and attending to the needs of victims.

As recommended by the USCCB, restorative justice is a viable alternative to incarceration. Also, evidence-based rehabilitative programs, based on what is called the "good lives model," can potentially partner well with restorative justice as a base for our criminal justice systems.[10] While incarceration unfortunately will remain necessary in some instances, use of restorative justice and rehabilitation could enable significant downscaling of our prison populations. As Catholics consider these alternatives, they should find that restorative justice and rehabilitation align well with the norms and values upheld by the sacrament of Penance and Reconciliation. Rather than being retributive and punitive, restorative justice and rehabilitation connect to the vision of forgiveness, humility, community, dialogue, healing, and service offered in this sacrament.

Because our crises of criminal and social justice are fundamentally intertwined, an adequate response to them cannot stop with criminal justice reform; we must also attend to the social injustices that mass incarceration both reflects and helps sustain and that are addressed in chapter 5 on a sacramental and liturgical basis. In attending to these social injustices, we must answer what kind of society we ought to become if we wish no longer to be the first genuine prison society. Michelle Alexander argues that our vision of a new kind of society depends upon a transformation of consciousness in which we recognize the human dignity of all persons and begin to care across barriers of race, ethnicity, gender, and class. Such a transformation would spark a multiracial movement for dismantling the first genuine prison society, the New Jim Crow, and mass incarceration.

Catholics and many other Christians experience in the Eucharist a transformation of consciousness; a vision of what a just society ought to look like; a call to defend human dignity especially among people who have been excluded through poverty, marginalization, and oppression. As the "source and summit" of our moral lives as Christians, the Eucharist beckons us toward justice

---

10. Tony Ward and Shadd Maruna, *Rehabilitation: Beyond the Risk Paradigm* (New York: Routledge, 2007).

both within the life of the church and in our public service of consecrating the world.[11] One aspect of this work for justice will be repenting of brokenness in our communal relationships and assuming personal responsibility for bringing about a new kind of society. Through Penance and Reconciliation, we may seek redemption from social sin, particularly through combined communal and private rites of this sacrament. Our penitential work will be necessary to unwind our criminal and social justice crises. The Eucharist feeds this work for justice as it nourishes hope that our vision of God's justice will ultimately reign. In response to liturgical and sacramental ethics, then, Catholics ought to join a multiracial—and interreligious—movement as an embodiment of our public service of consecrating the world in emulation of Jesus Christ, the Son of God, through the Holy Spirit. Only through such a movement will we be able to work toward a society in which everyone as a fully human person has access to conditions that foster the dignity, unity, and equality of all people.

Through this book, I hope that readers will come to care about people in prison as I have and to feel the same sense of urgency to act. For Catholics, I hope that as I appeal to liturgy and sacraments, you feel a similar compulsion to work for justice; for readers who are Christian, but not Catholic, I hope that I write about liturgy and sacraments in ways that foster possibilities for working together despite theological, ecclesiological, and practical differences between our denominations. Those with other religious commitments or no religious ties, I hope that I write about Catholicism in ways that show that Catholics share your commitment to justice. A movement to address our criminal and social justice crises must draw upon a multiracial and interreligious coalition. I intend this book to show why Catholics should participate in such a movement and how they could be good partners in such a coalition.

---

11. Second Vatican Council, *Sacrosanctum Concilium*, ¶10 and ¶14. See Austin Flannery, ed., *Vatican Council II: The Conciliar and Post Conciliar Documents*, vol. 1 (Northport, NY: Costello, 1998).

1

Our Crisis of Justice

Criminal justice systems in the United States are in crisis. Currently over 7.3 million adults in the United States are under some form of supervision, including probation, jail, prison, and parole, by state, local, or federal criminal justice systems.[1] At midyear 2009, nearly 1.6 million people were in prison, and nearly 800,000 were in jail.[2] These numbers represent a gross increase in the rate of incarceration in the United States over the last several decades. In 1972, the rate of incarceration in prisons was ninety-three people per hundred thousand U.S. residents. Over nearly forty years, this rate has increased by almost 540 percent; it was 502 people per hundred thousand U.S. residents in 2009 (these rates do not include jail inmates, who bring the overall rate of incarceration up to 762 people per hundred thousand).[3] Although the United States has less than 5 percent of the world's population, it holds nearly 25 percent of the world's incarcerated people.[4] The United States incarcerates its residents at higher rates than any other nation, and we incarcerate more people than any other nation (China, with an overall population more than four times as large as the U.S.

1. Heather C. West, "Prison Inmates at Midyear 2009—Statistical Tables," Bureau of Justice Statistics, U.S. Department of Justice, accessed July 21, 2010, http://bjs.ojp.usdoj.gov/content/pub/pdf/pim09st.pdf. In what follows, I draw on statistics that highlight the plight of prison and jail inmates. However, a larger proportion of the population of the United States experiences criminal justice systems through probation or parole. When we see statistics about incarceration rates, we really see only the proverbial tip of the iceberg of criminal justice systems.

2. Ibid. Jails differ from prisons in that the former typically confine only people prior to trial or sentencing and those who have been convicted of a misdemeanor, usually resulting in a sentence of less than one year. That is, jails are used for holding and restraining people temporarily while prisons generally have more permanent populations.

3. Ibid. "Key Facts at a Glance: Correctional Populations," Bureau of Justice Statistics, U.S. Department of Justice, http://bjs.ojp.usdoj.gov/content/glance/tables/corr2tab.cfm. See also Kathleen Maguire, ed., *Sourcebook of Criminal Justice Statistics* (table 6.28.2009), http://www.albany.edu/sourcebook/pdf/t6282009.pdf.

4. Adam Liptak, "U.S. Prison Population Dwarfs That of Other Nations," *New York Times*, April 23, 2008.

population, incarcerates the second-highest number of people at 1.6 million inmates, more than 700,000 fewer people than the United States).[5] In short, we have more people locked up in the United States and at higher rates than at any other time in our history and any other nation.

While these numbers are troubling enough to raise serious questions about our criminal justice systems, discrepancies related to race and ethnicity among prison and jail populations add greater urgency. Racial and ethnic minority populations are incarcerated at astounding rates in comparison with whites. At midyear 2009, the incarceration rate of black non-Hispanic men was six times that of the incarceration rate of white non-Hispanic men and nearly three times that of Hispanic men.[6] Although about 93 percent of people in state and federal prisons in 2009 were men, in recent years the incarceration rate of women has increased twice as quickly as that of men. While women are incarcerated at about a tenth of the rate of men, the population of incarcerated women reflects similar racial and ethnic disparities as the male inmate population.[7] Black non-Hispanic women are incarcerated at nearly four times the rate of white non-Hispanic women and over twice that of Hispanic women.[8] Increasing incarceration hits racial and ethnic minority populations in the United States especially hard.

In addition to racial and ethnic disparities, criminal justice systems in the United States are also marred by disparities related to socioeconomic status. Measures of the socioeconomic status of people in jail or prison are difficult to find; income and wealth are not noted upon incarceration as are sex and race. However, according to Marc Mauer of The Sentencing Project, "a 1997 survey of state inmates conducted by the Justice Department found that 68 percent of prisoners had not completed high school, 53 percent earned less than $1,000 in the month prior to their incarceration, and nearly one half were either unemployed or working only part-time prior to their arrest."[9] Another measure of socioeconomic status of inmates is whether they need publicly financed counsel.[10] In 1998, about two-thirds of federal felony defendants

5. Roy Walmsley, "World Prison Population List," 8th edition, International Centre for Prison Studies, King's College London, http://www.prisonstudies.org/info/downloads/wppl-8th_41.pdf.

6. See West, "Prison Inmates at Midyear 2009." The incarceration rate of black non-Hispanic men at midyear 2009 was 4,749 per 100,000; for white non-Hispanic men, it was 708 per 100,000; and for Hispanic men, it was 1,822 per 100,000.

7. Ibid. The incarceration rate for women at midyear 2009 was 131 per 100,000, versus 1,398 per 100,000 for men.

8. Ibid. The incarceration rate of black non-Hispanic women at midyear 2009 was 333 per 100,000; for white non-Hispanic women, it was 91 per 100,000; and for Hispanic women, it was 142 per 100,000.

9. Marc Mauer, *Race to Incarcerate*, 2nd ed. (New York: New Press, 2006), 178.

required public defense. In 1996, more than four-fifths of felony defendants in the seventy-five most populous counties in the United States required public defense. While conviction rates did not vary according to whether defendants had privately or publicly financed counsel, defendants with public defense were sentenced to prison or jail at higher rates and for longer sentences than those with private defense. In other words, persons with private defense are just as likely as those with public defense of being convicted. However, persons with private defense are less likely to be sentenced to jail or prison, instead given sentences that involve fines or probation, but no time behind bars. Criminal justice systems not only disproportionately incarcerate racial and ethnic minorities; they also tend to hold higher numbers of poor people behind bars.

These trends within adult criminal justice systems in the United States are also apparent within juvenile justice systems, which in many ways feed our prisons and jails through what the Children's Defense Fund calls the "cradle-to-prison pipeline."[11] On February 22, 2006, the last date of a census by the Office of Juvenile Justice and Delinquency Prevention (OJJDP), over 92,000 juvenile offenders were in "residential placement facilities."[12] According to the OJJDP, this number represents roughly how many juveniles occupy these facilities on "any given day." So, we could then expect about 15 percent of children in these facilities to be girls, and about 767 per hundred thousand black non-Hispanic children living in our country to be in a residential placement facility. The rate for Hispanic children was 326, and the rate for white non-Hispanic children was 170. Thus, the rate at which black children are placed in these facilities is about four-and-a-half times that of whites; the rate for Hispanics is about twice that of whites—statistics that echo patterns among adults.

More sixteen-year-olds than any other age group occupied residential placement facilities—about 25,000.[13] Sixteen-year-olds edged out seventeen-year-olds because thirteen states send seventeen-year-olds directly to adult criminal courts, and many other states allow for seventeen-year-olds to be sent to adult criminal courts via statutory exclusion or concurrent jurisdiction provisions. As a result, every year, over 200,000 youth under age eighteen are tried as adults.[14] During the 1990s, every state except Nebraska expanded

10. "Defense Counsel in Criminal Cases," Bureau of Justice Statistics, U.S. Department of Justice, bjs.ojp.usdoj.gov/content/pub/pdf/dccc.pdf.

11. "America's Cradle to Prison Pipeline," Children's Defense Fund, http://www.childrensdefense.org/child-research-data-publications/data/cradle-prison-pipeline-report-2007-full-highres.html.

12. For comprehensive statistics on juvenile justice in the United States, see "Statistical Briefing Book," Office of Juvenile Justice and Delinquency Prevention, U.S. Department of Justice, Office of Justice Programs, http://ojjdp.ncjrs.gov/ojstatbb/.

13. Ibid.

the number of children it sends through adult criminal justice systems rather than treat as juveniles. Thus, not only do our criminal justice systems disproportionately affect minority and impoverished individuals and communities; they also increasingly affect young people within these communities, blurring once well-established lines between youth and adults.

Together, these data suggest that as the reach of criminal and juvenile justice systems in the United States continues to expand, these systems grip certain groups of people in our society—especially racial and ethnic minorities and socioeconomically disadvantaged people, and increasingly, women and young people—more tightly than others. Being young, poor, black, and male greatly increases the likelihood that a person will be incarcerated. Sociologist Bruce Western found that twenty in one hundred black men born between 1965 and 1969 (men who were born at the dawn of the growth of our criminal justice systems) were imprisoned by their early thirties, in contrast with only about three in one hundred white men born in the same time period.[15] Class distinctions exacerbated the likelihood that young black men would be imprisoned. Nearly 60 percent of black men in this age group who dropped out of high school were imprisoned by their early thirties; only about 11 percent of white men who dropped out of high school were imprisoned by the same age. These numbers also represent a drastic change from previous generations. For white men born between 1945 and 1949, only 1.5 in one hundred were imprisoned by their early thirties. For black men in the same generation, only about eleven in one hundred experienced the same fate—still a significant racial disparity, but the disparity has grown over the last four decades despite other advances in civil rights for African Americans. This disparity continues to affect young black men in the United States. Western writes, "The stratification of incarceration by race and education produced extraordinary incarceration rates for young [age twenty to forty] black male [high school] dropouts by the end of the 1990s. Nearly a third were in prison or jail on a typical day in 2000, three times their incarceration rates just thirty years earlier."[16]

The current state of our criminal justice systems constitutes what social theorist David Garland calls "mass imprisonment," to distinguish incarceration

---

14. "2008 KIDS COUNT Message FACT SHEET: A Road Map for Juvenile Justice," The Annie E. Casey Foundation, http://www.aecf.org/KnowledgeCenter/
Publications.aspx?pubguid={29CFCA70-348B-416B-8546-63C297710C5D}.

15. Bruce Western, *Punishment and Inequality in America* (New York: Russell Sage Foundation, 2006), 24–28. These numbers actually *underestimate* the reach of our criminal justice systems for these men, as they do not include the risk of being jailed or otherwise placed under supervision.

16. Ibid., 17.

in the United States currently from incarceration in similar nations.[17] He describes two defining features of mass imprisonment. The United States clearly meets the first criterion: "a rate of imprisonment and a size of prison population that is markedly above the historical and comparative norm for societies of this type."[18] Data about the concentration of incarceration on young black men from socioeconomically disadvantaged backgrounds reveal that our society also fulfills the second feature: "Imprisonment becomes mass imprisonment when it ceases to be the incarceration of individual offenders and becomes the systematic imprisonment of whole groups of the population."[19] Because many, if not most, members of our society have never been to prison and may not know (or think they know) someone who has, the claim that imprisonment has become so common in the United States as to be a major part of the lives of many of our neighbors, to be systematically affecting whole groups of the population, may seem untenable. However, for young black men in large, impoverished urban centers and their families and friends,

> [i]mprisonment has become normalized. It has come to be a regular, predictable part of experience, rather than a rare and infrequent event. . . . It becomes part of the socialization process. Every family, every household, every individual in these neighbourhoods has direct personal knowledge of the prison—through a spouse, a child, a parent, a neighbour, a friend. Imprisonment ceases to be the fate of a few criminal individuals and becomes a shaping institution for whole sectors of the population.[20]

For these men, the typical life events of the young—education, military service, employment, marriage—have been circumscribed by the prison.

The problem of mass incarceration is not the problem alone of those sectors of the population most directly affected by our criminal justice systems. The crisis of these systems both *reflects* and *helps sustain* a broader crisis of social justice in the United States that marginalizes, disempowers, and endangers our neighbors. Catholic social teaching holds that social justice concerns the cultural, social, political, and economic requirements for treating all members of society as fully human persons and ensuring that each person has the resources

---

17. David Garland, "Introduction: The Meaning of Mass Imprisonment," in *Mass Imprisonment: Social Causes and Consequences*, ed. David Garland (Thousand Oaks, CA: Sage, 2001), 1–3.

18. Ibid., 1.

19. Ibid., 1–2.

20. Ibid., 2.

necessary to participate in the dignity, unity, and equality of all people. In the United States, racial, ethnic, and class inequality undermine social justice and fuel the crisis of our criminal justice systems. At the same time, our criminal justice systems contribute to the ongoing effects of these disparities in our society, exacerbating our failures to achieve social justice. Criminal and social justice are fundamentally intertwined. Addressing failures of criminal justice requires addressing failures of social justice, and vice versa. Social theorist Loïc Wacquant has argued that the state of mass incarceration in the United States has led to the creation of "*the first genuine prison society* of history,"[21] in contrast with merely a society with prisoners. If we wish for our society to no longer be distinguished by the practice of imprisonment, then we must rethink both what kind of society we would like to be and how we use prisons to maintain the inequalities within our society now. We must address our crises of criminal and social justice.

Becoming the First Genuine Prison Society

Demonstrating the link between social and criminal justice depends, in part, on understanding how the United States came to have the largest prison population and highest incarceration rate in our history and in the world. A naïve assessment of the reasons behind this shift might assume that we incarcerate more people because more people are committing crime in our society. If this were the case, then the argument that the crisis of our criminal justice systems reflects a crisis of social justice in the United States could not be supported. Rather our large prison populations would simply reflect a reality of criminality plaguing our society.

At least two bodies of evidence, however, show the faults of this assumption. First, while U.S. rates of incarceration are much higher than all other nations, our rates of crime do not differ significantly from other similar countries. While the United States is exceptional in its levels of lethal violence, perhaps due to relatively lax gun control laws, rates of nonlethal violence, property crime, and drug offending in the United States are comparable to rates in other Western industrialized democracies.[22] Some of these nations, such

21. Loïc Wacquant, "Deadly Symbiosis: When Ghetto and Prison Meet and Mesh," in *Mass Imprisonment*, ed. Garland, 82–120. Emphasis in original.

22. The key here is *lethal* violence. Other countries have similar rates of violence, but because of the accessibility of fire arms, violence in the United States is much more likely to result in death. For a thorough discussion of international comparisons of crime and incarceration rates, see James P. Lynch and William Alex Pridemore, "Crime in International Perspective," in *Crime and Public Policy*, ed. James

as England and Wales, the Netherlands, and Switzerland, have higher rates of crime overall, while nations such as Australia, Canada, and Sweden have roughly equivalent crime rates to those of the United States. Despite these similarities in crime rates, incarceration rates in the United States exceed those of all of these nations to a staggering degree. After the United States, the second-highest rate of incarceration among these nations is that of England and Wales with 152 people in prison per hundred thousand residents, leaving us with a rate at least 4.5 times that of similar nations with comparable crime rates.[23] This difference can be explained in part by higher rates of serious violent crimes in the United States, which virtually every nation punishes with longer prison terms; the argument would suggest that the higher rate of serious violent offenses in the United States contributes to our higher incarceration rates because we experience more crimes that call for longer punishments. However, the likelihood of being arrested for a drug, property, or nonlethal violent offense and sentenced to a long prison term in the United States, despite similar offending rates, contributes more significantly to higher rates of incarceration in our society. Because other nations find other means for responding to these offenses, their incarceration rates are not impacted by drug, property, or nonlethal violent offending as much as incarceration rates in the United States are. The punitiveness of our responses to crime—not exceptional crime rates in the United States—accounts largely for our exceptional incarceration rates.

A second body of evidence also shows that crime rates cannot explain incarceration rates in the United States. This evidence arises from the observation that the growth of incarceration rates over the last forty years has not coincided with increasing crime rates. While the beginning of our increased use of prisons may have reflected higher crime rates (or at least the *perception* of growing crime rates) in the late 1960s and early 1970s, Mauer notes, "A steadily increasing prison population has twice coincided with periods of increase in crime and twice with declines in crime."[24] The most dramatic

Q. Wilson and Joan Petersilia (New York: Oxford University Press, 2011), 5–52. For other discussions, see Alfred Blumstein, Michael Tonry, and Asheley Van Ness, "Cross-National Measures of Punitiveness," in *Crime and Punishment in Western Countries, 1980-1999*, ed. Michael Tonry and David P. Farrington (Chicago: University of Chicago Press, 2005), 347–76; and David P. Farrington, Patrick Langan, and Michael Tonry, eds., *Cross-National Studies in Crime and Justice* (Washington, DC: Bureau of Justice Statistics, 2004).

23. Walmsley, "World Prison Population List."

24. Mauer, *Race to Incarcerate*, 94. For a thorough, yet brief, discussion of the relationship between crime and incarceration rates—and why throwing more people in jails and prisons will not necessarily result in less crime—see Ryan S. King, Marc Mauer, and Malcolm C. Young, "Incarceration and Crime: A Complex Relationship," The Sentencing Project, http://www.sentencingproject.org/doc/publications/

decline began in the early 1990s and has persisted for the last twenty years. Crime rates therefore can explain only a small proportion of the growth in incarceration rates over the last four decades. Criminologists Alfred Blumstein and Allen Beck found that only 12 percent of the tripling of the national prison population between 1980 and 1996 can be explained by changes in crime rates; a greater likelihood of incarceration upon conviction and longer prison terms explain the remaining 88 percent of growth.[25] That is, we have more people in prison not primarily because of increased crime rates, but because we have a greater willingness than we used to as a society to imprison more people for longer periods of time.

A protest remains against this second body of evidence and its ability to disprove the notion that we incarcerate more people because more people are committing crime. Rather than examining crime data of the U.S. population in aggregate, this protest avers that since our criminal justice systems disproportionately affect young black men from disadvantaged socioeconomic backgrounds, the growth in incarceration rates could be explained if this sector of the population alone engaged in more crime than they used to do. It could be that the racial, ethnic, and class disparities in our criminal justice systems are legitimate because they reflect differences in criminal offending, not failures of social justice.

For this protest to have merit, young black men today must commit more crime than previous generations. Data from the National Longitudinal Surveys of Youth, however, show that this is not true.[26] Between 1980 and 2000, violent crime among poor black male youth, age fifteen to eighteen, dropped 21 percent; property crime dropped 68 percent; and drug dealing dropped 69 percent. While African-American men commit violent crimes at slightly higher rates than white men, the differences are not large enough to explain differences in incarceration rates.[27] Furthermore, most of the growth

inc_iandc_complex.pdf. See also Todd R. Clear, *Imprisoning Communities: How Mass Imprisonment Makes Disadvantaged Neighborhoods Worse* (New York: Oxford University Press, 2007), 15–48; Mauer, *Race to Incarcerate*, 92–129; William Spelman, "What Recent Studies Do (and Don't) Tell Us about Imprisonment and Crime," in *Crime and Justice: A Review of Research*, ed. Michael Tonry (Chicago: University of Chicago Press, 2000), 27:419–94; and Western, *Punishment and Inequality*, 168–88.

25. Alfred Blumstein and Allen J. Beck, "Population Growth in U.S. Prisons, 1980-1996," in *Prisons*, ed. Michael Tonry and Joan Petersilia (Chicago: University of Chicago Press, 1999), 17–62.

26. Cited in Western, *Punishment and Inequality*, 41.

27. Differences in violent offending between blacks and whites may be better explained by class than by race. Among young men who have steady employment or who live in a steady relationship, violent offending rates do not vary by race. Because of links between poverty and race, however, young black men are less likely to have the stabilizing forces of steady employment and relationships in their lives, and

in incarceration rates since the 1970s is due to the greater likelihood, first, that someone would receive a prison sentence for a drug crime and, second, that his prison sentence would be longer than it would have been in the past. The African-American proportion of arrests for drug crimes has increased, especially among juveniles, as low-income minority communities in inner cities are targeted for the enforcement of drug laws. As a result, in 2000, African Americans comprised 32 percent of total arrests (adult and juvenile) for drug possession and 47 percent of total arrests for drug selling. However, African Americans use and sell drugs at rates approximately proportionate to their representation in the general population. About 12 percent of drug users in 2000 were African American, and the vast majority of drug users buy from sellers of the same racial and ethnic background as themselves.[28] Rates of arrest of young black men for drug crimes far exceed their actual involvement in them. This disparity, along with more punitive sentencing, explains a significant proportion of the growing racial disparities in our incarceration rates over the last forty years. Against the protest that we have more young black men in prison because they are committing more crimes, these data instead indicate that we have more young black men in prison because we have become more willing to throw more of them in prison for longer periods of time than we, as a society, used to be.[29]

If crime rates in the United States, either of the aggregate population or of young black men in particular, cannot explain the current crisis of our criminal

any young man in such circumstances is more prone to violent offending. Thus, young black men are more likely to engage in violent offending because they are more likely to experience poverty than young white men. See Mauer, *Race to Incarcerate*, 176–86. See also Delbert S. Elliott, "Serious Violent Offenders: Onset, Development Course, and Termination—the American Society of Criminology 1993 Presidential Address," *Criminology* 32, no. 1 (1994): 1–21.

28. See Mauer, *Race to Incarcerate*, 157–76, for fuller discussion of the relationship between race and disparities in incarceration and crime rates. Also, Michael Tonry, *Punishing Race: A Continuing American Dilemma* (New York: Oxford University Press, 2011), 26–47, 59–76; and Western, *Punishment and Inequality*, 35–51.

29. Of course, we have been willing to exert other forms of social control on young black men in our history, beginning with slavery and moving to Jim Crow and segregation laws. Michelle Alexander ties the increased use of incarceration of African Americans to an effort to "ensure the subordinate status of a group defined largely by race." See *The New Jim Crow: Mass Incarceration in the Age of Colorblindness* (New York: New Press, 2012), 13. To say that we have become more willing to throw more young black men in prison for longer periods of time is not to say that we are now oppressing young black men in ways worse than we did in the past. It is to say that we are repeating patterns of social control, subordination, and oppression in *different* ways than we did in the past. What is new in our circumstances is our dependence on the prison as the primary means of social control.

justice systems, then we must look elsewhere for the cause of the creation of the first genuine prison society. Garland describes the difficulty of this task:

> Mass imprisonment was not a policy that was proposed, researched, costed, debated, and democratically agreed. America did not collectively decide to get into the business of mass imprisonment in the way that it decided to build the institutions of the New Deal, or the Great Society, or even the low-tax, low-spending, free-market institutions of Reaganomics. Instead, mass imprisonment emerged as the overdetermined outcome of a converging series of policies and decisions. . . . America has drifted into this situation, with voters and politicians, and judges and corporations willing the specific means without anyone pausing to assess the overall outcome.[30]

Understanding our drift into the crisis of our criminal justice systems requires consideration of the mixed and complicated history from which it arose.

SOCIAL AND CULTURAL FACTORS

Prior to the 1970s, the rate of incarceration in the United States hovered for decades around one hundred people per hundred thousand, with a high of 137 per hundred thousand in 1939.[31] Few Americans were concerned with crime as a major issue. Beginning in 1973, the incarceration rate started climbing. The initial growth of prison and jail populations at this time was probably due to climbing crime rates linked to the large number of adolescent and young adult baby boomers, although the extent of the crime boom of the late 1960s and early 1970s cannot be fully known because of limitations in the collection of crime statistics nationwide prior to the formation of the Law Enforcement Assistance Administration in 1968. Growing crime rates (or at least the *perception* of growing crime rates), alongside several other factors, contributed to greater anxiety about crime in the U.S. population during this period. Other factors include a heroin epidemic in many cities, sparked by Vietnam veterans returning from the war as addicts; numerous riots across the United States, especially with the stifling of many of the objectives of the civil rights movement; cases of police brutality that often accompanied these riots; rapid urbanization, particularly with many rural southern African Americans migrating to northern cities; and high-profile assassinations, notably

30. Garland, ed., *Mass Imprisonment*, 2.
31. Kathleen Maguire, ed., *Sourcebook of Criminal Justice Statistics* (table 6.28.2009), http://www.albany.edu/sourcebook/pdf/t6282009.pdf.

those of Martin Luther King Jr. and Robert Kennedy. In addition to these factors, the challenges brought by the civil rights movement and by the antiwar movement exacerbated an overall sense of social disorder, especially among white Americans. By the end of the 1960s, polls showed that 81 percent of the public believed that law and order in the United States had broken down and that the majority traced the roots of this failure to "Negroes who start riots" and "communists."[32]

Greater fear about crime and lawlessness coincided with an unprecedented shift among criminologists and criminal justice professionals concerning the purpose and effectiveness of criminal justice systems in responding to crime. Since the advent of the prison in the United States in the early nineteenth century, our criminal justice systems worked toward the goal of rehabilitation of criminal offenders. Beginning in the 1970s, the majority of criminologists and criminal justice professionals rejected rehabilitation as unattainable and began to emphasize deterrence and incapacitation—more punitive goals—as the purpose of criminal justice systems. Proponents of deterrence and incapacitation could justify their rejection of rehabilitation, in part, through appeal to a landmark 1974 study by criminologist Robert Martinson titled "What Works: Questions and Answers about Prison Reform."[33] Through a meta-analysis of studies of rehabilitative programs conducted between 1945 and 1967, Martinson concluded that "nothing works" to rehabilitate criminal offenders. This thesis drew widespread public attention—Martinson was even interviewed by *People* magazine in 1976—although the original study received significant, justifiable criticism. A 1976 panel for the National Academy of Sciences reviewed the work and concluded, "When it is asserted that 'nothing works,' the Panel is uncertain as to just what has even been given a fair trial."[34] In 1978, Martinson admitted that he had omitted pieces of research that would have shown that some rehabilitation practices are more effective than he had originally stated. Despite the weaknesses of the study, its "nothing works" thesis caught on as a sort of mantra among criminologists and criminal justice

32. Cited in Mauer, *Race to Incarcerate*, 52. For more detailed discussions of the historical factors contributing to the cultural context leading up to the growth of our criminal justice systems, see John Irwin, *The Warehouse Prison: Disposal of the New Dangerous Class* (Los Angeles: Roxbury, 2005), especially chapter 8; Mauer, *Race to Incarcerate*, 40–91; Tonry, *Punishing Race*, 77–143; Michael Tonry and Joan Petersilia, "American Prisons at the Beginning of the Twenty-First Century," in *Prisons*, ed. Tonry and Petersilia, 1–16; and Western, *Punishment and Inequality*, 52–66.

33. Robert Martinson, "What Works: Questions and Answers about Prison Reform," *Public Interest* 35 (1974): 22–54.

34. Quoted in Jerome G. Miller, "Is Rehabilitation a Waste of Time?," *Washington Post*, April 23, 1989.

professionals, a mantra that spread to policymakers and the general public. In response to questions of what could be done about crime and disorder, [the answer now became to use prisons more frequently for incapacitation and deterrence and to abandon rehabilitative practices.]

ghettos → jobless and institutional

ECONOMIC FACTORS

In conjunction with the cultural and social phenomena of growing anxiety about crime, often with racial undertones, and rejection of rehabilitation, economic factors also underlie the buildup of our criminal justice systems. The deindustrialization of cities contributed to the transformation of inner cities from what sociologist William Julius Wilson calls "institutional ghettos" (borrowing from historian Allan Spear) to "jobless ghettos."[35] Wacquant similarly describes this transformation as a shift from "communal ghettos" to "hyper-ghettos."[36] Institutional, or communal, ghettos were based largely on the segregation of black populations in our cities. While unjustly exclusionary, these ghettos also offered a measure of protection, solidarity, and autonomy among their residents, whose socioeconomic statuses ranged widely. African American lawyers, doctors, and ministers lived alongside and offered their services to African American working-class and poor families. Low-skilled, poorer residents, especially men, could typically find work near to home with relatively good blue-collar jobs in the industrial sector. Such jobs were often unionized and came with decent pay and comparatively strong benefits packages. Industrial workers in turn supported locally owned businesses in their neighborhoods, which provided myriad goods and services to residents. These businesses, alongside clubs, religious congregations, local newspapers, and other communal organizations, offered some level of informal social control in ghettos as well as some basic opportunities and resources that made for vibrant, even if still segregated and in many ways disadvantaged, neighborhoods.

The deindustrialization of inner cities triggered the demise of institutional ghettos beginning in the 1970s, brought on by increasing globalization, shifts toward higher-skilled jobs, and the suburbanization of employment. Deindustrialization resulted in fewer jobs for low-skilled men, leading to

35. William Julius Wilson, *When Work Disappears: The World of the New Urban Poor* (New York: Alfred A. Knopf, 1997).

36. Wacquant, "Deadly Symbiosis." For a more detailed history of economic factors linked to the creation of jobless, or hyper-, ghettos, see also Wilson, *When Work Disappears*; and Irwin, *The Warehouse Prison*, especially chapter 8.

increased bargaining power for corporations against unions. Those low-skilled men who could get jobs could expect lower wages, depleted benefits, and fewer hours. One of the most significant consequences of deindustrialization is a precipitous drop in real wages for low-skilled workers since 1970. The best employment many residents of ghettos could find was in the growing service sector, which tends to hire more women, pay them less, and offer little stability. Furthermore, most service sector jobs were located outside of cities in new suburbs. Formerly thriving businesses in ghetto neighborhoods collapsed as industrial workers were laid off and could no longer afford to patronize local groceries, barbershops, and hardware stores. Suburban service sector jobs proved difficult for ghetto residents to hold given the distances they had to travel to and from work, often using public transportation. While deindustrialization killed jobs in inner cities, many middle-class African American residents left the ghettos in the late 1960s and early 1970s, liberated to move to more affluent neighborhoods by the advances of the civil rights movement. The confluence of deindustrialization with the loss of many middle-class residents resulted in the creation of jobless ghettos, or hyper-ghettos, in which the poorest members of our society are isolated from the rest of the population, left with few economic, political, or social resources. Poverty is concentrated in inner-city neighborhoods largely populated by African Americans. Between 1970 and 1990, the number of "ghetto poverty census tracts" (those with poverty rates exceeding 40 percent) doubled. Seven out of eight of the people living in these tracts in 1990 were minority group members.[37]

In themselves, these changes to ghetto neighborhoods should not necessarily feed into our growing criminal justice systems. However, the transformation of inner-city neighborhoods into jobless ghettos increased their level of what sociologists call "social disorganization." A trajectory within criminological theory rooted in the seminal work of Clifford Shaw and Henry McKay examines the relationship between social disorganization and community characteristics such as poverty, ethnic heterogeneity, and residential mobility.[38] Residents of neighborhoods with these characteristics tend to have little human capital, or "the personal resources that an individual brings to the social and economic marketplace," such as education or job and social skills.[39] They also have sparse social networks, which provide them with little access to

---

37. Wilson, *When Work Disappears*, 14.

38. Clifford R. Shaw and Henry D. McKay, *Juvenile Delinquency and Urban Areas* (Chicago: University of Chicago Press, 1942).

39. Todd R. Clear, *Imprisoning Communities*, 76.

new resources. As a consequence, their communities as a whole have little social capital, or a limited "capacity of [their] networks to provide goods for people within these networks."[40]

With weakened human and social capital along with sparse social networks, members of these communities may also experience lessened "collective efficacy."[41] On one hand, they have less ability to work together to address problems faced by the community as a whole, particularly as community members may not agree on what the problems are or how to fix them. On the other hand, institutions outside of the formal social control of the state, such as families, voluntary social groups, businesses, or religious organizations, may not have the wherewithal to sustain order and compliance with communal norms through informal social controls. As a consequence, the social disorganization of these communities may result in higher crime rates, especially higher rates of violence and the presence of "overt drug markets" in public spaces.[42]

A core community of hard-working, law-abiding residents remains in these neighborhoods, but they do not have the power to control the minority of people who are shooting guns and selling drugs on street corners to white people driving into the neighborhood from the suburbs. Criminologist and co-chair of the National Network for Safe Communities David Kennedy describes the fate of these neighborhoods in the period following the deindustrialization of inner cities:

> There was nothing inevitable about the crack epidemic that took these neighborhoods down. But it was inevitable that when it hit, it would hit here hardest. It was, especially, where young men whose present and future both offered next to nothing were most likely to think that standing on a corner and selling it was a good and reasonable choice, and where the reeling community around them would be least able to keep them in check.[43]

40. Ibid., 80.

41. "Collective efficacy" is originally the term of Robert Sampson and colleagues. See Robert J. Sampson, Stephen W. Raudenbush, and Felton Earls, "Neighborhoods and Violent Crime: A Multilevel Study of Collective Efficacy," *Science* 277 (August 1997): 918–24.

42. David Kennedy, *Don't Shoot: One Man, A Street Fellowship, and the End of Violence in Inner-City America* (New York: Bloomsbury, 2011).

43. Ibid., 142. For ethnographic descriptions of life in these neighborhoods and the tensions between the numerically predominant law-abiding residents and the relatively few residents engaged in illegal activities, see Mary Pattillo McCoy, *Black Picket Fences: Privilege and Peril among the Black Middle Class*

Although young white and black men commit crime at roughly the same rates (with the exception of serious violent offenses) the dynamics within jobless ghettos enable violent, property, and especially drug offenses to take place in the open, in abandoned buildings and dilapidated street corners. Arrests of young black men in these neighborhoods are then also much easier for police, particularly when compared with the challenges of enforcing drug laws when the suburban trade takes place behind the closed doors of ranch houses. These neighborhoods easily become seen as the core of a "crime problem" in the United States, and their images can be easily manipulated to support a "war on crime" or a "war on drugs" that demonizes their residents.

With the spread of ghettos and the increasing isolation of their residents, the perception that "bad neighborhoods" are getting worse has perhaps exacerbated the sense of anxiety about law and order in our society. Sociologist Paul Jargowsky summarizes the effects of this perception:

> The geographic size of a city's ghetto has a large effect on the perception of the magnitude of the problem associated with ghetto poverty. How big an area of the city do you consider off limits? How far out of your way will you drive not to go through a dangerous area?[44]

The spread of ghettos and the isolation of their residents make it easier to point to these "bad neighborhoods" as hotbeds of crime, especially when we add racial, ethnic, and class stereotypes about criminality to the mix. People living outside these neighborhoods—perhaps particularly people working in law enforcement—come to see the residents of these communities as irredeemably bad. No one can be trusted; everyone is a criminal, or at least, a potential criminal. When operating on these assumptions, the best thing to do seems to be to stop and search anyone who seems suspicious (that is, anyone who is young, black, and male) and to arrest anyone who commits even the slightest infraction. Kennedy critically summarizes the response of our criminal justice systems to residents of jobless ghettos: "all we can do is occupy them, stop everybody, arrest everybody we can . . . send all the men to prison."[45]

(Chicago: University of Chicago Press, 1999) and Elijah Anderson, *Code of the Street: Decency, Violence, and the Moral Life of the Inner City* (New York: Norton, 1999).

44. Quoted in Wilson, *When Work Disappears*, 14–15.

45. Kennedy, *Don't Shoot*, 18.

never political issue! *POLITICAL FACTORS*

The economic factors rooted in the deindustrialization of our inner cities have helped to feed political agents touting "tough on crime" policies since at least the early 1970s. Political efforts to combat crime were furthered also by the cultural and social phenomena of a growing sense of anxiety about crime and the rejection of rehabilitation as a viable response to crime. Cultural, social, economic, and political factors thus coalesced in the early 1970s into forces for more punitive criminal justice systems.

Prior to 1964, crime had never been a significant political issue, especially on the national stage. It had been viewed as a local problem with local solutions. Barry Goldwater introduced this issue to national politics in his 1964 presidential campaign, running ads that called for political leaders "to restore proper respect for law and order in this country."[46] Despite Goldwater's loss, Richard Nixon picked up the call to address "crime in the streets" in his 1968 run for the presidency. He replaced Lyndon Johnson's war on poverty with new wars on crime and drugs. Other conservative Republicans followed Nixon's lead, viewing the "tough on crime" stance with its often thinly veiled racial rhetoric as part of a winning platform for wooing disaffected southern Democrats to the party. In all levels of government, but especially in the states, Republican political leadership resulted in more punitive criminal justice systems: "There is strong evidence that imprisonment rates have grown faster under Republican governors. Accounting for state effects shows that imprisonment rates are about 14 percent higher under Republicans than under Democrats."[47] Not to be outdone, Democrats joined the charge against crime and drugs, especially after the failure of Michael Dukakis's 1988 presidential bid, which was brought down by George H. W. Bush's infamous Willie Horton advertising campaign. Bill Clinton then declared in his own campaign, following the execution of Ricky Ray Rector in Arkansas in the weeks before for the New Hampshire primary, that he refused to be outflanked on the right by accusations of being soft on crime. At least since the early 1990s, both political parties have fully waged battles in the wars on crime and drugs in order to win votes.

Mass incarceration emerged from the convergence of these social, cultural, economic, and political factors. Several specific policies, enacted on both state and federal levels, combined to create our crisis of criminal justice. To be clear:

46. To see some of Barry Goldwater's campaign advertising, see the archive of presidential television campaigns from Eisenhower to Obama at the Museum of the Living Image website, under the title "The Livingroom Candidate," http://www.livingroomcandidate.org/.

47. Western, *Punishment and Inequality*, 71.

this crisis is the result primarily not of high crime rates, but of policy decisions to which politicians, academics, criminal justice professionals, and voters have consented. Among these policies are mandatory minimum and determinate sentences that have replaced indeterminate sentences, which provided judges and parole boards more freedom to respond to the particular circumstances of each case.[48] First instituted in New York with the passage of the Rockefeller Drug Laws in 1973, by the mid-1990s, thirty-five other states and the federal government had enacted mandatory minimum sentences. The demise of indeterminate sentencing also brought about the end of the parole board in many states, beginning with Maine in 1976. By 2000, thirty-three states had eliminated or abolished parole. Many states also created sentencing commissions that established sentencing guidelines based on the severity of offense and an offender's criminal history alone. These guidelines limited the power of judges to respond to mitigating circumstances for individual offenders, increasing the severity of punishment in many cases. By the early 1990s, twenty-two states and the federal government had sentencing guidelines established by such commissions (the federal guidelines were found unconstitutional by the U.S. Supreme Court in 2005). Other policies such as three-strikes and truth-in-sentencing laws followed.

Together these policies resulted in greater likelihood of being incarcerated upon conviction and of being sentenced to a longer prison term. Even though most of these policies have no explicit racial or class-based prejudices, they resulted in greater disparities in sentencing, with young, poor black men more likely to be caught up in our criminal justice systems. Most of these disparities are the result of police disproportionately arresting black people for drug crimes in comparison with whites and relative to their actual involvement in drug use and trade. Furthermore, black people arrested for drug crimes are more likely than whites to be convicted and imprisoned.[49] Since most of the crime policies developed over the last forty years primarily focus on creating more punitive responses to drug crimes, these policies exacerbate the problems with arrest, conviction, and sentencing, thus generating a crisis in these systems.

Beneath this crisis lies a failure to treat all members of our society as fully human persons and to ensure that each person in our society has the resources

48. Both sides of the political spectrum criticized indeterminate sentencing. On the right, indeterminate sentencing was viewed as too soft on crime. On the left, critics worried that indeterminate sentencing offered few protections against the biases of judges and parole boards. Both sides thought that determinate sentencing was preferable because it more consistently punished offenders—but the two sides worried about inconsistency in sentencing for very different reasons.

49. See Tonry, *Punishing Race*, 47–52, 67–76.

necessary to participate in the dignity, unity, and equality of all people. Racial, ethnic, and class disparities evident in these factors fuel the crisis of our criminal justice systems. That is, our criminal justice crisis reflects a crisis of social justice in our society. But further and in turn: our criminal justice crisis also helps sustain a social justice crisis that marginalizes, disempowers, and endangers our neighbors.

EFFECTS OF CRIMINAL JUSTICE ON SOCIAL JUSTICE

Despite the problems of social justice underlying our criminal justice crisis, one argument for maintaining, or even augmenting, our incarceration rates might be that a more punitive response helps to decrease crime. Advocates of this position often cite the drop in crime rates since the 1990s as evidence that despite all of the problems, our criminal justice systems make the majority of us safer. From this perspective, the relationship between social and criminal justice may be irrelevant if incarcerating more people can improve the quality of life for the rest of us. Of course, incarcerating certain people does make us safer and helps to combat crime. Putting a serial killer in prison does ensure that fewer people will be murdered and is likely the best course of action available. However, putting in prison a man who got in a bar fight or a boy who sells drugs on the street corner does not necessarily mean that barroom brawls will be deterred or that another boy will not take over the neighborhood drug trade. Although our use of prisons often has been justified by theories of deterrence and incapacitation, prisons do not deter or incapacitate offenders in uniform or necessarily effective ways.[50] Most evidence suggests that while

50. On the effectiveness of incarceration for *deterring* crime, see Robert Apel and Daniel S. Nagin, "General Deterrence: A Review of Recent Evidence," in *Crime and Public Policy*, ed. Wilson and Petersilia, 411–36; Anthony N. Doob and Cheryl Marie Webster, "Sentence Severity and Crime: Accepting the Null Hypothesis," in *Crime and Justice: A Review of Research*, ed. Tonry, 30:143–95; Don M. Gottfredson, "Effects of Judges Sentencing Decisions on Criminal Careers," in *NIJ Research in Brief* (Washington, DC: U.S. Department of Justice, 1999); Timothy A. Hughes, Doris James Wilson, and Allen J. Beck, *Reentry Trends in the United States: Inmates Returning to the Community After Spending Time in Prison* (Washington, DC: Bureau of Justice Statistics, 2006); Patrick Langan and David Levin, *Recidivism in Prisoners Released in 1994* (Washington, DC: Bureau of Justice Statistics, 2002); Paula Smith, Claire Goggin, and Paul Gendreau, *The Effects of Prison Sentences and Intermediate Sanctions on Recidivism: General Effects and Individual Differences* (Ottawa: Public Works and Government Services of Canada, 2002); and Michael Tonry, "Learning from the Limits of Deterrence Research," *Crime and Justice* 37, no. 1 (2008): 279–311. On the effectiveness of incarceration for *incapacitation*, see Raymond V. Liedka, Anne Morrison Piehl, and Bert Useem, "The Crime-Control Effect of Incarceration: Does Scale Matter?" *Criminology and Public Policy* 5 (2006): 245–76; Alex R. Piquero and Alfred Blumstein, "Does

prison may deter some offenders from committing crime in the future, or at least, incapacitate them for the present, the effects of prison on crime rates are minimal. Sociologist Bruce Western found that at best 10 percent of the drop in crime rates between 1993 and 2001 could be explained by increased incarceration.[51] The remaining 90 percent could be explained by factors such as a booming economy, declines of crack cocaine markets, lesser prevalence of drug use, changes in policing practices toward "community policing," and what is called the "younger-sibling effect," in which young people growing up in the 1980s rejected the criminal paths of their elders.[52] Moreover, while incarceration has minimal deterrent and incapacitative effects, the experience of prison may in fact be criminogenic.[53] People leaving prison may be more likely to commit crime upon release than if they had experienced other responses to their wrongdoing because prison itself can foster crime. The ineffectiveness of incarceration for most offenders should concern us because most of the people in prison are not serial killers who will spend the rest of their lives behind bars. Rather, most people in prison committed nonviolent property or drug crimes, and 95 percent—currently over 600,000 people per year—will return to our communities.[54]

At the same time, our extreme reliance on incarceration and other punitive responses to crime helps sustain, and even worsens, problems of social justice in our society. Putting people in prison costs money. In fiscal year 2009, the states spent $52.3 billion on corrections, more than four times what they spent in 1987, $12 billion.[55] If not for severe revenue shortfalls due to the recession, the costs would likely have been much larger; spending on corrections grew

Incapacitation Reduce Crime?" *Journal of Quantitative Criminology* 23, no. 4 (2007): 267–85; William Spelman, "The Limited Importance of Prison Expansion," in *The Crime Drop in America*, ed. Alfred Blumstein and Joel Walman (New York: Cambridge University Press, 2000), 97–129; and Franklin E. Zimring and Gordon Hawkins, *Incapacitation: Penal Confinement and the Restraint of Crime* (New York: Oxford University Press, 1995).

51. Western, *Punishment and Inequality*, especially chapter 7. See also Clear, *Imprisoning Communities*, chapter 2 and Mauer, *Race to Incarcerate*, chapters 5 and 6.

52. For a thorough discussion of each of these factors, see Mauer, *Race to Incarcerate*, 98–112.

53. Tonry, "Learning from the Limits of Deterrence Research," 279–311.

54. For a full discussion of prisoner reentry, see Jeremy Travis, *But They All Come Back: Facing the Challenges of Prisoner Reentry* (Washington, DC: Urban Institute Press, 2005).

55. For information on current state expenditures, see National Association of State Budget Officers, *State Expenditure Report: Fiscal Year 2009* (Washington, DC: NASBO, 2010). For an overview of past expenditures see "One in 100: Behind Bars in America," Pew Center on the States, http://www.pewcenteronthestates.org/uploadedFiles/
8015PCTS_Prison08_FINAL_2-1-1_FORWEB.pdf.

6.2 percent in fiscal year 2008, but only 0.9 percent in fiscal year 2009.[56] Beyond the budget allowances for corrections, understanding the true costs of mass incarceration must also account for lost opportunities. The money spent on corrections by our federal and state governments cannot be spent on other measures that may be more effective at improving our communities and ensuring that each member of our society has access to resources necessary for achieving their full human personhood. On average, states spent 6.8 percent more of their general fund dollars on corrections in fiscal year 2007 than they did twenty years earlier. As the portion of state budgets devoted to corrections has increased, less money has been spent on other expenditures such as higher and early childhood education and public health. Moreover, as a larger portion of corrections budgets has been devoted to prisons, fewer dollars could be directed to alternatives, such as mental healthcare, substance abuse treatment, or community corrections, which are often more effective than prison at reducing recidivism and making our communities safer. We have made our prisons more robust while decreasing the viability of other social institutions that better foster the dignity, unity, and equality of all of our community members.

PERMANENT EXCLUSION OF EX-PRISONERS

Aside from financial costs, our criminal justice crisis has severe consequences for the lives of ex-prisoners, including limited employment and educational opportunities, exacerbated poverty, and loss of civil rights. While people entering prison often have poor employment records, their work possibilities are even more limited upon release. These limitations are caused by many factors, including employers' unwillingness to hire former offenders, especially in financial and service sectors and with jobs that involve direct customer contact; the stagnation of prisoners' work skills while locked up; and the loss of networks outside of prison that could help ex-prisoners find and hold a job.[57] Because of these barriers, most ex-prisoners enter a secondary labor market characterized by temporary, insecure, and low-income work that provides little opportunity for advancement. As a result, ex-prisoners' hourly wages are about 15 percent lower than their wages prior to imprisonment, and their annual earnings are reduced by 30 to 40 percent. Furthermore, their wage growth

56. See NASBO, *State Expenditure Report.*

57. Harry J. Holzer, Steven Raphael, and Michael A. Stoll, "Will Employers Hire Former Offenders?: Employer Preferences, Background Checks, and Their Determinants," in *Imprisoning America: The Social Effects of Mass Imprisonment*, ed. Mary Pattillo, David Weiman, and Bruce Western (New York: Russell Sage Foundation, 2004), 205–43.

over time is stagnant.[58] These effects are long-lasting. Youth detained in a correctional facility before age twenty experience higher unemployment and receive lower wages than their peers ten years after incarceration. Ex-prisoners lose about 40 percent of their lifetime incomes due to the ongoing effects of incarceration. Among African-American men, these effects have increased poverty rates by as much as 4 percent. The effects of incarceration on the employment opportunities of ex-prisoners constitute a hidden cost of our crisis of criminal justice: "The lifetime lost earnings that results from a prison record doubles the cost of incarceration measured by correctional budgets,"[59] as ex-prisoners are less able to support themselves and to contribute to their families, communities, and society.

Not only do ex-prisoners experience fewer and worse employment opportunities and higher rates of poverty due to incarceration, several policy decisions in recent years inhibit their abilities to escape these deleterious effects. The 1994 Violent Crime Control and Law Enforcement Act abolished prisoner access to Pell Grants, which had previously been used to provide higher education to people while in prison. People convicted of felony drug crimes cannot receive federal financial aid for higher education after release from prison. Following the 1996 Personal Responsibility and Work Opportunity Reconciliation Act, they also lost access to welfare benefits and food stamps. Such policy measures decrease the likelihood that ex-prisoners will be able to build a life outside of crime, particularly as these bans also decrease access to substance abuse treatment (welfare benefits traditionally had been used to pay for room and board in rehabilitation facilities). The 1996 Housing Opportunity Program Extension Act and the 1998 Quality Housing and Work Responsibility Act further limited access to public housing for people with criminal records—and anyone, such as their children, who might live with them. Together these policies establish several roadblocks for people who have

58. Western, *Punishment and Inequality*, 108–30. See also Richard B. Freeman, "Crime and the Employment of Disadvantaged Youth," in *Urban Labor Markets and Job Opportunity*, ed. George Peterson and Wayne Vroman (Washington, DC: Urban Institute Press, 1992); John Hagan and Ronit Dinovitzer, "Collateral Consequences of Imprisonment for Children, Communities, and Prisoners," in *Prisons*, ed. Tonry and Petersilia, 121–62; Bruce Western and Katherine Beckett, "How Unregulated Is the U.S. Labor Market? The Penal System as a Labor Market Institution," *American Journal of Sociology* 104 (1999): 1030–60; Bruce Western, Jeffrey R. Kling, and David F. Weiman, "The Labor Market Consequences of Incarceration," *Crime and Delinquency* 47 (2001): 410–27; and Bruce Western, Becky Pettit, and Josh Guetzkow, "Black Economic Progress in the Era of Mass Imprisonment," in *Invisible Punishment: The Collateral Consequences of Mass Imprisonment*, ed. Marc Mauer and Meda Chesney-Lind (New York: New Press, 2002), 165–80.

59. Western, *Punishment and Inequality*, 129.

been released from prison and who want to improve their situations through employment, education, drug or alcohol treatment, or access to safe and affordable housing. For ex-prisoners, especially those convicted of drug crimes, there is no social safety net.[60]

In addition to these effects, most prisoners experience a loss of civil rights, and for many of them, this loss continues even after completing their sentences. Forty-eight states, excluding Maine and Vermont, do not allow people in prison to vote. Thirty-five disenfranchise felons on parole, and thirty-one disenfranchise felons on probation. Twelve states permit disenfranchisement of people with felony records for periods after they have completed their sentences; four states disenfranchise ex-prisoners for life. Disenfranchisement policies for ex-prisoners make the United States exceptional among industrialized Western democracies; no other similar nation disenfranchises ex-prisoners for any period, let alone for life. The result of these policies is that currently about 5.85 million Americans do not have the right to vote, 2.6 million of whom have completed their criminal sentences and 2.23 million of whom are African-American men. Three out of ten of the next generation of African-American men can expect to be disenfranchised at some point in their lifetimes.[61] Disenfranchisement policies, along with the practice of counting prisoners in the U.S. Census toward the districts where they are imprisoned rather than the districts from where they came, contribute to the underrepresentation in government of urban areas, particularly those most harmed by poverty. Census and disenfranchisement policies have also likely affected the outcomes of elections. Sociologists Christopher Uggen and Jeff Manza have surmised that disenfranchisement laws affected the outcomes of at least seven U.S. Senate races between 1970 and 1998, preventing Democratic control of the Senate from 1986 to 2000. Allowing ex-felons permanently disenfranchised in Florida to vote probably would have changed the outcome of the 2000 presidential election.[62] While disenfranchisement laws limit the civil

60. For a more detailed discussion of these policies, see Gwen Rubinstein and Debbie Mukamal, "Welfare and Housing: Denial of Benefits to Drug Offenders," in *Invisible Punishment*, ed. Mauer and Chesney-Lind, 37–49.

61. "Felony Disenfranchisement Laws in the United States," The Sentencing Project, http://www.sentencingproject.org/doc/publications/fd_bs_fdlawsinusMar11.pdf.

62. Christopher Uggen and Jeff Manza, "Lost Voices: The Civic and Political Views of Disenfranchised Felons," in *Imprisoning America*, ed. Pattillo, Weiman, and Western, 165–204. See also Elizabeth A. Hull, *The Disenfranchisement of Ex-Felons* (Philadelphia: Temple University Press, 2006); Marc Mauer, "Mass Imprisonment and the Disappearing Voters," in *Invisible Punishment*, ed. Mauer and Chesney-Lind, 50–58; Christopher Uggen and Jeff Manza, *Locked Out: Felon Disenfranchisement and American Democracy* (New York: Oxford University Press, 2008); and Christopher Uggen and Michelle

rights of many prisoners and ex-prisoners, they affect all Americans, as the voices of the citizenry as a whole are not taken into full account.

HARMING FAMILIES

Beyond the effects of incarceration on the lives of individual prisoners, even after being released, our turn to punitiveness in our criminal justice systems also affects the families that prisoners leave behind. Admittedly, these effects on families are not necessarily unidirectional. The incarceration of an abusive, disruptive, or neglectful family member may result overall in positive outcomes for a family. However, in the majority of cases, the removal of a family member has serious negative consequences for other family members, especially the children of the incarcerated. Indeed, family members may suffer more because of incarceration than prisoners do. Sociologist Donald Braman, reflecting on ethnographic interviews with children of prisoners, writes, "The dramatic increase in the use of incarceration over the last two decades has in many ways missed its mark, injuring the families of prisoners often as much as and sometimes more than criminal offenders themselves."[63]

Of course, as incarceration rates have increased, so have the numbers of people left behind in our communities. At midyear 2007, 52 percent of state prisoners and 63 percent of federal prisoners reported having minor children.[64] An estimated 1.7 million minor children, or 2.3 percent of the U.S. population under eighteen years of age, have a parent in prison. Over the last two decades, the number of parents in state and federal prison increased 79 percent, and the number of minor children with incarcerated parents increased 80 percent. The majority of parents in prison are fathers, but just as growth in the rate of incarceration of women has outpaced growth in the rate for men, so has the growth in the number of mothers in prison outpaced that of fathers. Since 1991, the number of children with mothers in prison has risen 131 percent, while that of children with fathers in prison has risen 77 percent. The effects of racial and ethnic disparities in our criminal justice systems can also be seen in the

Inderbitzin, "The Price and the Promise of Citizenship: Extending the Vote to Nonincarcerated Felons," in *Contemporary Issues in Criminal Justice Policy: Policy Proposals from the American Society of Criminology Conference*, ed. Natasha A. Frost, Joshua D. Freilich, and Todd R. Clear (Belmont, CA: Cengage/ Wadsworth, 2010), 61–68.

63. Donald Braman, "Families and Incarceration," in *Invisible Punishment*, ed. Mauer and Chesney-Lind, 118.

64. Lauren E. Glaze and Laura M. Maruschak, "Parents in Prison and Their Minor Children," Bureau of Justice Statistics, U.S. Department of Justice, http://bjs.ojp.usdoj.gov/content/pub/pdf/pptmc.pdf.

populations of children with parents in prison. Black children at midyear 2007 were seven-and-a-half times more likely than white children to have a parent in prison, and Hispanic children were more than two-and-a-half times more likely than white children to have a parent in prison. Most parents in prison committed nonviolent drug or property offenses, not violent crimes.

The effects of incarceration on families and children are difficult to parse, and the research on this topic has been limited. On one hand, research on the effects of incarceration has focused more on issues such as recidivism than on families and children. On the other hand, many factors that might contribute to the incarceration of a family member, such as poverty, mental illness, or substance abuse, may have similar effects on families and children as incarceration. This overlap makes it difficult to say that incarceration of a family member is itself the direct cause of any difficulties with families or children of prisoners. In addition, the complexity of family dynamics makes it difficult to draw straightforward conclusions. For example, family arrangements before, during, and after incarceration shape the effects of incarceration. A child who lived with her mother prior to her mother's arrest, who was placed in foster care with strangers and separated from her siblings during her mother's incarceration, and who returned to her mother only after long-fought custody battles might face a certain set of likely outcomes. A child who lived with both of his parents prior to his father's arrest, who stayed with his mother and siblings during his father's time in prison, and who welcomed his father home after release would face another set of likely outcomes. Add other factors such as ages of children, parental involvement before incarceration, and histories of abuse or neglect, substance abuse, poverty, relational conflict, and mental illness, and it becomes increasingly challenging to say much with certainty about the effects of incarceration on the family members of people in prison.

Nevertheless, some common or likely effects can be deduced from available data and various theoretical frameworks for understanding family structure and child development. For example, the majority of families with an incarcerated parent will probably experience greater poverty while the parent is in prison, and in all likelihood, after the parent is released as well. About half of parents in prison (52 percent of mothers and 54 percent of fathers) provided the primary financial support for their children prior to incarceration.[65] While their parents are in prison, children—and their caretakers—lose this source of economic support. As shown above, the earning potential of ex-prisoners is greatly decreased after incarceration. Lower levels of economic support for children of prisoners thus probably continue even after their parents have

65. Ibid.

completed their sentences. Family members of prisoners may also experience a loss of emotional support as well as greater social stigma from extended family, friends, neighbors, school officials, co-workers, employers, and others who learn about their family member's incarceration. This stigma may make it less likely that struggling families seek needed assistance from others and may increase their sense of isolation, humiliation, and shame.

Incarceration may also contribute to difficulties in maintaining familial relationships with imprisoned family members as well as to disruption of family organization. Several barriers make it challenging to remain in contact with someone in prison, including the high cost of collect phone calls from prisons, inconvenient visiting hours, invasive security procedures, and long distances between a prisoner's family home and the prison. The last barrier may be particularly onerous for incarcerated mothers and their families as fewer women's prisons means that women in prison are on average much farther from home (about 160 more miles) than men in prison.[66] With difficulties in maintaining regular contact, prisoners may find that their roles within their families, especially as parents, change. They have little direct say over the day-to-day rearing of their children. Children's caretakers may become gatekeepers of the relationship between parent and child as they must determine whether and how often to visit or to accept collect phone calls. Parents may miss important milestones in their children's lives, including first steps, first days of school, or first dates, and children may miss the guidance of caring adults in their lives as they reach these milestones. For fathers in prison, contact with their children often depends on remaining in good relationship with their children's mothers. However, even controlling for demographic characteristics, economic variables, relationship skills, and fathers' potential history with violence and substance abuse, incarcerated men are much less likely to remain in good relationship with the mothers of their children than men who have not.[67] In some cases, those in which parents may have been abusive, disruptive, or neglectful, these barriers may provide welcome respite for fragile families. In

66. Jeremy Travis and Michelle Waul, "Prisoners Once Removed: The Children and Family of Prisoners," in *Prisoners Once Removed: The Impact of Incarceration and Reentry on Children, Families, and Communities*, ed. Jeremy Travis and Michelle Waul (Washington, DC: Urban Institute Press, 2003), 20.

67. Bruce Western, Leonard M. Lopoo, and Sara McLanahan, "Incarceration and the Bonds between Parents in Fragile Families," in *Imprisoning America*, ed. Pattillo, Weiman, and Western, 21–45. See also Kathryn Edin, Timothy J. Nelson, and Rechelle Paranal, "Fatherhood and Incarceration as Potential Turning Points in the Criminal Careers of Unskilled Men," in *Imprisoning America*, ed. Pattillo, Weiman, and Western, 46–75.

other cases, these broken relationships between parents and children may have long-term negative consequences.

Most of these negative consequences are borne by the children of incarcerated parents. Some of these outcomes may be the result, in part, of belonging to any family struggling with poverty or the mental illness or substance abuse of a family member, but they may also be attributed to the incarceration of a parent. They may also vary with the developmental age of the child. Nonetheless, Jeremy Travis and Michelle Waul draw on literature on child development and trauma to try to understand how children might respond to the incarceration of a parent, and conclude, "*Children always experience the loss of a parent as a traumatic event*, regardless of the circumstances surrounding the parent's departure (death, divorce, moving away, or incarceration)."[68] Parental incarceration can then be linked to the effects of trauma on a child, including lowered self-esteem, depression, emotional withdrawal, inappropriate or disruptive behaviors, and the inability to form attachments with others. Depending on the developmental age of the child, incarceration of a parent could also be related to separation anxiety, survivor guilt, developmental regression, inability to cope with future trauma, rejection of behavioral boundaries, and intergenerational crime and incarceration.[69] With these effects on children, our punitive turn with incarceration may be helping to create a new generation of young people who are likely to face time behind bars, just as their parents did.

---

68. Travis and Waul, "Prisoners Once Removed," 16. Emphasis in original.

69. See Travis, *But They All Come Back*, chapter 6, especially p. 141. For more on effects of incarceration on children and families, see Donald Braman and Jennifer Wood, "From One Generation to the Next: How Criminal Sanctions Are Reshaping Family Life in Urban America," in *Prisoners Once Removed*, ed. Travis and Waul, 157–88; Hagan and Dinovitzer (1999); Creasie Finney Hairston, "Prisoners and Their Families: Parenting Issues during Incarceration," in *Prisoners Once Removed*, ed. Travis and Waul, 259–82; Elizabeth I. Johnson and Jane Waldfogel, "Children of Incarcerated Parents: Multiple Risks and Children's Living Arrangements," in *Imprisoning America*, ed. Pattillo, Weiman, and Western, 97–131; Anne M. Nurse, "Returning to Strangers: Newly Paroled Young Fathers and Their Children," in *Imprisoning America*, ed. Pattillo, Weiman, and Western, 76–96; Ross D. Parke and K. Alison Clarke-Stewart, "The Effects of Parental Incarceration on Children: Perspectives, Promises, and Policies," in *Prisoners Once Removed*, ed. Travis and Waul, 189–232; Beth E. Richie, "The Social Impact of Mass Imprisonment on Women," in *Invisible Punishment*, ed. Mauer and Chesney-Lind, 136–49; and Western, *Punishment and Inequality*, chapter 6.

THE BREAKDOWN OF COMMUNITIES

When the effects of incarceration on individuals and families are considered in aggregate, it becomes apparent that incarceration also affects the well-being of whole communities, especially when we tend to concentrate incarceration on the residents of just a few impoverished, minority, urban neighborhoods. One of the assumptions about the use of incarceration in response to crime is that it accomplishes a sort of "addition by subtracting."[70] That is, by removing unwanted elements from a community, that community is improved. In recent years, as the effects of mass incarceration have been concentrated on just a few communities, many scholars have begun asking whether this formulation can be so simple. The communities from which people in prison come and to which they return are not evenly distributed across the landscape. Most often people in prison come from and return to those counties that contain the central city of a metropolitan area.[71] Within those cities, they come from and return to the most vulnerable and impoverished neighborhoods, those neighborhoods in which concentrated disadvantage leaves few resources and little resiliency among residents—the jobless ghettos, in Wilson's terminology. Some of these neighborhoods have as many as one in four adult male residents in jail or prison on any given day and one in eight adult male residents entering jail or prison in any given year.[72] As a result, these neighborhoods experience constant flux among their residents, adding instability to already tenuous community dynamics. The concentration of mass incarceration, increased use of prisons and jails, may actually have adverse effects on communities.

Criminologist Todd Clear, along with his colleague Dina Rose, has led the way over the last decade in trying to understand the effects of concentrating mass incarceration on particular communities.[73] He argues, "Concentrated incarceration in . . . impoverished communities has broken families, weakened the social-control capacity of parents, eroded economic strength, soured

70. Todd R. Clear, "The Problem with 'Addition by Subtraction': The Prison-Crime Relationship in Low-Income Communities," in *Invisible Punishment*, ed. Mauer andChesney-Lind, 181–93.

71. Travis, *But They All Come Back*, 281.

72. Clear, "Addition by Subtraction."

73. Ibid. Also, Dina R. Rose and Todd R. Clear, "Incarceration, Social Capital, and Crime: Examining the Unintended Consequences of Incarceration," *Criminology* 36, no. 3 (1998): 441–79; Dina R. Rose and Todd R. Clear, "Incarceration, Reentry, and Social Capital: Social Networks in the Balance," in *Prisoners Once Removed*, ed. Travis and Waul, 313–42; Todd R. Clear, Dina R. Rose, Elin Waring, and Kristen Scully, "Coercive Mobility and Crime: A Preliminary Investigation of Concentrated Incarceration and Social Disorganization," *Justice Quarterly* 20, no. 1 (2003): 33–64; Todd R. Clear, *Imprisoning Communities*; and Todd R. Clear, "The Effects of Higher Imprisonment Rates on Communities," *Crime and Justice* 37, no. 1 (2008): 97–132.

attitudes toward society, and distorted politics; even, after reaching a certain level, it has increased rather than decreased crime."[74] To support their argument connecting concentrated incarceration to higher crime rates, Clear and Rose draw upon the social disorganization theory of Shaw and McKay described above. According to this theory, lack of human and social capital along with sparse social networks results in communities that struggle with high levels of poverty, ethnic heterogeneity, and residential mobility having lessened collective efficacy in addressing problems and lessened informal social control over their residents. These factors contribute to social disorganization that decreases the capacity of the majority of residents who are law-abiding to work together to control crime or to call on the resources of law enforcement outside of the community for help. Clear and Rose add to this model the insight that the concentration of mass incarceration, with its constant movement of people in and out of jails and prisons, in and out of the same neighborhoods, entails a sort of "coercive mobility" that may worsen the dynamics of social disorganization, and therefore, increase crime in certain communities.

The viability of Clear and Rose's hypothesis is still under test. While they have found some evidence supporting it in studies done in Tallahassee, James Lynch and William Sabol have found only mixed results in their studies of Baltimore neighborhoods.[75] Currently the Collaborative Project on Concentrated Incarceration is testing the hypothesis in ten other cities. About this project, Jeremy Travis, the president of John Jay College of Criminal Justice, observes,

> If the replication studies confirm the original findings, then our country will have to face a sobering reality. Not only has our national experiment in the increased use in incarceration resulted in profound harms to individual prisoners, their families, their communities, the pursuit of racial justice, and our democracy, but a primary rationale for these policies—that they would reduce crime—has turned out to be flawed.[76]

It may be the case not only that prisons do not reduce crime rates and may in fact be criminogenic in individual instances, but also that the concentrated use of imprisonment on residents of certain neighborhoods creates the social

74. Clear, *Imprisoning Communities*, 5.

75. James P. Lynch and William J. Sabol, "Effects of Incarceration on Informal Social Control in Communities," in *Imprisoning America*, ed. Pattillo, Weiman, and Western, 135–64.

76. Travis, *But They All Come Back*, 299.

conditions that foster more crime within the communities that prisoners leave behind.

Even if the argument that concentrated incarceration may lead to higher crime rates ultimately cannot be proven, many other negative effects of mass incarceration on communities remain. Negative effects on families add up to have aggregate effects on their neighborhoods. The concentration of mass incarceration contributes to neighborhoods with many more women than men as the male population cycles in and out of jail and prison. Those men that are around the neighborhood often do not seem like "marriage material," especially if they have criminal records, thereby lessening long-term, stable relationship prospects for young women and contributing to their toleration of inappropriate and even harmful relationships. Men in these circumstances may be less committed to building long-term relationships with women, given the larger number of women available to them. These dynamics between men and women may result in increased rates of sexually transmitted infections, unplanned pregnancy, and domestic violence.[77] Women with children are more vulnerable to the loss of financial and emotional support from their partners, contributing to more family instability, which in turn leads to increased risks of poor school performance by children and contact with juvenile justice systems. As long-term relationships and marriage can contribute to withdrawal from criminal activity for men, one effect of the disproportionate number of women compared to men in communities marked by concentrated incarceration may be higher rates of recidivism. The lack of income from two parents may lead to higher poverty rates. Furthermore, the absence of men limits adult supervision of young people in a neighborhood and may result in fewer role models for children. Of course, some of these men may not always be the best role models for children, but they may make some positive contributions to their communities as well, such as escorting vulnerable people in the neighborhood, serving as guards, and discouraging truancy.[78]

The concentration of mass incarceration also affects the economic viability of a community. Time in prison or jail depletes human capital, making it more

77. Rucker C. Johnson and Steven Raphael, *The Effects of Male Incarceration on Dynamics of AIDS Infection Rates Among African-American Women and Men* (Berkeley: Goldman School of Public Policy, University of California, 2005); and James C. Thomas and Elizabeth Torrone, "Incarceration as Forced Migration: Effects on Select Community Health Outcomes," *American Journal of Public Health* 96, no. 10 (2005): 1–5.

78. Sudhir Alladi Venkatesh, "The Social Organization of Street Gang Activity in an Urban Ghetto," *American Journal of Sociology* 103, no. 1 (1997): 82–111. Also, Pattillo McCoy, *Black Picket Fences*; and Anderson, *Code of the Street*.

difficult for people to succeed in the labor market after release. When people leaving jail or prison return to only a few neighborhoods that are already weak economically, fewer residents of these communities as a whole are able to find and retain jobs. As a result, more families are impoverished and may become dependent on welfare, which in turn leads to greater isolation of women with children from wider society. Because many people who go to prison engage in both legal and illegal work prior to incarceration, their removal results in the loss of legitimate workers from the economy. With the loss of legitimate adult workers, young people in those communities may lose access to jobs as they lose contacts with potential mentors as well as links with the working world. Moreover, if the concentration of mass incarceration does contribute to higher crime rates, then it may also contribute to lower property values, decreasing the wealth of a community overall and the likelihood that people would invest in a neighborhood. Mass imprisonment therefore may make already bad conditions in hyper-, or jobless, ghettos much worse.

Beyond these economic problems, the weakened political clout of these neighborhoods caused by disenfranchisement policies and the divvying of governmental representation based on U.S. Census data (again, in which prisoners are counted toward where they are incarcerated rather than where they are from) decreases the likelihood that residents will be able to change these conditions on their own. Prisoners are counted in the Census where they are imprisoned, resulting in the population of the communities where they come from being undercounted. The population of communities that have prisons, in turn, is exaggerated, while a large number of people in these communities cannot vote and have interests that lie in other political jurisdictions. "Prison-based gerrymandering" dilutes the political power of communities with a large number of residents who have been incarcerated while boosting the political power of communities that have prisons, affecting municipal, county, state, and federal elections.[79] Added to this lack of representation is lessened collective efficacy, caused by social disorganization in jobless ghettos. Without the social cohesion within a neighborhood necessary to work together for the common good, residents of these communities often are not empowered to demand

79. The effects of prison-based gerrymandering are best documented by the Prison Policy Initiative. See "Prisoners of the Census," Prison Policy Initiative, http://www.prisonersofthecensus.org/; and "Prisoners and the Census Count," Redrawing the Lines, http://www.redrawingthelines.org/prisonersthecensuscount. See also Eric Lotke and Peter Wagner, "Prisoners of the Census: Electoral and Financial Consequences of Counting Prisoners Where They Go, Not Where They Come From," *Pace Law Review* 24, no. 587 (2004): 587–607; and Peter Wagner, "Breaking the Census: Redistricting in an Era of Mass Incarceration," *William Mitchell Law Review* 38, no. 4 (2012): 1241–60.

more from their government and to address the problems they face because of the overlapping effects of concentrated poverty and the concentration of mass incarceration.

WHAT TYPE OF SOCIETY DO WE WISH TO CREATE?

The effects of mass incarceration in the United States on individuals, families, and communities have helped sustain, and even worsen, a social justice crisis that marginalizes, disempowers, and endangers our neighbors. Mass incarceration not only reflects social injustice; it also contributes to conditions in which some members of our society (and not only prisoners) are not treated as fully human persons and are not vested with the resources necessary to participate in the dignity, unity, and equality of all people. Those people who are excluded from the common good of our society due to our justice crises are disproportionately members of racial or ethnic minority groups from socioeconomically disadvantaged backgrounds. They are also increasingly women and children, many of whom are being pushed through a cradle-to-prison pipeline that may ensure that our social and criminal justice crises in the United States will get worse before they get better. Social and criminal justice in our society are fundamentally intertwined, so any effort to address either must address both.

As we contend with our justice crises, we must also reckon with the large number of people who gain from the status quo. While the rise of mass incarceration was not driven by profit motive, groups whose livelihoods depend in part on the maintenance of large prison and jail populations tend to support the continuation of policies and practices that undergird mass incarceration. Mauer describes the situation well: "The growth of the system itself serves to create a set of institutionalized lobbying forces that perpetuate a societal commitment to imprisonment through the expansion of vested economic interests."[80] He estimates that over 700,000 people work in our criminal justice systems as prison and jail guards, administrators, service workers, and other personnel. Civil rights advocate Michelle Alexander notes that if Mauer counted other people working in the bureaucracy surrounding prisons and jails, the estimated number of people employed because of mass incarceration would rise above two million.[81] As more people find work in criminal justice systems, they tend to resist penal reform, and organization in unions can enable them to muster enough political clout to maintain their positions.[82] In addition to

80. Mauer, *Race to Incarcerate*, 10.
81. Michelle Alexander, *The New Jim Crow*, 230.

people in our criminal justice systems, many rural communities bank on prisons (usually foolishly) as engines of growth after losing the manufacturing and agricultural jobs that once drove their economies.[83] Many members of these communities fear the loss of prison populations as they believe it would lead to the failure of yet another local industry.

Other groups that would likely oppose the end of mass incarceration include prison profiteers, such as correctional HMOs that provide healthcare (usually of poor quality) to people in prisons and jails; manufacturers of gear used in our criminal justice systems, including Tasers, electronic monitors, guns, and body armor; the U.S. military, which depends on cheap prison labor to make equipment for soldiers; and industries that similarly exploit prison labor and that often make goods for local, state, and federal governments.[84] Private prisons have also become more prominent, and their long-term viability as for-profit corporations depends upon an ever-increasing number of incarcerated people.[85] The largest private prison corporation in the United States is the Corrections Corporation of America (CCA), a publicly traded business. CCA

82. Joshua Page discusses the power of the California Correctional Peace Officers Association in propping up mass incarceration in California even as state leaders worked to reform the state's penal system. See "Prison Officer Unions and the Perpetuation of the Penal Status Quo," *Criminology and Public Policy* 10, no. 3 (2011): 735–70; and *The Toughest Beat: Politics, Punishment, and the Prison Officers Union in California* (New York: Oxford University Press, 2011).

83. On the limitations of this economic strategy for rural communities, see Terry Besser and Margaret Hanson, "The Development of Last Resort: The Impact of New Prisons on Small Town Economies," *Journal of the Community Development Society* 35 (2004): 1–16; Susan Blankenship and Ernest Yanarella, "Prison Recruitment as a Policy Tool of Local Economic Development: A Critical Evaluation," *Contemporary Justice Review* 7 (2004): 183–98; Gregory Hooks, Clayton Mosher, Shaun Genter, Thomas Rotolo, and Linda Lobao, "Revisiting the Impact of Prison Building on Job Growth: Education, Incarceration, and County-Level Employment," *Social Science Quarterly* 91, no. 1 (2010): 228–44; Tracy Huling, "Building a Prison Economy in Rural America," in *Invisible Punishment*, ed. Mauer and Chesney-Lind, 197–213; Ryan King, Marc Mauer, and Tracy Huling, "An Analysis of Economics of Prison Sitings in Rural Communities," *Criminal Public Policy* 3 (2004): 453–80; and Clayton Mosher, Gregory Hooks, and Peter B. Wood, "Don't Build It Here: The Hype Versus the Reality of Prisons and Local Employment," in *Prison Profiteers: Who Makes Money from Mass Incarceration*, ed. Tara Herivel and Paul Wright (New York: New Press, 2007), 90–97.

84. Each of these practices is described in more detail in *Prison Profiteers*, ed. Herivel and Wright. See also Joel Dyer, *The Perpetual Prisoner Machine: How America Profits from Crime* (Boulder, CO: Westview, 2000); and Judith A. Greene, "Entrepreneurial Corrections: Incarceration as a Business Opportunity," in *Invisible Punishment*, ed. Mauer and Chesney-Lind, 95–113.

85. On private prisons, see Michael A. Hallett, *Private Prisons in America: A Critical Race Perspective* (Urbana: University of Illinois Press, 2006); Charles H. Logan, *Private Prisons: Cons and Pros* (New York: Oxford University Press, 1990); Donna Selman and Paul Leighton, *Punishment for Sale: Private Prisons,*

boasts that it currently maintains 90,000 prison beds, making it "the fifth-largest corrections system in the nation, behind only the federal government and three states."[86] In early 2012, the company approached forty-eight states with an offer to purchase and take over management of government-run prisons so long as the state could guarantee that it would supply enough prisoners for 90 percent occupancy for twenty years or more, depending on the terms of the contract.[87] To generate profits, businesses like CCA rely upon filling prisons and jails with more people and keeping them there for longer periods of time. As we confront our criminal and social justice crises, we will need to respond to the reality that many people now benefit from mass incarceration.

Because of the relationship between social and criminal justice, work for greater justice must move beyond questions about guilt and punishment, about costs and benefits, about profits and losses, about deterrence, retribution, and incapacitation. If we want no longer to be the first genuine prison society of history, we, as a society, must consider these questions contextually and systematically, without taking an atomistic view of the problems of criminal justice. We must begin to engage in more thoughtful reflection about our character, beliefs, and actions. We must reconsider what kind of a people we want to be and what we want our communities to be like. We must examine what holds us together and what breaks us apart, what barriers prevent us from achieving a common good in which social and criminal justice can be positively related and in which no one is treated as less than a fully human person. To move toward this sort of reflection, however, we must also move beyond "factual analyses that argue that the cost-benefits of mass imprisonment are quite modest, particularly with other policy options."[88] While such analysis is important for understanding our crisis of criminal justice, these "instrumental considerations . . . are but one component in the development in criminal justice policy."[89] Rather, "the first step [in addressing mass incarceration] involves expanding the discussion of crime policy beyond the day-to-day debates on the relationship between prison and crime to more fundamental concerns about the type of society we wish to create."[90]

Big Business, and the Incarceration Binge (Lanham, MD: Rowman & Littlefield, 2010); and David Shichor, *Punishment for Profit: Private Prisons/Public Concerns* (Thousand Oaks, CA: Sage, 1995).

86. "About CCA," Corrections Corporation of America, http://www.cca.com/about/.

87. A copy of the letter is available at http://big.assets.huffingtonpost.com/ccaletter.pdf.

88. Marc Mauer, "The Causes and Consequences of Prison Growth in the United States," in *Mass Imprisonment*, ed. Garland, 10.

89. Ibid.

90. Ibid., 13.

In this discussion, religious voices will have much to say about these questions. The next chapter examines Catholic responses to our criminal justice crisis.

2

Catholic Responses to Our Criminal Justice Crisis

While our criminal justice systems are in crisis, their current state is fundamentally intertwined with a crisis of social justice in the United States. On one hand, our criminal justice systems reflect numerous injustices that mar our society. The creation of mass incarceration is the result of economic, cultural, political, and social factors coalescing into a drive for more punitive criminal justice systems. On the other hand, these systems help sustain social injustices that marginalize, disempower, and endanger our neighbors. Because of particular policy decisions, money has been funneled away from education, mental healthcare, substance abuse treatment, job training, and other efforts that could contribute to the well-being of members of our society. Criminal justice systems have limited employment and educational opportunities for those caught up in them, as well as exacerbated poverty and curtailed civil rights. These effects extend beyond people convicted of crime to affect family members, friends, neighborhoods and communities, and ultimately, society as a whole. The burden of these crises, however, is not borne evenly by everyone in our society; our failures of criminal and social justice disproportionately affect members of racial and ethnic minority groups and people who have been socioeconomically disadvantaged. As a result of these interlocking problems, these members of our society are not treated as fully human persons who are due the resources necessary to participate in the dignity, unity, and equality of all people.

Any adequate response to our circumstances must move beyond questions about criminal justice alone to consider its relationship with social justice. Not only must we ask how we ought to respond to individuals who commit crime and to their victims. We must also examine the broader social, economic, political, and cultural contexts of victims and offenders as well as of our society as a whole. Our responses to victims and offenders depend in part upon our understanding of the kind of people we want to be and what we want our communities to be like. Our responses depend upon our character, beliefs, and actions about the type of society we wish to create. Given these concerns, our responses will depend in part upon our religious worldviews.

In recent years, Christian theologians have entered into the conversation about our criminal justice crisis, offering reflections on how Christianity could offer alternative ideologies and practices of criminal justice, which then might support substantial institutional and social reform. Lee Griffith and Christopher Marshall, for example, each have written surveys of biblical texts that address these issues.[1] Timothy Gorringe in *God's Just Vengeance* offers a history of the relationship of penal ideology to Christian theology, especially Anselm's satisfaction theory of atonement, and the effects of this ideology upon criminal justice practices.[2] In *The Protestant Ethic and the Spirit of Punishment*, T. Richard Snyder connects certain Protestant theologies of sin and grace to American interpretations of crime and redemption.[3] Mark Lewis Taylor indicts what he calls "the prison–industrial complex" (borrowed from Christian Parenti[4]) and calls Christians to stand with "the executed God" against the racist and classist imperial dominance of our criminal justice systems.[5] James Samuel Logan offers a constructive Christian social ethics of "good punishment" based in what he calls a "politics of ontological intimacy" with people in prison as an alternative framework for our current criminal justice systems.[6] Each of these texts is important for initiating conversations among Christians about our criminal justice crises. Beyond these contributions, on a popular level, Charles Colson and his organization, Prison Fellowship, have worked toward the creation of

1. Lee Griffith, *The Fall of the Prison: Biblical Perspectives on Prison Abolition* (Grand Rapids: Eerdmans, 1993). Also, Christopher D. Marshall, *Beyond Retribution: A New Testament Vision for Justice, Crime, and Punishment* (Grand Rapids: Eerdmans, 2001).

2. Timothy Gorringe, *God's Just Vengeance: Crime, Violence, and the Rhetoric of Salvation* (Cambridge: Cambridge University Press, 1996).

3. T. Richard Snyder, *The Protestant Ethic and the Spirit of Punishment* (Grand Rapids: Eerdmans, 2001).

4. Christian Parenti, *Lockdown America: Police and Prisons in the Age of Crisis* (London, New York: Verso, 1999). Parenti rejected the term "prison–industrial complex" shortly after the publication of his book. For a discussion of his reasons, see Theodore Hamm, "Our Prison Complex," *The Nation*, October 11, 1999, 23. Mike Davis coined "prison–industrial complex" in his article "Hell Factory in the Field: A Prison Industrial Complex," *The Nation*, February 20, 1995, 229. The foremost theorist and critic of the prison–industrial complex is Angela Davis. Her critique is summarized well in a 1997 speech, which is available on CD, *The Prison-Industrial Complex* (Oakland, CA: AK Press, 2001).

5. Mark Lewis Taylor, *The Executed God: The Way of the Cross in Lockdown America* (Minneapolis: Fortress Press, 2001).

6. James Samuel Logan, *Good Punishment? Christian Moral Practice and U.S. Imprisonment* (Grand Rapids: Eerdmans, 2008).

Christian-based prisons and programs that have become models for several state criminal justice systems.[7] Notwithstanding these contributions, we must recognize that this conversation is still limited and its participants few.

One limitation of the conversation among Christians about our intertwined criminal and social justice crises is the lack of Catholic voices. While Protestants have been relatively active participants in discussions about criminal justice, Catholics have remained somewhat muted, with a few notable exceptions. Some Catholics have reflected on criminal justice by going back to core theoretical concepts such as justice and punishment, exploring the contributions of Catholic tradition for understanding these ideas in modern society. Peter Karl Koritansky and Kathryn Getek Soltis provide examples of this approach.[8] The church hierarchy, particularly the United States Conference of Catholic Bishops (USCCB), provides another Catholic response to our criminal justice crisis. The bishops published a document in 2000, titled *Responsibility, Rehabilitation, and Restoration: A Catholic Perspective on Crime and Criminal Justice*, advocating rehabilitative and restorative reforms for criminal justice systems in the United States.[9] A third voice comes from Catholic historian Andrew Skotnicki, who has been an adamant detractor from the bishops' proposal, criticizing the bishops for not fully understanding debates within contemporary criminology and for failing to draw upon traditional Catholic resources for criminal justice.[10] He advocates instead a return to the model of monastic and ecclesiastical prisons as "the normative means of punishment" in Catholic tradition.[11] The bishops and Skotnicki present opposing views of appropriate Catholic responses to criminal justice crises in the United States.

This chapter explores the contours of the conversation among Catholics about criminal justice in the United States. I maintain that any adequate response to our criminal and social justice crises will fully account for the current unique realities of mass incarceration in the United States. It must attend

7. Prison Fellowship, www.prisonfellowship.org.

8. Peter Karl Koritansky, *Thomas Aquinas and the Philosophy of Punishment* (Washington, DC: Catholic University of America Press, 2012). Kathryn Getek Soltis, "Just Punishment? A Virtue Ethics Approach to Prison Reform in the United States" (Ph.D. diss., Boston College, 2010).

9. United States Conference of Catholic Bishops, *Responsibility, Rehabilitation, and Restoration: A Catholic Perspective on Crime and Criminal Justice* (Washington, DC: United States Conference of Catholic Bishops, 2000). Available online at http://www.nccbuscc.org/sdwp/criminal.shtml.

10. Andrew Skotnicki, "Foundations Once Destroyed: The Catholic Church and Criminal Justice," *Theological Studies* 65 (2004): 812.

11. Andrew Skotnicki, *Criminal Justice and the Catholic Church* (Lanham, MD: Rowman & Littlefield, 2008). See especially chapter four, "Prison as the Normative Means of Punishment," 73–114.

to the conditions that foster crime, but also respond to the ways in which our criminal justice crisis both reflects and sustains social injustices. In addition, from a Catholic perspective, a faithful response will draw upon core religious and moral teachings of our tradition, while engaging in dialogue with other communities and traditions about the type of society we ought to create.

The first section of this chapter compares the works of Koritansky and Soltis. While a well-grounded theory of punishment is important for critiquing our criminal justice systems and offering more just correctives, Koritansky's Thomistic approach remains limited because it does not clarify how to apply Aquinas's theory to our context. Soltis, in contrast, provides a useful reassessment of Aquinas's discussion of the virtue of legal justice as a basis for her critique of the failures of our criminal justice systems, particularly the ideologies and practices of prisons. The next two sections turn to the bishops and Skotnicki. I find that both the bishops' and Skotnicki's efforts fail because they do not acknowledge fully the ways in which our criminal and social justice crises are fundamentally intertwined. Furthermore, Skotnicki draws upon aspects of Catholicism that few Catholics would recognize as part of their moral and religious tradition. Without recognizing the connections between social and criminal justice, and without relating the core insights of Catholic tradition to our particular circumstances, these Catholic efforts will not provide sufficient resources for a more just future.

Thomistic Theories of Criminal Justice: Peter Karl Koritansky and Kathryn Getek Soltis

One strategy for responding to our criminal justice crisis is to go back to basic theoretical concepts undergirding criminal justice to determine the justification and purpose of these systems. With clearer theoretical grounding, we may then be better able to determine what our criminal justice systems ought to be doing and how they ought to be achieving their objectives. On the face of it, this strategy would seem to have merit as our current systems are marred by a lack of philosophical clarity about their practices, which results in a hodgepodge of rehabilitative, retributive, and incapacitative practices in their operation. Writing in 1990, social theorist David Garland reflected,

> For nearly two decades now those employed in prisons, probation, and penal administration have been engaged in an unsuccessful search to find a "new philosophy" or a new "rationale" for punishment. They have been forced to rethink what it is they do,

and to reopen foundational questions about the justifications and purposes of penal sanctions, without so far having found a suitable set of terms upon which to rebuild an institutional identity.[12]

In light of this confusion about basic theoretical concepts upon which our criminal justice systems are built, a strategy that responds to our crisis of criminal justice by examining and clarifying these concepts would be worthwhile.

PETER KARL KORITANSKY AND A THOMISTIC APPROACH TO PUNISHMENT

Peter Karl Koritansky offers one example of this strategy in his text, *Thomas Aquinas and the Philosophy of Punishment*. He responds to the weaknesses of modern philosophies in providing a justification for punishment. Friedrich Nietzsche and Michel Foucault in particular have explored these weaknesses, both arguing that punishment cannot be justified in either utilitarian or retributive terms.[13] Tracing utilitarian justifications of punishment to Jeremy Bentham and retributive justifications to Immanuel Kant, Koritansky explains the pitfalls of these modern philosophies and proposes returning to the premodern thought of Thomas Aquinas as a corrective.

Koritansky's criticism of a utilitarian theory of punishment is that it can simultaneously allow for too much and too little punishment because of its lack of concern with connecting punishment to justice.[14] On one hand, because punishment is doled out, according to utilitarianism, depending upon whether it will have good consequences such as rehabilitation, deterrence, or protection of society, it seems that it may be permissible to reject the punishment of a criminal if none of these consequences will be achieved; the state has no duty to punish, even if only to render a wrongdoer's just deserts. On the other hand, punishing an innocent person seems permissible with utilitarianism if doing so may result in good consequences, perhaps by deterring others from committing the crime of which the innocent person was falsely accused. Koritansky rejects both Bentham's and H. L. A. Hart's formulations of a utilitarian philosophy of punishment because of their failures to relate punishment to justice.

In contrast with utilitarians, Kant disallows considerations of the consequences of punishment, or for that matter, of any action, in his moral philosophy.[15] Rather he maintains that all criminals must be punished for one

12. David Garland, *Punishment and Modern Society: A Study in Social Theory* (Chicago: University of Chicago Press, 1990), 6.

13. Koritansky, *Thomas Aquinas*, 2–3.

14. Ibid., 11–38.

punishment

reason only: they deserve punishment. This philosophy seems to avoid the issues of too little or too much punishment; one's punishment may only be as severe as one's offense, but no less severe. For Kant, according to the principle of proportionality, punishment must also correspond directly with the offense in a literalistic "eye-for-an-eye" way. Koritansky levels two critiques against retributivism. First, the principle of proportionality, especially as interpreted by Kant, yields absurd results. Is it just to respond to rape with rape, for example? "Unfair advantage theorists" have responded to this issue by suggesting that punishment should not return the crime unto the criminal, but instead remove the "unfair advantage" gained by the criminal relative to other citizens by committing the crime. The assumption with this stance is that criminals have gained some "benefit" in the criminal commission. For these theorists, the unfair advantage is neither any material benefit gained (such as the proceeds from robbery) nor any pleasure gained (such as the sexual pleasure from rape). Rather the unfair advantage comes from the breaking of law itself, to which other citizens hold themselves accountable. This argument leads to Koritansky's second criticism: it is unclear how criminal actions constitute a benefit to the criminal himself. He asks, "Can the mere performance of an action prohibited by law, considered independently from that action's material benefits or any pleasure derived from it, constitute a meaningful benefit?"[16]

In response to the shortfalls of utilitarianism and retributivism, both theories rooted in modern philosophies of political society, Koritansky turns to the premodern perspective of Thomas Aquinas on both punishment and political society.[17] One key of Thomistic philosophy is its teleological character (although Aquinas is not a consequentialist, in contrast with utilitarians). Rather his ethics depend upon the understanding that all things ought to be directed toward their appropriate ends. The justice of punishment then depends on whether it is directed toward the end of teaching an offender to live justly through the means of specific deterrence and rehabilitation.[18] Ideally

15. Ibid., 39–67.

16. Ibid., 66.

17. Ibid., 103–32.

18. Specific and general deterrence differ in their assumptions about *who* is deterred by punishment. On one hand, specific deterrence supposes that punishment deters the offender, the person being punished, from reoffending. Slapping the hand of a toddler reaching into a cookie jar deters her from trying to sneak cookies again. On the other hand, general deterrence supposes that punishment deters anyone who witnesses the punishment. Slapping the hand of a toddler reaching into a cookie jar deters her brother from trying to sneak cookies: "Sister didn't get away with it; why should I even try?" Koritansky finds that the justice of a punishment depends on whether it deters offenders from reoffending, not on whether it deters anyone else from violating the law.

punishment results in an offender's recommitment to the common good. Aquinas allows a role for retribution, but only secondarily, following the "medicinal" qualities of punishment. [The purpose of punishment ought never to be punishment itself.] Retributive punishment ought only to be used as a means of thwarting the offender's misdirected will and of informing the wills of members of the community who might choose to emulate him (that is, of general deterrence).

Although Aquinas would agree with utilitarians that punishment ought to be directed toward rehabilitation and specific deterrence primarily, he does not fall into the utilitarian trap of simultaneously allowing for too much and too little punishment. Koritansky argues that Aquinas manages to avoid the problems of utilitarianism because of his emphasis on the role of punishment in correcting the will of the offender.[19] It would be unjust to punish someone who did not have an errant will, as it would be unjust not to punish someone who did have errant will. Koritansky suggests that by stressing the focus of punishment on the will of the offender, rather than on the criminal act alone, Aquinas ensures that justice and punishment will not be disconnected. Aquinas also avoids the problems of retributivism in this way.[20] Rather than resorting to a strange Kantian principle of proportionality that answers bad act with bad act, Aquinas's philosophy of punishment attends to the degree to which an offender's will requires correction. Koritansky writes, "What matters, then, is not the *kind* of crime committed, but the *degree* to which the criminal's will encroached upon the common good in the commission of the crime."[21] Furthermore, Aquinas need not explain how an offender benefited from an offense since the punishment is given to repair the offender's will, not to even the score.

While Koritansky recommends Aquinas's philosophy of punishment, he also recognizes some impediments to applying it as the theoretical basis for a modern criminal justice system.[22] Aquinas's philosophy of punishment is rooted, in part, in his philosophy of political society, which is decidedly medieval. Modern readers may want to correct Aquinas on a few points, particularly with respect to his view of the inviolable and inalienable dignity of the human person. The difficulty of Aquinas's perspective on this point is apparent in Koritansky's chapter on capital punishment, in which he argues that John Paul II's papal encyclical *Evangelium Vitae* is reconcilable with Thomistic ethics

19. Koritansky, *Thomas Aquinas*, 191–94.
20. Ibid., 194–96.
21. Ibid., 195. Emphasis in original.
22. Ibid., 4, 198.

although the two seem to disagree about the legitimacy of the death penalty.[23] Koritansky comments extensively on *Summa Theologiae* II-II, 25.6 (ad. 2), in which Aquinas seems to compare serious sinners to a dog. Koritansky writes, "Rather than arguing that a serious sinner has sunk to the level of a dog, deserves to be shown no charity, and may be killed, therefore, Aquinas is saying that the sinner, though resembling a dog, retains his dignity and may be killed in spite of this fact for the sake of, and out of love for, the common good."[24] This defense of Aquinas may not be entirely satisfactory as it seems to indicate that some people may legitimately be sacrificed—killed—for the common good. However, at least in more recent Catholic social teaching, the realization of the common good depends upon the recognition of the inviolable dignity of the human person and upon the effort to achieve human flourishing for all members of our communities.[25] At least on this point, Koritansky might have more readily argued for the validity of this modern advancement in Catholic ethics.

Aside from difficulties within a Thomistic philosophy of punishment, we might also ask whether Koritansky's approach is adequate for addressing our criminal and social justice crises. To be fair, it seems that considering how Aquinas's perspective might apply to our current criminal justice systems in a concrete manner is not a goal of Koritansky in this text. Nevertheless, he does set out this project as an answer to the failure of modern philosophies of punishment that in many ways undergird our criminal justice systems. Moreover, it may be important to discern the scope of a project such as his in order to understand how far the reevaluation of basic theoretical concepts in light of Catholic tradition can take us in responding to our own context. Keeping Koritansky's expressed purposes in mind, his project seems inadequate for our purposes in at least three ways.

First, it is unclear how a Thomistic philosophy of punishment would translate into practices of criminal justice in a modern society. What sorts of punishments would we use to correct the wills of offenders? How would we know the wills of offenders in order to correct them? How would we punish

23. Ibid., 182–90.

24. Ibid., 189.

25. See, for example, the discussion of the common good in the *Catechism of the Catholic Church*, ¶1905–12, 1929–33. In *Evangelium Vitae*, Pope John Paul II significantly limits the validity of using the death penalty (although he still allows it in "very rare, if practically non-existent" cases in which there were no other means of protecting society). Admittedly, he does not rule out the death penalty on principle, but he still does seem to push back on the identification of any human person as a dog to be put down by insisting on the inalienability of our human dignity. See Pope John Paul II, *Evangelium Vitae*, ¶56.

offenders who may have wills turned decisively against the "common good" (however we understand that term in modern societies), but who commit only minor offenses, such as cutting off the heads of parking meters, like the eponymous hero of *Cool Hand Luke*?

Second, Koritansky does not examine the relationship between failures in realizing the common good as a society and the creation of criminal justice systems. This issue is connected to the limitations of Aquinas's medieval philosophy of political society. By using a Thomistic framework without offering corrections or additions to that framework in light of modern circumstances, the interconnection of social and criminal justice remains beyond the scope of Koritansky's argument.

Finally, because Koritansky focuses on punishment rather than justice, the broader concern of Aquinas, many questions about the relationship of punishment to other important concepts remain unexamined. For example, one significant question about punishment is whether we ought to be merciful, and if so, under what conditions. The issue of mercy receives scant attention in Koritansky's text; he seems much more concerned with establishing the duty to punish than with understanding when we should not do so. Mercy makes an appearance only in passing as a marker of the superiority of Aquinas's framework to Kant's.[26] Koritansky provides a thorough and clear discussion of Aquinas's philosophy of punishment, but his consideration of the basic theoretical concepts upon which our criminal justice systems are built does not prove adequate for answering our criminal and social justice crises.

KATHRYN GETEK SOLTIS AND THE VIRTUE OF LEGAL JUSTICE FOR PRISONS

Kathryn Getek Soltis embarks on a project similar to Koritansky's work, but in her dissertation, "Just Punishment? A Virtue Ethics Approach to Prison Reform in the United States," she avoids many of the weaknesses of his project for our purposes. She describes the models that currently shape our criminal justice systems based upon retribution, rehabilitation, and incapacitation (the latter two values being rooted in utilitarianism). Soltis finds fault with all three of these models because they each fail to accomplish the good of both society as a whole and its individual members, especially offenders. While rehabilitation best meets these ends among the three models, it also fails because it tends to reduce the moral agency of offenders, treating them as clients or patients, and thus limits the capacity of this model to serve their good and that of their communities.

26. Koritansky, *Thomas Aquinas*, 195–96.

To correct for the influence of these models on our criminal justice systems in general and our prisons in particular, Soltis suggests basing a new model of justice upon Aquinas's discussion of the virtue of legal justice, "an orientation toward the common good."[27] While Aquinas bases his understanding of criminal justice upon commutative justice, concerned with the justice of exchanges, including the punitive exchange of harm for harm through restitution and retaliation, Soltis recommends Aquinas's legal justice as a better foundation for criminal justice. The virtue of legal justice orients us toward a teleological vision of what is necessary for the flourishing of individual human persons and of human societies. Drawing upon this vision, the justification of punishment is neither retributive nor utilitarian. Rather punishment is justified insofar as it can reorient the offender toward the common good and teach him to inhabit the virtue of legal justice.

While Soltis retrieves Aquinas's thought for this recommendation, she does not do so uncritically and offers three important corrections to Aquinas. First, instead of thinking of the virtue of justice as a perfection of the power of the will, Soltis suggests thinking of it as the perfection of human relationships. With this shift, we must acknowledge the necessity of relationality for the formation of the virtues.[28] Second, Soltis maintains the inviolability and inalienability of human dignity, even among those who have committed crimes and are perhaps vicious.[29] Without this stance, the sacrifice of guilty individuals for the common good remains a possibility in Aquinas's thought, as seen above in the discussion of Koritansky. Soltis wants to eliminate this possibility because she recognizes that the common good depends upon the well-being of each of a community's members and that all individuals belong ultimately to God. To uphold the limitations of punishment based on human dignity, Soltis reminds us, "God's purposes are fundamental, and they trump the purposes of the body politic."[30] Even if it would be easier to dispense with people who have violated the law and harmed others, we cannot do so because they are God's and the common good cannot be truly common unless it includes everyone. Finally, Soltis draws upon Aquinas's notion of "fraternal correction" to argue that justice requires the correction not only of the sin (as would be achieved by commutative justice), but also of the sinner.[31] Aquinas describes punishment as "medicinal," but allows for the medicine to benefit only the broader community (for example, as a

27. Ibid., 4.
28. Ibid., 112–14.
29. Ibid., 114–21.
30. Ibid., 118.
31. Ibid., 121.

general deterrent). Soltis insists that the "medicine" of punishment must treat the one being punished in a way that "recognizes the sinner as a member of the community and corrects the sinner in order to reorient her toward the good of the community."[32]

To shape her specific recommendations for prison reform, Soltis draws upon the insight of virtue ethics that "to be just one must perform just acts."[33] The performance of just acts must be in a context that emphasizes the reestablishment of relationships and upholds the moral agency of offenders who must habituate the virtue of legal justice. Soltis provides numerous concrete recommendations for the reform of prisons so that they may become institutions where prisoners can become more just. She suggests that we ought to imprison only those people who commit crimes that harm the good of the community, who have made a habit of injustice, and who demonstrate a willful rejection of the common good; such requirements would significantly depopulate our prisons, as most offenders have committed drug offenses rooted in "self-regarding vices," such as drug addiction.[34] For cases in which incarceration remains necessary, prisons ought to provide peer advocacy and support, educational opportunities, and meaningful work for the people in them. Correctional officers and staff ought to be empowered to be more than hall monitors and security specialists so that they can foster just relationships within the prison. Soltis also suggests building relationships between the community outside of the prison and the community inside. People outside of prison must have relationships with people inside, for example, by visiting and offering programs to prisoners. Prisoners can also be given opportunities to serve the broader community while still in prison. To inform these efforts, Soltis draws critically on the resources of cognitive and behavioral training, restorative justice, criminological literature on "virtuous prisons," and prisoner reentry programs as starting points for enabling prisons and prisoners to become more just. Furthermore, she provides several examples of prisons that already use some of these initiatives behind their walls.

Soltis avoids many of the weaknesses of Koritansky's project for our purposes. She does not appropriate Aquinas's philosophy uncritically, offering several corrections to his thought in its application to modern contexts. She more readily connects her theoretical perspective to specific practices of criminal justice in our society. By beginning her project with the broader concept of justice, Soltis more thoroughly connects the related notions of

32. Ibid., 124.
33. Ibid., 1.
34. Ibid., 133–37.

justice, punishment, and mercy. Finally, she clearly and explicitly recognizes the relationship between social and criminal justice. She concludes her chapter on the application of justice as virtue to prisons in the United States by exploring how prisons could be loci for unraveling the ties between our criminal and social justice crises. She recognizes, first, that prisons currently exploit social injustices in order to perpetuate the hold that they have on our criminal justice systems. From this recognition that our criminal justice crisis reflects a crisis of social justice, she also describes ways in which our prisons help sustain social injustices, drawing on data similar to that described in the first chapter. In light of the ways that social and criminal justice are fundamentally intertwined, Soltis suggests that prisons work with organizations outside of their walls to promote social justice. She concludes,

> The prison as an institutional moral agent will only be effective in making men and women more just if it is simultaneously working for the transformation of society as well. Indeed, many of the opportunities for inmates to serve the wider community through just action are also expressions of the prison's own orientation for the common good. Ultimately, for the purpose of the prison to be fully enacted, just individuals must be offered the chance to reintegrate into a just community.[35]

Unlike any of the other authors discussed in this chapter, Soltis understands the links between our crises of social and criminal justice, and her response provides tools for addressing both crises.

CATHOLIC THEORETICAL INSIGHTS INTO CRIMINAL JUSTICE

Consideration of Koritansky's and Soltis's discussions of Thomistic theories of criminal justice offers some insight into the norms of punishment within Catholic tradition. Although Koritansky does not critique Aquinas rigorously about willingness to sacrifice individual offenders for the sake of the common good, Soltis's correction of Aquinas in light of modern developments in Catholic social teaching upholds the necessity of recognizing the inalienability and inviolability of human dignity for all persons, including people who have violated the law and harmed others. Acknowledgment of human dignity places limits upon extreme punishment and inflicting pain for the sake of causing pain on offenders. It also requires treating offenders as moral agents responsible for their wrongdoing, but who can redirect their wills toward better lives that

---

35. Ibid., 248–49.

serve the common good. The achievement of the common good is not possible without maintaining human dignity, even for people who have committed crime.

Punishment cannot be justified in utilitarian or retributive terms, from a Catholic perspective. Rather the justification of punishment is that the person has violated the common good and that a response from the community is necessary to restore the well-being of all community members, especially victims, and to enable offenders to reorient themselves to the common good. Reorientation will require internal reform by the offender and social reintegration of the offender into the community.

With this justification, the purpose of punishment can never be punishment itself. Both Soltis and Koritansky note Aquinas's description of punishment as "medicinal." The medicine of punishment ought to provide some cure for the ills of society as a whole and for the ills of its individual members. We ought to evaluate practices of punishment according to their capacity to restore the health of our communities and their individual members. The purpose of punishment is to teach people who have done wrong to live justly again, to serve the common good. Through accomplishing these ends, people who have violated the law and harmed others can then be reintegrated fully into our society.

The Bishops on Crime and Criminal Justice

The United States Conference of Catholic Bishops (USCCB) composed *Responsibility, Rehabilitation, and Restoration* in 2000 to build upon Pope John Paul II's message earlier that year, *Jubilee in Prisons*.[36] This statement was the first document issued by the bishops about crime and criminal justice since the 1970s, when they released two documents concerning these issues. In many ways, *Responsibility, Rehabilitation, and Restoration* echoes the themes of these previous church documents, while adapting to the circumstances of crime and criminal justice in the United States in the twenty-first century. The previous documents are interesting in comparison with *Responsibility, Rehabilitation, and Restoration* because they were written as the buildup of our criminal justice systems began and reflect idiosyncrasies of the time, such as the strength of the prisoners' rights movement beginning toward the late 1960s and upset with the Watergate scandal as an example of the deleterious social effects of white-collar crime.

36. Pope John Paul II, *Jubilee in Prisons*, The Vatican, accessed May 24, 2010, http://www.vatican.va/holy_father/john_paul_ii/messages/documents/hf_jp-ii_mes_20000630_jubilprisoners_en.html.

"Rebuilding Human Lives," written in 1973, focuses on prison reform.[37] From the text, it seems that awareness of mistreatment of prisoners, which at the time was often publicized through prison protests and riots, precipitated the writing of this statement. The bishops state at the outset, "The numerous reports issued by representatives of [suspects and convicted criminals], coupled with incidents of violence in correctional institutions across the nation, have aroused many consciences."[38] They continue by noting that "the poor, the disadvantaged minorities, and the 'losers' of our society" disproportionately occupy our prisons: "We may need to examine whether we may not have a 'poor man's' system of criminal justice."[39] The bishops recognize the interrelationship of criminal and social justice, and the possibility that social injustices taint our ability to carry out criminal justice prompts their writing. They encourage their readers to examine the justice of the system as a whole rather than focus only upon how to respond to individual wrongdoers. They maintain,

> [I]t is necessary that we not only visit individuals confined in prison but 'visit' the correctional system itself. Our concern for correctional institutions does not exist in isolation from other related issues. The injustices and inequities that plague our society affect both the incidence of crime and the administration of correctional institutions.[40]

In order to "rebuild human lives," the bishops argue that we must examine not only individual wrongdoing and its correction, but also the systemic context in which wrongdoing and correction take place.

The bishops proceed to offer recommendations for reform according to which sorts of reforms will best realize what they deem to be the proper ends of a criminal justice system: punishment, but also incapacitation, general and specific deterrence, and especially, rehabilitation of offenders. They also emphasize the necessity of recognizing that prisoners are human beings, "created in the image and likeness of God and endowed with free will," whose basic rights and dignity cannot be violated.[41] With these goals and principles in view, the bishops suggest several reforms "to insure [*sic*] protection for all

37. Catholic Bishops of the United States, "Rebuilding Human Lives," *Origins* 3 (1973): 344–50.
38. Ibid., 344.
39. Ibid., 344.
40. Ibid., 345.
41. Ibid., 346.

the civil rights of confined offenders in an atmosphere of human compassion conducive to reconciliation and rehabilitation."[42] Among their many recommendations, they suggest locating prisons nearer to urban centers so that prisoners may be closer to family and friends, providing education and vocational training to prisoners, creating a national bill of rights for prisoners, and instituting common living standards across prisons. With these suggestions, they also comment, "Significant achievement in the reform of our correctional system will benefit society more than it will benefit the reformed criminal."[43] While they view the reform of prisons as having a positive effect on society as a whole, and therefore see some links between criminal and social justice, the bishops do not provide recommendations for social reforms that might in turn break our society's dependence on the prison. That is, although the bishops recognize that we may have a "poor man's" system of criminal justice, their recommendations focus mainly on making prisons better places to live, not on the inequities in our society that may create prisons filled with poor men in the first place. Of course, much of the canon of Catholic social teaching addresses social injustice more broadly; nevertheless, discussing the relationship of broader social justice reforms to criminal justice reforms could clarify the full extent to which social and criminal justice are intertwined.

In contrast with "Rebuilding Human Lives," the 1978 Catholic Conference statement, "A Community Response to Crime," attends to the "war against crime."[44] With this document, the conference turns its attention from the experiences of offenders to the effects of crime on victims and communities. Here again, it recognizes that the burden of crime and criminal justice is borne unevenly in our society. The authors write, "We are shocked by the level of crime in our nation and the human suffering it leaves in its wake. Our concern is intensified by the fact that the impact of crime falls disproportionately on the weakest in our society—the poor, the minorities, and the elderly."[45] While the conference notes the uneven burden of crime and criminal justice, it also acknowledges that many significant crimes are not committed by marginalized people, but by white-collar workers and government officials (the historical proximity of this document to Watergate is most apparent here).

The conference describes numerous factors contributing to high rates of crime, including a lack of moral leadership in business, government, media,

42. Ibid., 347.
43. Ibid., 349.
44. United States Catholic Conference, "A Community Response to Crime," *Origins* 7 (1978): 593–604.
45. Ibid., 595.

and the church; the breakdown of families and neighborhoods; the toleration of materialism and greed; the loss of personal responsibility for one's action; and economic and social deprivation. As it cites both individual- and social-level causes of crime, the conference makes individual- and social-level recommendations for confronting crime. The authors write, "Any effective response to crime ought to focus on improving our community life, on strengthening our families and neighborhoods, on rooting out economic deprivation and social injustice, and on teaching basic values of personal responsibility, human dignity, and decency."[46] With these emphases, the conference begins to correct the shortcomings of "Rebuilding Human Lives" by addressing the causes of crime based in social injustices. Their concern with the ways in which social and economic deprivation lead to crime can be seen in their section on the role of the church in responding to crime and problems of criminal justice. The conference suggests that local churches provide educational, employment, and recreational activities for youth; support community efforts for improved housing, infrastructure, and public services; offer assistance to victims of domestic violence; and sponsor programs to monitor courts to ensure that the legal rights of defendants are upheld. It also recommends public policy changes that dioceses should support, such as providing full employment and living wages, decent housing, quality education, and adequate medical care.

"A Community Response to Crime" thus makes advances beyond "Rebuilding Human Lives" in terms of recognizing the ways in which social injustice fosters crime and making recommendations to improve the well-being of all members of our society. Both documents also make important contributions by highlighting the ways in which lessening the harms caused by our criminal justice systems may improve society as a whole; that is, they acknowledge that injustices in our criminal justice systems can contribute to social injustice more broadly. In these ways, they move toward fuller recognition of the interconnection of social and criminal justice. Nevertheless, both documents rest on an assumption that makes it difficult to apply their analysis and recommendations to our current crisis. The assumption is that social injustice only indirectly leads to growth of our criminal justice systems by fostering crime; as crime rates climb, so do incarceration rates. As demonstrated in the previous chapter, however, crime rates and incarceration rates are largely independent of each other. That chapter suggests that social injustice has directly contributed to the growth of our criminal justice systems through political, social, economic, and cultural dynamics; our criminal justice crisis

46. Ibid., 595.

reflects a crisis of social justice, unmediated by the effects of social injustice on crime. Since our crisis of criminal justice is directly affected by social injustices, regardless of the crime rate, a comprehensive response to crime as well as to our criminal and social justice crises must attend also to the ways in which social injustice underlies the creation of our prison society. If the authors of these documents attended to this dynamic, then they might recommend, for example, revisions to laws that lead to incarcerating more people for longer periods of time in addition to efforts to alleviate social and economic deprivation. To their credit, the authors acknowledged many of the complexities of the relationships among crime, criminal justice, and social justice in the 1970s, before our criminal justice systems began their descent into our current crisis. On this side of the crisis, we need something more than these documents offer in terms of recommendations for action.

While these two documents provide precedents for *Responsibility, Rehabilitation, and Restoration,* the bishops' 2000 statement ought also to be read in conjunction with Pope John Paul II's message for the *Jubilee in Prisons,* written in 2000 as well. The papal text addresses issues concerning prisons worldwide and so does not directly remark upon the unique conditions of criminal justice systems in the United States. This document was one of a series of papal messages delivered to commemorate the millennium as a year of Jubilee. John Paul II begins the message by describing the salvation offered by Christ to all people, including people in prison, whom Christ brings back into the fold as a Good Shepherd in search of lost sheep. Jesus accompanies the prisoner on a journey of return to God by "giving meaning" to the time spent behind bars, reminding prisoners that even this "time belongs to God."[47] The recognition of God's dominion over all time leads John Paul II to point out that there are limitations to the dominion that public authorities hold over prisoners. It also leads him to the conclusion that prisoners must not view time in prison as a waste, but as an opportunity to recognize God's dominion in their lives.

These observations are the basis for John Paul II's call for change with the Jubilee. First, prisoners must use the experience of incarceration to change their own lives. John Paul II assumes a pastoral tone. He writes that the Jubilee is a time "to right injustices committed, to mitigate excesses, and to recover what might otherwise be lost," but furthermore also "*to strive to find new paths of redemption* in every personal and social situation."[48] John Paul II's

---

47. John Paul II, *Jubilee in Prisons.*
48. Ibid., emphasis in original.

recommendation for redemption underlies his call for prisons to work toward rehabilitation of prisoners rather than merely enacting vengeance.

In addition to prisoners, John Paul II recognizes the need for change in society more broadly during the Jubilee. More ought to be done, he argues, to conform "the penal system both to the dignity of the human person and to the effective maintenance of public order."[49] More ought to be done to prevent crime and to redeem criminals, but John Paul II acknowledges that prisons may not be the best tools for achieving these goals. The pope concludes his message with an appeal to governments to provide a sort of clemency by "fostering initiatives which will lay a solid basis for a genuine renewal of both attitudes and institutions."[50] In particular, "this includes giving more consideration to penalties other than imprisonment," but also making prison a place where prisoners can prepare to reenter the rest of the world through job training, psychological assistance, charitable works, and spiritual guidance.[51] Where prisons remain, they should conform to regulations that respect the dignity of their inmates, such as allowing contact with family and friends, decreasing violence, ensuring religious freedom, and attending to prisoners with serious or terminal illnesses.

Inspired by John Paul II's Jubilee message, *Responsibility, Rehabilitation, and Restoration* is an effort by the USCCB to apply the pope's general insights for prisons and prisoners worldwide to the particular circumstances of the United States. Building upon a commitment to the common good rooted in Catholic social teaching, the bishops' statement reflects a tension within all Catholic approaches to dealing with crime, punishment, and justice. On one hand, Catholic tradition insists that criminal behavior that harms others and violates the rights of human persons cannot be tolerated. On the other hand, the church also upholds the inherent dignity of all children of God, including victims and offenders, and maintains that every person bears the potential for redemption and restoration to full relationship with both God and neighbor. These two beliefs lead the bishops to conclude, "The common good is undermined by criminal behavior that threatens the lives and dignity of others and by policies that seem to give up on those who have broken the law."[52] In light of this conclusion, the bishops hope in this statement to find some resolution to this tension and some response rooted in Catholic tradition to the crisis in U.S. criminal justice systems: "We are convinced that our tradition and our faith

49. Ibid.
50. Ibid.
51. Ibid.
52. USCCB, *Responsibility*.

offer better alternatives [than more prisons and more executions] that can hold offenders accountable and challenge them to change their lives; reach out to victims *and* reject vengeance; restore a sense of community and resist the violence that has engulfed so much of our culture."[53]

The bishops begin by describing current problems with crime and criminal justice in the U.S. context. Their general conclusion is that "the status quo is not really working—victims are often ignored, offenders are often not rehabilitated, and many communities have lost their sense of security."[54] The bishops recognize that crime has steadily fallen beginning in the 1990s for a variety of reasons, including new policing strategies, economic prosperity, and fewer young people. Nevertheless, large numbers of people are still victims of crime, and crime victims are disproportionately members of marginalized and vulnerable populations, such as racial and ethnic minorities, people who are socioeconomically deprived, and children. The bishops also highlight differences in punishment in the United States in comparison with similar nations, particularly our inordinately high rates of incarceration caused by policies such as "three strikes," "zero-tolerance" for drug offenders, and mandatory minimum sentences. They note that the expense of incarcerating people at such high rates diverts money from other public concerns such as education, health and human services, and infrastructure development as well as from other methods of responding to wrongdoers, such as probation and community treatment. Just as members of marginalized and vulnerable populations are more likely to be victims of crime, so are they more likely to be caught up in our criminal justice systems. The bishops describe how prisons are disproportionately populated with members of racial and ethnic minorities, people with mental illnesses, and immigrants as well as people with substance abuse problems and little education. Finally, they note that our criminal justice systems have become more punitive since the 1970s as the emphasis of these systems has shifted away from rehabilitation.

At this point, it is important to note some strengths and weaknesses in the bishops' description of our criminal justice crisis. First, they seem to recognize that our criminal justice systems have grown independently of crime rates, and that crime rates have fallen for reasons other than our reliance on incarceration. Second, they explore ways in which our criminal justice crisis sustains social injustices, as the money spent on prisons cannot be spent on more productive means of promoting human dignity in our society and as these systems disproportionately affect vulnerable and marginalized populations. They miss,

53. Ibid.
54. Ibid.

however, the ways in which social, cultural, economic, and political factors contribute to the creation of our prison society—they miss the fact that our criminal justice crisis also reflects a social justice crisis, independent of the effects of social injustice on crime. This oversight has significant effects on the bishops' policy recommendations found later in *Responsibility, Rehabilitation, and Restoration.*

From their brief description of criminal justice systems in the U.S. context, the bishops turn to resources from the "scriptural, theological, and sacramental heritage" of the Catholic Church to build a framework for their response, which they hope allows them to "move away from the so-called 'soft' and 'tough' approaches to crime and punishment offered by those on opposite ends of the political spectrum."[55] The bishops find support for their *via media* within Old Testament traditions that demonstrate God's justice and mercy in the context of the covenant community and the extension of these traditions in the New Testament with the life, death, and resurrection of Jesus Christ. In the life of Jesus Christ, they find the roots of the tension described above between upholding the inherent dignity of all people and holding offenders accountable as Jesus both battled oppression and called for the transformation of sinful lives. The bishops also note that Jesus himself was a prisoner who called his disciples to visit the imprisoned (Matthew 25). In addition to scriptural sources, the bishops draw upon Catholic social teaching to justify their stance. They particularly cite the value of human life, the recognition of human dignity, the importance of participation in family and community for human beings, the option for the poor and vulnerable, and the principles of subsidiarity and solidarity as offering direction for Catholic responses to crime, justice, and punishment. Finally, the bishops suggest, "Our sacramental life can help us make sense of our paradoxical approach to crime and punishment."[56] While they mention the Eucharist in passing, they find that the sacrament of Penance[57] provides the fundamental Catholic model for "taking responsibility, making amends, and reintegrating into the community."[58] From these resources of Catholic heritage, the bishops conclude that although punishment of wrongdoers is justified in Catholic tradition, punishment must always be meted out for the purposes of

---

55. Ibid.
56. Ibid.
57. Here I follow the bishops' use of "Penance" to name this sacrament, rather than "Reconciliation." In the Catechism of the Catholic Church ¶1440–49, this sacrament is referred to as "Penance and Reconciliation," following the introduction of the latter term in the Second Vatican Council.
58. USCCB, "Responsibility."

internal reform and reintegrating offenders into the community—never for the sake of punishment itself.

Based upon this framework, the bishops propose several policy directions for a Catholic response to our criminal justice crisis in the United States. They maintain that while some people will inevitably need to be removed from society for public safety, from a Christian perspective, punishment ought to be directed not toward incapacitation, deterrence, or retribution, but always toward rehabilitation and restoration of offenders to community and, when possible, toward restitution for victims. Punishment ought not be for the sake of punishment itself. Reforms of criminal justice systems need to be accompanied by work for crime prevention and social justice, especially poverty reduction. The church ought to lead these efforts, in part, by promoting a culture of life rather than a culture of violence. The bishops also support efforts to meet the needs of victims of crime and communities, particularly through restorative justice programs. Offenders must have access to spiritual guidance as well as to treatment for mental illness and substance abuse when necessary. Finally, the bishops advocate a variety of community alternatives to incarceration that may reduce incidents of crime, including community policing, neighborhood watch, and "broken windows" policing. They conclude that together these policy directions navigate the way between the insistence that we cannot ignore criminal behavior and the recognition that all people, including criminal offenders, are children of God created for responsible, rehabilitated, and restored relationship with God and neighbor: "We believe a Catholic ethic of responsibility, rehabilitation, and restoration can become the foundation for the necessary reform of our broken criminal justice system."[59]

To evaluate the adequacy of the bishops' recommendations for our unique context, we must determine whether they respond to the conditions that foster crime as well as acknowledge ways in which our criminal justice crisis both reflects and helps sustain social injustices that marginalize, disempower, and endanger our neighbors. The difficulty with "Rebuilding Human Lives" and "A Community Response to Crime" was that neither accounted for ways in which our criminal justice crisis directly reflects a crisis of social justice in our society. Of course, the bishops may have been especially prescient had they recognized this connection in the 1970s. The question, however, is whether they made this connection in 2000 and corrected this oversight in light of developments in our context since the previous documents were written.

On the face of them, many of the bishops' recommendations seem to provide the necessary corrective. For example, the bishops advocate "rejecting

59. Ibid.

simplistic solutions such as 'three strikes and you're out' and rigid mandatory sentencing."[60] The reason they give for this recommendation is that such strategies are ineffective for reducing crime and that we need more flexible, accountable, and community-based solutions that emphasize treatment and restoration. With this policy recommendation and its justification, the bishops respond to conditions that foster crime. Nevertheless, in their justification, the bishops do not acknowledge the ways in which "three strikes" and mandatory minimum sentencing reflect and help sustain social injustice. As a result, the bishops fail to offer other good—and important—reasons for rejecting these policies. One reason depends, in part, on the recognition that these policies arose from a political drive for more punitive sentencing in the United States. This drive gained traction because of economic dynamics that led to the creation of jobless ghettos along with cultural and social dynamics such as growing fear of crime and people in "bad neighborhoods." These political, economic, and social factors unfortunately coincided historically with the cultural and criminological rejection of rehabilitation as a goal for criminal justice. Another reason for rejecting these policies is that, probably more than any other policies, they have led to the incarceration of more people for longer periods of time for nonviolent drug and property offenses, and thus, they underlie the catastrophic expansion of our criminal justice systems. These policies are the main policies that contribute to the marginalization, disempowerment, and endangerment of large sectors of our population. In short, the bishops should reject these policies not only because they are ineffective at reducing and preventing crime, but also—and more fundamentally—because they are built on and perpetuate social injustice. The bishops' recommendation is an important step, but in terms of advocating for comprehensive reforms, these recommendations should be based upon questions of justice, not questions of effectiveness alone. Effectiveness is important—but it ought not to be our only consideration when recommending reforms for our criminal justice systems.

Another example may help demonstrate how the bishops' recommendations still fail to acknowledge fully the ways in which crises of social and criminal justice are fundamentally intertwined, independent of problems with crime. Their second recommendation is to "promote serious efforts toward crime prevention and poverty reduction," because "socio-economic factors such as extreme poverty, discrimination, and racism are serious contributors to crime."[61] Of course, they are right—but they do not

60. Ibid.
61. Ibid.

recognize that extreme poverty, discrimination, and racism have helped create mass incarceration regardless of the crime rate. The bishops would perhaps take a different, more prophetic stance against the social injustices that our criminal justice systems reflect and help sustain if they were to recognize this interrelationship more fully. They might, for example, call upon politicians to refrain from fear-mongering "war-on-crime" language with racist overtones to win elections. They might decry the ways in which we have constructed a "cradle-to-prison" pipeline that shuttles young minority males from jobless ghettos to school suspensions to juvenile hall, and ultimately, to prison. They might call for the divestment of funds from prison industries. They might recognize the need for a social movement to dismantle the structures that have made us the first genuine prison society. And they would do so because that is what social and criminal justice demands.

AN ARGUMENT FOR PRISONS: ANDREW SKOTNICKI

While my criticisms of the bishops concern the adequacy of their account of crime and criminal justice in the United States, particularly their understanding of how these phenomena relate to social justice, another Catholic author, historian Andrew Skotnicki, offers additional critiques of *Responsibility, Rehabilitation, and Restoration* in his article, "Foundations Once Destroyed," which he later expands in his book, *Criminal Justice and the Catholic Church*. Skotnicki's criticisms are twofold. First, he argues that the bishops do not engage sufficiently the insights of criminologists and therefore make suggestions that are counterproductive to their goals of rehabilitation and restorative justice. Second, Skotnicki maintains that the bishops should reconsider their recommendations of rehabilitation and restorative justice as he finds that they ignore the importance of prisons in Catholic tradition. While I find that Skotnicki's first criticism is warranted to a limited degree, his second criticism is flawed practically, morally, and theologically.

Skotnicki first argues that the bishops "lack analytical depth concerning contemporary criminology,"[62] resulting in their advocacy of policies that exacerbate the punitiveness and racial, ethnic, and class bias of criminal justice systems. He writes, "The Catholic bishops of the United States have found themselves in the rather strange position of advocating a number of policies that are hallowed by the very forces to which they have expressed opposition."[63] Skotnicki cites movements for "penal harm" and "social control" within

62. Skotnicki, "Foundations Once Destroyed," 812.
63. Ibid.

contemporary criminology as the forces in opposition with the bishops' position. These movements developed since the 1970s as a backlash against rehabilitation as the prior working ideology of criminal justice systems in the United States. With penal harm, Skotnicki finds an increase in punitive responses to crime, in which punishment in itself is the final end of strategies for dealing with offenders. He describes the accompanying movement for social control as "a systems management approach that 'aggregates' the individual, understanding him or her solely as a member of a group, uncoupled from social history and subjective interpretations, and defined in terms of risk."[64] With social control, Skotnicki finds an emphasis on incapacitation based on one's racial, ethnic, and class background (that is, "risk level"), which results in "the detecting, monitoring, and control of a permanent criminal class."[65] In *Responsibility, Rehabilitation, and Restoration*, Skotnicki detects what he sees as a turn to incapacitation incongruous with Catholic tradition in the bishops' use of the phrase "protection of society," and he claims that the bishops' call for the development of alternatives to incarceration plays into plans by penal harm and social control theorists "to 'downsize' the traditional prison in favor of creating virtual penal colonies in many poor urban neighborhoods."[66]

To a limited degree, Skotnicki's first criticism of the bishops is warranted, although it does not entirely undermine their recommendations for reforms of our criminal justice systems. On two points in particular, the bishops need to reconsider their recommendations in light of contemporary criminology. First, whenever one proposes alternatives to incarceration, one must also beware of what criminologists call "net widening," in which new strategies for responding to offenders are not used instead of incarceration, but in addition to it. For example, electronic ankle monitors have been touted as a means for keeping track of offenders so that they do not need to be sent to jail or prison. However, they are often used to tack on a few years of supervision by criminal justice systems after inmates have been released into the community, thereby adding to the burden of offenders' sentences when they would have previously been monitored much more loosely or not at all.[67] The bishops do not acknowledge the danger of net widening in their statement, and a word of warning about the risks of proposing alternatives to incarceration would be appropriate.

64. Ibid., 814.
65. Ibid.
66. Ibid., 815.
67. See Graeme Wood, "Prison Without Walls," *The Atlantic*, September 2010, www.theatlantic.com/magazine/archive/2010/09/prison-without-walls/8195, for a compelling description of the use of electronic monitors in our criminal justice systems.

Second, Skotnicki fairly cautions about the possibility of inadvertently supporting the creation of "virtual penal colonies of racial and ethnic minorities" with respect to at least one of the bishops' recommendations: the use of the "broken windows" model of policing, which they mention briefly as an example of an alternative community-based effort at crime control. With this model, first formulated by James Q. Wilson and George L. Kelling,[68] minor infractions of the law result in stiff penalties, based on the hope that increased public order on the streets will deter more serious crimes because potential offenders have the sense that they will inevitably get caught by a proactive police force. Broken windows policing was the guiding model of policing in New York City under the administration of Mayor Rudy Giuliani and has since been criticized for both its ineffectiveness and its contribution to the breakdown of relationships between police and minority communities.[69] The recommendation of broken windows policing by the bishops reflects lack of attention to contemporary criminology.

Skotnicki's first criticism, however, does not seem to get at the heart of his problem with the bishops' approach to crime, justice, and punishment. The central issue that Skotnicki raises against the bishops—and his second criticism—is that he finds in their call for rehabilitation and restoration "an insufficient appreciation for the foundational importance of the prison and the essential element of the 'time' sentence as contributing factors in the dynamic of punishment and renewal."[70] He argues that Catholic tradition has long insisted that prisons are necessary to inspire contrition in those offenders who feel no remorse and that, in these cases, some level of retribution is necessary to bring about offenders' cooperation with rehabilitation and restoration. The bishops, Skotnicki avers, ignore the tradition of Roman Catholicism that has held that "the principal vehicle for connecting the Church's belief in the legitimacy of punishment with its desired end of reconciliation has been the prison."[71] Skotnicki's main problem with the bishops' approach to crime, justice, and

68. James Q. Wilson and George L. Kelling, "Broken Windows: The Police and Neighborhood Safety," *The Atlantic Magazine*, March 1982, http://www.theatlantic.com/magazine/archive/1982/03/broken-windows/4465/.

69. For further discussion of "broken windows" policing, see Bernard E. Harcourt, *Illusion of Order: The False Promise of Broken Windows Policing* (Cambridge, MA: Harvard University Press, 2001); George E. Kelling and Catherine M. Coles, *Fixing Broken Windows: Restoring Order and Reducing Crime in Our Communities* (New York: Touchstone, 1996); and Gary Stewart, "Black Codes and Broken Windows: The Legacy of Racial Hegemony in Anti-Gang Civil Injunction," *The Yale Law Journal* 107 (1998): 2249–79.

70. Skotnicki, "Foundations Once Destroyed," 810.

71. Ibid., 800.

punishment, in sum, is that the bishops do not see that a truly Catholic approach to these issues must include prisons as the normative means of punishment.

Skotnicki develops his argument for prisons in a Catholic theory of criminal justice most fully in his book, *Criminal Justice and the Catholic Church*. He organizes his presentation of this theory around four questions that he argues any theory of criminal justice must answer, and his answers to the first three by and large agree with what the Catholic bishops in the United States might say as well as with Koritansky's and Soltis's interpretations of Thomistic ethics. Skotnicki's main area of disagreement with other Catholic authors lies in his answer to the final question, which he spends most of his effort addressing. Nevertheless, Skotnicki's responses to all four questions depend upon one another, so full understanding of his argument requires consideration of each question in turn.

The first question is, *Who are the offenders?* Skotnicki suggests that our images of the people who commit crime shape our penal ideologies and practices. He writes, "When the prisoner is imaged as a political or social threat, as morally repugnant, or, simply put, as a means to an end, virtually any punishment is possible."[72] Drawing on resources in both scripture and Catholic tradition, Skotnicki argues that Catholics must reject these images and instead "see the prisoner . . . [as] the battered body of Jesus."[73] Identifying prisoners with Jesus Christ ought to lead all Christians, in Skotnicki's view, to compassionate care, rather than to limitless punishment. We will then recognize prisoners as human persons—sinful, but still bearing the image of God. Skotnicki continues by proposing a concomitant image for "those who design, operate, or at least underwrite the penal complex with their political and moral support."[74] For this image, he notes that the Catholic Church has viewed itself in this role "as the father/mother who loves the child who is punished."[75] From this conclusion, Skotnicki seems to suggest that everyone outside of prisons—church, state,

72. Skotnicki, *Criminal Justice*, 20.

73. Ibid., 21.

74. Ibid., 23.

75. Ibid. On this latter point, I suspect that the bishops might raise some questions about Skotnicki's ecclesiology. Skotnicki seems to assume an ecclesiology that does not distinguish between the roles of church and state, presuming that both church and state ought to relate to criminals as a parental figure. My concern with this ecclesiology, in part, is that it does not adequately conceive of the sacramental quality of the church described in *Lumen Gentium* and *Gaudium et Spes*, which suggest that while the church is involved in the world, it also embodies a separate reality linked to the Church of Christ, and as this reality, the church ought serve as a light to the world. This separation is part of the basis for the prophetic stance of the church sometimes in opposition to the state—a stance that is much needed in our responses to our criminal justice crisis.

Christian, and citizen (he seems never to differentiate these positions)—ought to assume the role of a loving, disciplinarian parent in relationship with the prisoner as Christ.

Skotnicki's second question, *What is the justification for punishing criminal offenders?*, he answers in two parts. First, he draws upon Augustine and Aquinas to show that Catholic tradition holds that the state has a moral obligation to punish people who violate the law because of its duties to maintain order and to establish justice in society for the common good. The efforts of the state to realize order and justice, however, will always be limited:

> We cannot expect the state to assume full responsibility for criminal justice. Despite its critical role and the legitimacy of its desire for order, justice is found, finally, only in Christ and in love . . . . This leads to the need for creating a "mystical" space wherein God's design can be accomplished in a way that is outside the gaze and understanding of human judges and human authorities.[76]

Skotnicki's observations about the limitations of the state in redeeming people who violate the law inspire the second part of his answer to this question: the ultimate justification of punishment is neither order nor justice, but atonement. Based on Anselm's substitutionary model of atonement, Skotnicki argues that Christ transformed the meaning of punishment by willingly becoming a prisoner: "Christ, who bore his captivity humbly and prayerfully, in silence, obedience, and fidelity, becomes the model for the repentant prisoner."[77] Punishment is ultimately justified, according to Skotnicki, because it may lead prisoners on an internal journey toward repentance, which potentially results in God's forgiveness and liberation. He thus summarizes his interpretation of a Catholic answer to the question of the justification of punishment: "[T]he social ethic of Catholicism favors state-sponsored retributive intervention [for order and justice] but, principally, the true work of criminal justice must be internal to the process itself and contained in the heart of the individual offender."[78]

In light of this justification for punishment, Skotnicki presents his response to a third question: *What is the end at which forcible intervention aims?* He contextualizes his answer to this question within Catholic interpretations of the end toward which all of human life aims, the experience of God's grace. In light of this end, Skotnicki proposes two purposes of punishment. First, punishment

76. Ibid., 45–46.
77. Ibid., 49.
78. Ibid., 51.

ought to aim for social reintegration of offenders with full restoration to the community after a period of enforced exile. Second, it ought to lead to internal reform, resulting in the liberation and reconciliation of offenders with God and neighbor.[79] Together these ends correspond with the justification of punishment, as social reintegration and internal reform of prisoners ought to contribute to order and justice in society as well as to atonement of offenders with God. The achievement of these ends, according to Skotnicki, also requires viewing prisoners as Christ and nonprisoners assuming the role of loving, disciplinarian parents. These images place limits on punishment so that it can achieve its proper ends and so that punishment is not for the sake of punishment itself. Skotnicki writes, "When viewed in light of the imprisoned Christ, punishment is not absolute and closed as advocates of retribution would contend, or simply a means to a desired social state of affairs, as those who favor deterrence or incapacitation would contend, but always part of the ongoing narrative of a life touched by grace and designed for human and spiritual fulfillment."[80]

Skotnicki's responses to these first three questions do not present perspectives significantly different from those of the U.S. bishops or of Thomistic ethics; his disagreements with the bishops and other Catholic authors arise with his fourth question: *By what means will the end of punishment be accomplished?* Through a historical survey of the formation of Western penal systems, Skotnicki argues that Catholic tradition upholds the prison as the normative means of punishment. He finds that penal systems in the West are rooted in the development of, first, monastic prisons and, later, ecclesiastical prisons under the jurisdiction of the church from the late patristic period through the Middle Ages. These prisons, Skotnicki argues, were centered upon the monastic ideal that "the cell is a place for people serious about finding their true identity and rooting out the influences and impulses that lead to alienation from self, from others, from nature, and from God."[81] Drawing upon this elevation of isolation as a means for self-reform within monasteries, the church created monastic and ecclesiastical prisons as alternatives to secular punishments, which typically used prisons merely as holding cells in anticipation of "real" punishments (usually corporal or monetary in nature). Prisons became "the

79. Although he draws on Aquinas for his argument, Skotnicki's conclusions about the end of punishment notably differ from those of both Koritansky and Soltis, both of whom argue that the end of punishment in Aquinas's thought is the reorientation of the offender's will toward the common good. Skotnicki's interpretation places an explicitly theological spin on the end of punishment.

80. Skotnicki, *Criminal Justice*, 58.

81. Ibid., 135.

basic disciplinary apparatus in the church and, by extension, in Western jurisprudence"[82] with the development of canon law in the twelfth and thirteenth centuries. The Catholic Church continued to use monastic and ecclesiastical prisons throughout the next few centuries in religious criminal justice systems that ran parallel to secular systems. Skotnicki admits that the use of these prisons for punishment throughout the history of the church was "ambiguous" and that "prisoners in Catholic institutions often did not 'live happily.'"[83] Nevertheless, he finds virtue in the Catholic use of prisons where the image of the prisoner as Christ was maintained along with the justification of atonement and the ends of internal reform and social reintegration, and he suggests that monastic and ecclesiastical prisons were often recognized, even by offenders, as more merciful and humane than secular punishments.[84] Skotnicki seems to view the pinnacle of Catholic influence upon Western penal systems as the creation of the penitentiary in the early nineteenth century in the United States by Quaker reformers who drew upon monastic and ecclesiastical models to create secular prisons, building upon the idea "that the combination of work, silence, prayer, and spiritual counsel could mend what was wrong in the human heart."[85] Based upon his historical account, Skotnicki concludes, "Imprisonment is then not the only means to bring the offender back to personal well-being and normal social interaction but, criticisms and misuse notwithstanding, it is clearly the preferred means to accomplish the ends of criminal justice unique to the Catholic tradition."[86]

Skotnicki's second criticism of the bishops' stance on rehabilitation and restoration is thus that the bishops have ignored what he views as the primary means of punishment in a Catholic theory of criminal justice: the prison. The only means of tying together the threads of a Catholic understanding of crime, punishment, and justice, in Skotnicki's view, is the use of time sentences in prisons so that prisoners may come to recognize their wrongdoing and seek reconciliation with God and neighbor. Skotnicki fears that the bishops have lost sight of the value of incarceration as punishment, and he seems to stake a lot on this argument. He writes, "The question that undoubtedly arises in the mind of the reader is whether the theory outlined here . . . can work in practice. The material presented . . . suggests that if the idea of confinement cannot work, then the entire monastic system, *as well as Catholic anthropology and spirituality,*

82. Ibid., 87–88.
83. Ibid., 101. See also 95–97.
84. Ibid., 91–92.
85. Ibid., 122–23.
86. Ibid., 137.

is in question, not to mention its penitential ethos."[87] Skotnicki seems to believe that if the prison cannot work as the means of achieving social reintegration and internal reform of prisoners, then it may be that the entirety of Catholic tradition—not just his theory of criminal justice—is undermined.

The stakes that Skotnicki places in his theory of criminal justice ought to lead to questions not only about whether it can work in practice, but also about whether prisons really are the normative means of punishment within Catholic tradition. The former question concerns the effectiveness of prisons in terms of social reintegration and internal reform of prisoners. In failing to answer this question fully, Skotnicki himself is guilty of his first criticism of the bishops—lack of analytical depth concerning contemporary criminology. He presents no criminological evidence that prisons in the United States—or anywhere else, for that matter—are effective. He does not account for criminological data that suggest that about two-thirds of released prisoners in the United States are rearrested within three years of reentry into the community, half are reconvicted, and one-quarter resentenced to prison for a new crime.[88] Nor does he account for data that indicate that recidivism does not seem to correspond to the length of a prisoner's sentence. Prisoners serving five years in prison are as likely to reoffend as prisoners serving one year in prison, and while those who serve between five to ten years may be less likely to reoffend, the decrease in recidivism in this group is explained mostly by prisoners "aging out" of criminal behavior.[89] Modern U.S. prisons clearly do not "work" as far as Skotnicki's stated ends for criminal justice systems are concerned.

With respect to this question, however, Skotnicki might respond that he would not expect to achieve these ends in modern U.S. prisons as they do not practice what he is preaching; these prisons are therefore not a true test of his theory. Given the praise he gives to Quaker penitentiaries, a reader might then suppose that those penal institutions would offer a fair test of Skotnicki's theory. While recidivism data are not available for these institutions, Charles Dickens visited the United States in 1842 in order to see their innovations firsthand. Skotnicki is clearly aware of Dickens's writings on this subject, as he cites them in both *Criminal Justice and the Catholic Church* and an earlier book based upon

87. Ibid., 137. Emphasis mine.

88. "Recidivism," Bureau of Justice Statistics, U.S. Department of Justice, accessed July 26, 2010, http://bjs.ojp.usdoj.gov/index.cfm?ty=tp&tid=17. Note that these figures do not include released prisoners who returned to prison for parole violations.

89. Marc Mauer, "The Hidden Problem of Time Served in Prison," *Social Research* 74, no. 2 (2007): 701–6.

his dissertation, *Religion and the Development of the American Penal System.*[90] Although he draws upon Dickens's visit, as well as that of Alexis de Tocqueville, to praise penitentiaries, Skotnicki fails to mention that neither Dickens nor Tocqueville was pleased with what he found. Dickens wrote,

> The system here is rigid, strict, and hopeless solitary confinement. I believe it, in its effects, to be cruel and wrong. In its intentions, I am well convinced that it is *kind, humane, and meant for reformation*; but I am persuaded that those who devised this system of Prison Discipline, and those benevolent gentlemen who carry it into execution, *do not know what they are doing.* I believe that few men are capable of estimating the immense amount of torture and agony which this dreadful punishment, prolonged for years, inflicts upon its sufferers.[91]

Dickens was not alone in his criticism of penitentiaries. Recognition of their failure grew throughout the nineteenth century, leading to the creation of "reformatories" in their place, beginning in the 1870s. The historical record thus suggests that even early penitentiaries did not realize in practice Skotnicki's theory of criminal justice. To the question of whether a theory of criminal justice that uses prisons as normative means of punishment can work, any level of intellectual honesty requires the answer that *it never has before.* Skotnicki writes, "The theory that I present carries no weight if it cannot be redeemed in human experience."[92] Both contemporary criminology and the historical record suggest that Skotnicki's theory may then carry no weight.[93]

90. Skotnicki, *Criminal Justice*, 122. Also, *Religion and the Development of the American Penal System* (Lanham, MD: University Press of America, 2000), 142.

91. Charles Dickens, *American Notes*, introduction by Christopher Lasch (Gloucester, MA: Peter Smith, 1842/1968), 120. Emphasis mine.

92. Skotnicki, *Criminal Justice*, 7.

93. In *Just Punishment,* Soltis helpfully notes that Skotnicki holds a minority viewpoint on the efficacy of penitentiaries. She writes, "Ultimately, Skotnicki argues that the decline of the penitentiary should be attributed to surrounding conditions rather than inefficacy of the formal guiding principles of the separate and silent systems; in his view, silence, work, and moral/religious training were never demonstrated to be unsuccessful" (46). To reach this conclusion, Skotnicki draws on Carl E. Schneider, "The Rise of Prisons and the Origins of the Rehabilitative Ideal," *Michigan Law Review* 77 (1979): 707–46. See also Skotnicki's *Religion and the Development of the American Penal System*, note 5 on p. 148. Both Skotnicki and Schneider depart from the majority of evidence from the time period of penitentiaries in which critics like Dickens saw a strict dependence on religious ideology causing a failure to restore prisoners to society as healthy and contributing citizens.

With this conclusion, Skotnicki may worry that the failure of his theory on practical grounds destabilizes the whole of Catholic tradition. Such could be the case, however, only if he is correct that incarceration is foundational within a Catholic theory of criminal justice, and here we must ask whether prisons really are the normative means of punishment within Catholic tradition, whether they represent well our core religious and moral teachings. In the following chapters, I contend that few Catholics would view the prison as a redemptive, or even an accurate, representation of their tradition. Rather the sacraments lie at the center of Catholic faith and practice, and in the sacramental life, particularly in the practices of the Eucharist and Penance, we may find a stronger foundation for a Catholic theory of criminal justice—one that supports the call of the bishops of the United States for responsibility, rehabilitation, and restoration.

Before proceeding to that argument, however, one more critique ought to be leveled against Skotnicki's project. Suppose that he is correct that incarceration is foundational within a Catholic theory of criminal justice. Also, allow for the sake of argument that Skotnicki could be correct that prisons can be effective means for achieving the ends of social reintegration and internal reform of prisoners when the proper image of the prisoner as Christ and justification of imprisonment as being for atonement as well as for the maintenance of order and establishment of justice in society are upheld. Even if Skotnicki is correct on both of these points, touting the virtues of prisons in a context such as ours where crises of social and criminal justice are so tightly bound together strikes me as shortsighted at best and deeply irresponsible at worst. In a society marked by mass incarceration, particularly of members of racial and ethnic minorities, Skotnicki's argument for prisons seems to support the ongoing caging of our citizens. Perhaps his argument is intended as a call for reform of our prisons to make them more humane, but this intention is not apparent in any of Skotnicki's texts. Even if he is trying to argue for reform, recommendations based on his answers to the four questions for a theory of punishment ignore the ways in which our criminal justice systems reflect and sustain social injustice. "More prisons" is not a good response to our problems because it will only exacerbate our problems as the first genuine prison society. "Better prisons" alone is also not a good response because it fails to account for the broader social context in which even better prisons will continue to perpetuate social injustice.[94] Because Skotnicki never attends to the interconnections of criminal and social justice and instead examines a theory of

94. The strength of Soltis's argument in comparison with Skotnicki's is that she argues not only for prison reform, but also for downscaling our prison populations and for addressing the social injustices that contribute to and are exacerbated by mass incarceration.

criminal justice in a contextual vacuum, his recommendations—even if based in Catholic tradition and even if effective at bringing about social reintegration and internal reform—cannot provide sufficient resources for a different, more just future.

CONCLUSION

Any adequate response to mass incarceration in the United States must satisfy several criteria, beginning with an accurate assessment of the nature of our criminal and social justice crises. It will, first, account for the ways in which criminal and social justice in our society are fundamentally intertwined. Such a response will not only address the conditions that foster crime. It will also attend to the ways in which social injustice helped create our criminal justice crisis independently of crime rates and, in turn, the ways in which mass incarceration continues to help sustain social injustice. It will provide insight into the unique realities of our criminal and social justice crises in the United States in light of our history and in comparison with the rest of the world. Furthermore, it will offer resources for responding to crime and individual wrongdoing.

A response from a Catholic perspective ought also to draw upon the heart of our religious and moral tradition. Among the authors discussed in this chapter a consensus can be found about certain aspects of Catholic tradition with respect to issues of justice. Each author upholds (to some degree) the human dignity of all persons, including people who commit crime. Human dignity places a limitation upon punishment. The recognition of human dignity requires the acknowledgment of moral agency of people who violate the law and harm others. This acknowledgment is the basis for holding individuals responsible for their actions and for enabling them to choose to change their lives for the common good. Punishment cannot be justified for the sake of punishment itself or for utilitarian purposes alone. Rather the justification of our responses to wrongdoers must be that such responses can serve the common good by restoring the well-being of all community members, including victims and offenders. The common good requires the maintenance of order and establishment of justice in society in addition to the realization of the good of each individual member of society, which may entail the repair of broken relationships or atonement. Punishment ought to be "medicinal," providing the means of achieving internal reform and social reintegration of people who commit crime and harm others.

Despite this important consensus, with the exception of Soltis, none of the Catholic authors writing about our criminal justice systems have managed to satisfy all of these criteria, especially in terms of accurately assessing our crises of justice. Reflections on criminal justice that go back to core theoretical concepts such as justice and punishment, such as Koritansky's consideration of Aquinas's philosophy of punishment, lack grounding in the unique context of current criminal justice systems in the United States. Soltis corrects for this oversight in her application of Aquinas's virtue of legal justice to prison reform. The USCCB offers some important guidance about Catholic resources for reassessing our criminal justice systems. Nevertheless, they take a less prophetic stance than is necessary to address our justice crises. Finally, Skotnicki provides an argument that fails on practical, theological, and moral grounds. Prisons have never achieved the ends that he identifies for them, and I doubt that they could succeed in their general use. But beyond the question of the effectiveness of his recommendations, it seems ill advised to tout the virtues of the prison as a solution to mass incarceration. Although Skotnicki agrees with the other authors discussed here regarding the human dignity of people who commit crime and the justification and purposes of punishment, his turn to ecclesiastical and monastic prisons is out of touch with our intertwining crises of justice. Moreover, Skotnicki's appeals to these means of punishment oddly places these institutions at the center of Catholic moral and religious tradition, when it seems doubtful that many Catholics would recognize them as related to the heart of their faith and practice.

In light of the weaknesses of Catholic contributions to solutions to our criminal and social justice crises, it seems that we need to generate a new response. In addition to satisfying the criteria enumerated here, this response should begin with reconsideration of what truly lies at the heart of Catholic moral and theological tradition. I argue that Catholics see the sacraments and liturgy as that heart—not monastic and ecclesiastical prisons. By drawing upon liturgical and sacramental ethics, we may find resources that may undergird an adequate response to our crises of justice.

3

A Liturgical and Sacramental Approach to Justice

Sacramentality—the idea that "everything is, in principle, capable of embodying and communicating the divine"[1]—lies at the heart of Catholic tradition. While many other Christians share this perspective, sacramentality has particular influence upon Catholic liturgical practices and theological beliefs. With the belief that everything has the potential to reveal God, Catholics also maintain that Jesus Christ, who is the ultimate sacrament, instituted specific, tangible signs of God's grace, disclosing the hidden reality of salvation in the world. The *Catechism of the Catholic Church* delineates how the seven sacraments recognized by Catholics touch all key moments of life from birth through death, thereby consecrating human existence.[2] Sacramentality thus draws connections between our natural and spiritual lives, revealing human unity with the holy. Each sacrament in the church entails a liturgy, or rite, through which God's grace is conveyed to its recipient.

Since the sacraments consecrate our lives, Catholics (and other Christians who maintain a sacramental life) believe that the sacraments form who we are. The sacraments initiate Christian community; they sanctify our particular callings; and they offer healing when fallenness draws us away from both spiritual and physical wholeness. Through participation in the sacraments in our liturgy, Catholics believe we are drawn "into the compelling love of Christ" and that we are "set on fire" as "grace is poured forth on us."[3] We are sanctified, pulled closer to God, and called into activities in the world that share this grace. The formative character of the sacraments suggests that our sacramental lives relate to our moral lives. The disclosure of the hidden reality of salvation in the world, the revelation of God's grace through a sign instituted by Jesus

1. Richard P. McBrien, *Catholicism*, study edition (San Francisco: HarperCollins, 1981), 731.
2. See *Catechism of the Catholic Church*, ¶1210.
3. Second Vatican Council, *Sacrosanctum Concilium*, ¶10.

Christ influences our perceptions of reality, and our new perceptions ought to influence how we act in response to the challenges of our world. The rehearsal of the vision of salvation and grace through the liturgy of the sacraments should help us to envision the world, our selves, and our neighbors as God does. In taking on this vision in our sacramental lives, we are formed to see and act in certain ways in our moral lives.

The hidden reality of salvation in the world revealed in the sacraments is the coming in fullness of God's reign, inaugurated in the life, death, and resurrection of Jesus Christ. Although we cannot know the full reality of God's reign in our own time and place, from the ministry of Jesus Christ we can know that one of its distinguishing markers is justice. If we are formed through the liturgy of the sacraments to envision reality as God does, then one aspect of the moral formation of the sacramental life is that we are called to seek God's justice in the world as we witness the in-breaking of God's reign in our own time and place. In this way, sacramentality, morality, and the pursuit of justice are linked to each other.

The liturgy of the sacraments provides a starting point in Catholic tradition for theological and moral reflection about justice. Liturgical and sacramental ethics offer resources for discerning an adequate Catholic response to our criminal and social justice crises. Examination of specific sacraments and the liturgical practices associated with them illumines the ways that Christians should be formed in work for justice. In particular, the Eucharist, the paradigmatic practice of Christian sacramental life for Catholics and many Protestants, offers a framework for critiques of social injustice. As the Eucharist grounds practices of Penance and Reconciliation, these sacraments also provide a model for responses to individual wrongdoing, and thus, resources for examining criminal justice.

Relating sacraments and liturgy to ethics and the pursuit of justice, however, can involve some significant difficulties. Among these difficulties are privatization and politicization of worship; pluralism both within the church and beyond it; injustice within church practices and institutions; and issues concerning whether and how participation in sacrament and liturgy can be morally formative. This chapter begins by elucidating these challenges to sacramental and liturgical ethics, and then proposes an interpretation of sacraments and liturgy that can alleviate these difficulties while providing a basis for linking the sacraments and liturgy to the moral life of Christians generally and their pursuit of justice in particular. From this framework, I explore how the disclosure of grace and salvation in the Eucharist and Penance ought to form our visions of justice in the world with respect to both social injustice and individual wrongdoing. By forming our visions of justice in this way, liturgy and sacraments, which are clearly more central to Catholic tradition than ecclesiastical and monastic prisons (*contra* Skotnicki), offer resources for responding to our criminal and social justice crises.

CHALLENGES TO LITURGICAL AND SACRAMENTAL ETHICS

Several difficulties arise when trying to construct a sacramental ethic, or more broadly, a liturgical ethic, first and foremost, differences among Christians about what constitutes liturgy and sacrament. Christians disagree about the role of sacraments in worship, their definition, their number, and who administers them. These disagreements have played themselves out for centuries, and in many ways, lie at the center of ongoing denominational divisions among Christians, especially within the Western church. Differences in liturgical style and practice also divide Christians across denominations, or even within particular congregations and denominations. If Christians cannot agree about liturgy and sacraments, then it seems liturgy and sacraments would be poor resources for Christian moral discernment.

Another issue with sacramental and liturgical ethics is that privatization of Christian worship practices specifically, and religion generally, within many contexts makes it appear that sacraments and liturgy offer little insight or inspiration for addressing injustice. As a result of these dynamics, religion is seen as a sphere for becoming acquainted with one's "authentic self" or "inner truth" rather than as an arena that transforms one's self and one's relationships in response to God's grace.[4] Liturgy becomes an instrument of self-improvement, "a resource for getting in touch with the inward God or for celebrating inwardly constituted faith," and it loses its public, political, and communal valence.[5] Congregations become appendages of "lifestyle enclaves" in which

---

4. These dynamics are apparent in the classic sociological work of Robert Bellah and his co-authors in *Habits of the Heart: Individualism and Commitment in American Life* (Berkeley: University of California Press, 1985). Christian Smith offers an interesting perspective on these dynamics among youth in the United States in *Soul Searching: The Religious and Spiritual Lives of American Teenagers* (New York: Oxford University Press, 2009). For discussions of how these dynamics relate to liturgical and sacramental ethics, see William T. Cavanaugh, *Torture and Eucharist* (Malden, MA: Blackwell, 1998), especially 207–21; Roger Mahoney, "The Eucharist and Social Justice," *Worship* 57, no. 1 (1983): 52–61; and M. Francis Mannion, "Liturgy and the Present Crisis of Culture," *Worship* 62, no. 2 (1988): 98–123.

5. Mannion, "Liturgy," 106. For additional discussion of the problems of privatization of worship, see Ralph A. Keifer, "Liturgy and Ethics: Some Unresolved Dilemmas," in *Living No Longer for Ourselves: Liturgy and Justice in the Nineties*, ed. Kathleen Hughes and Mark R. Francis (Collegeville, MN: Liturgical, 1991), 68–83.

people of similar economic class and social status gather on a weekly (or monthly, or yearly) basis. Religion, in this view, at best, offers little more than an empty morality, and at worst, recapitulates the morality of the secular world, which too often bases discernment of justice upon the whims of political, economic, social, or cultural power. If religion is privatized, we ought not to look to liturgy and sacraments for guidance about who we ought to become and how we ought to respond to the injustices of the world.

While privatization of religion is one danger to liturgical and sacramental ethics, disagreement about the politicization of worship is another face of this danger. This disagreement is based on the common assumption that while "ethics is political, worship is (or should be) apolitical," resulting in divergent senses about the relationship among liturgy, sacraments, ethics, and justice.[6] On one side lies a sort of "religious ritualism" that emphasizes "smells and bells" without recognizing that our rituals are nothing to God unless we "let justice roll down like waters and righteousness like an ever-flowing stream."[7] From this perspective, worship concerns the "otherworldly," and properly so. The introduction of ethics to liturgy and sacraments can result in little more than themed worship services that alter the substance of worship. On the other side are people who design such services and who often have a sense that politics must be introduced to religious practices that focus too much upon the otherworldly. What they fail to see is that "we gather for worship to celebrate not an idea by a Person, not what we can, should, or will do but what God has done and continues to do for us in Jesus, dead and risen."[8] Although these two sides differ on whether to politicize worship practices, they share the notion that worship and politics—and along with it, ethics—are separated. The separation of worship and ethics would seem to suggest that exploring sacramental and liturgical ethics as a basis for working for justice would be a fruitless venture.

Yet another difficulty with constructing liturgical and sacramental ethics is the question of how to respond to pluralism both within the church and beyond church walls. Constructing such an ethic prior to the modern period, in the days of medieval Christendom, would not confront the same sort of problem. However, we now live in a world of religious, philosophical, ideological,

6. Stanley Hauerwas and Samuel Wells critique the quoted perspective in "Christian Ethics as Informed Prayer," in *The Blackwell Companion to Christian Ethics*, ed. Stanley Hauerwas and Samuel Wells (Malden, MA: Blackwell, 2004), 6.

7. Amos 5:24; cf. Isa. 1:10-17 and Mic. 6:6-7. See H. Kathleen Hughes's discussion of these divergent senses in "Liturgy and Justice: An Intrinsic Relationship," in *Living No Longer for Ourselves*, ed. Hughes and Francis, 36–51.

8. Ibid., 38.

social, cultural, and political diversity, a new situation with modernity that many welcome, despite its complexities. If liturgical and sacramental ethics seek to apply Christian practices to the problems of the world, people outside of the church may not readily agree about the intention, direction, or value of this work. Theologian William Everett writes, "The problem with Christian liturgy, with its biblical roots, is that it seeks to do more than legitimate an ecclesiastical institution or to dispose individuals to move into society. It also seeks to bring about some kind of new and perfect society under God's governance."[9] Any liturgical or sacramental ethics that propose the "Christianizing" of society will rightfully face serious, valid, and important opposition. Yet if the aim of Christians is not to "Christianize" society, it remains unclear what Christians propose to do in response to injustice. Even within the church, it may be difficult to generate consensus about how to concretize the work of the church in the world, or how to "apply" the liturgy and sacraments to our circumstances. Themed worship services threaten to divide communities in which disagreements often remain unexpressed. Meanwhile the deeper social, cultural, political, economic, and moral implications of celebrating "one bread, one body" are left unexplored. A challenge to liturgical and sacramental ethics is to find ways to express the work of the church community in response to worldly problems while still respecting the individual consciences both of its members and of people outside of the church in a pluralistic world.

Such work is especially difficult when the inner liturgical and sacramental life of the church fails to embody justice itself, particularly amidst the ongoing realities of racial, ethnic, gender, class, and sexual discrimination and disparity. Theologian Kenneth Himes recommends "examining in an empirical way what actually happens at sacramental celebrations," to uncover what they communicate about our society and how the broader social context shapes the message of the liturgy.[10] He suggests attending to who plays which roles and who is excluded both from particular roles and from the community entirely. When we examine the actual practices of our rituals, we may become more aware of how they may "constrict [the] grace-filled potential" of our liturgies and sacraments, depending on whether they reinforce or subvert unjust patterns of human interactions in our society.[11] People with positions of privilege may not readily recognize injustice in the pews, but the sense of alienation among

9. William Everett, "Liturgy and Ethics: A Response to Saliers and Ramsey," *Journal of Religious Ethics* 7, no. 2 (1979): 208.

10. Kenneth R. Himes, "Eucharist and Justice: Assessing the Legacy of Virgil Michel," *Worship* 62 (1988): 216.

those people who are marginalized within our churches ought to inspire us all to address the divisions that keep us from becoming fully the body of Christ. Moral theologian Margaret Farley observes,

> Those who continue to be marginalized in the church (whether because of sex or race or class or whatever) are acutely aware that we have never adequately asked what it means to worship together as equals. We have not yet worked out patterns of authority that fully satisfy the gospel norms. We have not yet found creative answers to questions of roles, degrees, and forms of participation in liturgy. We violate in our symbols and structures of worship both our teaching regarding the church as *koinonia* and our teaching regarding social justice in the world.[12]

If the church fails to embody justice in its sacramental and liturgical life, it may be difficult to discern how the sacraments and liturgy may serve as the basis for ethics that argue for the embodiment of justice in the world.

Finally, apart from the dynamics of the church in the modern world and the difficulties of injustice within the church, the simple problem of the meaning of participation in ritual presents several issues for liturgical and sacramental ethics. Many forays into liturgical and sacramental ethics have built upon the idea that our ritual lives in church communities ought to shape Christians to become people who bear certain virtues in response to God's grace conveyed in worship. Ethicist Paul Ramsey, for instance, writes, "*lex orandi lex credendi lex bene operandi*," tying together creed, prayer, and well-doing as the basis for the formation of Christian moral character and agency.[13] Liturgical theologian Don Saliers responds to Ramsey by suggesting that worship is a "characterizing activity": "When worship occurs, people are characterized, given their life and their fundamental location and orientation in the world."[14] From this location and orientation, people derive their actions from "the inner logic of the Christian moral life."[15] The link between worship

11. Susan Ross, *Extravagant Affections: A Feminist Sacramental Theology* (New York: Continuum, 1998), 13.

12. Margaret Farley, "Beyond the Formal Principle: A Reply to Ramsey and Saliers," *Journal of Religious Ethics* 7, no. 2 (1979): 195. Several African American Catholic theologians make similar arguments to Farley's. See M. Shawn Copeland, *Enfleshing Freedom: Body, Race, and Being* (Minneapolis: Fortress Press, 2010); Diana L. Hayes, *Standing in the Shoes My Mother Made: A Womanist Theology* (Minneapolis: Fortress Press, 2011); and Bryan N. Massingale, *Racial Justice and the Catholic Church* (Maryknoll, NY: Orbis, 2010).

13. Paul Ramsey, "Liturgy and Ethics," *Journal of Religious Ethics* 7, no. 2 (1979): 139–71.

and ethics in the creation of Christian character is essentially the driving insight of *The Blackwell Companion to Christian Ethics*, edited by Stanley Hauerwas and Samuel Wells.[16] Within Catholic theology, the premise is also apparent in the significant work of Virgil Michel in the liturgical reform movement of the early twentieth century.[17] Despite this common theme, anyone who has sat through a Sunday service in almost any church might wonder how much character formation took place, especially as churchgoers often go through the motions of the ritual with little reflection upon how they have been given a fundamental location or orientation in the world. Moreover, poorly enacted worship services may test the capacity of liturgy and sacraments to form well even the most devout participants, despite doctrine that maintains that the efficacy of a sacrament is independent of the merit of those who administer it. As Saliers admits, "Worship is . . . necessarily normative. At the same time, not all who participate in its language and action are shaped by it."[18] Or as Margaret Farley observes, "The human spirit is as often dulled, distracted, burdened as it is touched and awakened, freed in faith and hope. Far from 'building up' the body of Christ, common worship often paralyzes it."[19] If churchgoers find it difficult to participate meaningfully in weekly services (and I think almost everyone has shared in this experience at some point), then it is difficult to make strong claims about how liturgy and sacraments actually dispose individuals to become virtuous, let alone how worship creates communities that may bring about a more just world in response to God's grace.

A More Expansive View of Liturgy and Sacrament

Even with these caveats, liturgy and sacraments can and should serve as a basis for understanding Christian ethics. They are after all the central practices of

14. Don E. Saliers, "Liturgy and Ethics: Some New Beginnings," *Journal of Religious Ethics* 7, no. 2 (1979): 175.

15. Ibid., 178.

16. See Hauerwas and Wells, *The Blackwell Companion to Christian Ethics*.

17. For discussion of Michel's legacy in Catholic theology, see Himes, "Eucharist and Justice." Also, Paul Marx, *Virgil Michel and the Liturgical Movement* (Collegeville, MN: Liturgical, 1957). While many of Michel's contributions can be found in his many editorials in *Orate Fratres*, some key articles of his include "With Our Readers," *Orate Fratres* 5 (1930–31): 430–31; "The Liturgy the Basis of Social Regeneration," *Orate Fratres* 9 (1934–35): 536–45; and "The Scope of the Liturgical Movement," *Orate Fratres* 10 (1935–36): 485–90. See also "Are We One in Christ?," *Ecclesiastical Review* 81 (1934): 395–401 and *The Christian in the World* (Collegeville, MN: Liturgical, 1939).

18. Saliers, "Liturgy and Ethics," 176.

19. Farley, "Formal Principle," 192.

Christians, especially Catholics, and so lie at the heart of our moral lives. With respect to widely ranging, sometimes conflicting, views about what constitutes a sacrament or what liturgy entails, a more expansive approach to defining liturgy and sacrament may be helpful for grounding an ethic accessible to a wide range of Christians regardless of denominational divisions. Moreover, taking a broader view of liturgy and sacraments may also help address the other challenges to liturgical and sacramental ethics such as privatization and politicization of worship, pluralism, injustice within the church, and problems with the meaning of participation in liturgy and sacraments. A broad view begins with the recognition that liturgy is not simply a rubric of words and actions for worshiping together and that sacraments cannot be reduced simply to a particular list of signs of God's grace instituted by Christ. More expansive accounts of liturgy and sacraments allow us to reflect upon the fundamental beliefs and practices underlying these aspects of our faith and to engage more readily in ecumenical conversations about how they relate to ethics.

The term "liturgy" comes to us from the Greek *leitourgia*, meaning "public service," while the term "sacrament" comes from the Latin *sacrare*, meaning "to consecrate."[20] The public service of *leitourgia* can refer to the gathering of the church, of the *ekklesia*, in prayer (as opposed to private devotion), but it refers more basically to the service rendered by the *ekklesia* unto others, especially unto the poor, oppressed, and marginalized. The liturgy, then, is the work of the church, of the assembly of Christians scattered throughout the world, in the service of God and neighbor in our own time and place, emulating the servanthood of Jesus Christ in anticipation of God's full reign.[21] We celebrate the sacraments in our liturgy, and the grace of God is made perceptible to us human beings through their signs, thus consecrating human life. Anything that discloses the hidden reality of salvation is sacramental. The seven sacraments recognized by the Roman Catholic Church are seen as instituted by Jesus Christ, but the emphasis upon sacramentality in Catholic tradition draws us to look more widely for God's grace in our world. The public service of the church, the liturgy, revolves around the sacraments. In this capacity, the church does not draw us out of the world but more deeply into it in anticipation of the ultimate mystery of God's reign. Moral theologian Susan Ross writes, "What is celebrated in the sacraments is not an otherworldly reality, but rather what the Christian community strives for: a community in which all eat and

---

20. David L. Stubbs provides a helpful discussion of the meaning of *leitourgia* in "Liturgy and Ethics, or Liturgy Is Ethics," *Reformed Review* 57, no. 3 (2004): 1–12.

21. See *Catechism of the Catholic Church*, ¶1070–72.

drink together at a common table, in which justice is a reality, in which the sacramental lives of Christians reflect and inspire their lives 'in the world.'"[22] More than a rubric or a list, liturgy and sacraments comprise the work of the church in consecrating the world in emulation of Jesus Christ, the Son of God, through the Holy Spirit by serving God and neighbors, particularly victims of injustice. Engaging in this work is the worship of God. This more expansive understanding of liturgy and sacraments, while rooted in Roman Catholicism, concurs with the beliefs and practices of many other Christians.

This understanding of liturgy and sacraments provides a framework for responding to the challenges to liturgical and sacramental ethics. First, this interpretation suggests that Christian worship that only endeavors to help participants realize their authentic selves within a lifestyle enclave fails to become truly liturgical and sacramental. Such practices do not render the public service of the *ekklesia* unto others, especially unto the poor, oppressed, and marginalized. They do not consecrate the world, making the grace of God perceptible to human beings. Where celebration of liturgy and sacraments fails in these ways, Christians ought to refocus their worship practices away from the pursuit of one's inner truth alone and toward the praise of the transcendent God who entered the world to establish God's reign, embodied proleptically in the church. With this refocus, Christians move from concern with one's authentic self toward the transformation of one's self and one's communities in response to God's call for justice. We ought to reclaim our faith and its practice from privatization, or else "the liturgy loses its power to embody a vision of social transformation, and its ability to elicit commitment to the social project is vitiated."[23] We ought to emphasize the public service of liturgy consecrating the world in anticipation of God's reign as we participate in the religious practices that nurture our souls.

The move away from privatization of liturgy and sacraments suggests that Christians must reclaim the public, political, and communal valence of worship. People on either side of the divide about the politicization of worship assume falsely that liturgy and sacraments are apolitical and thus have nothing to do with ethics. Neither acknowledges that worship is already political, that participation in liturgy and sacraments already challenges the principalities and powers of this world, and that liturgy and sacraments do more than merely collect discrete individuals in pursuit of inward truth—they create a new sort of community bound together in a common public work. By creating this community, liturgy and sacraments provide a foretaste of God's reign. Liturgy

22. Susan Ross, *Extravagant Affections*, 63.

23. Mannion, "Liturgy," 107.

and sacraments do not draw us out of political and moral troubles, but more deeply into the world, presenting an alternative vision of who ultimately rules over us all. Drawing on Orthodox theologian Alexander Schmemann, William Cavanaugh writes,

> The original sense of *leitourgia* was "an action by which a group of people become something corporately which they had not been as a mere collection of individuals." The emphasis here is the *externality* of the liturgy to individual bodies, the way it incorporates individuals into the body of Christ. But to participate in a communal and public discipline of bodies is already to be engaged in direct confrontation with the politics of the world.[24]

Of course, the church always fails to live up to the visions of God's reign. The visions upheld in liturgy and sacraments, however, hold these ideals before us as an alternative to the politics and ethics that now reign. Liturgy and sacraments always already are political acts.

The challenges of pluralism must be met with acknowledgment of the limits of liturgical or sacramental ethics. As liturgy and sacraments create a people, the *ekklesia*, so liturgical and sacramental ethics are the ethics of that people. While the ultimate hope of the people who participate in liturgy and sacraments is the full realization of God's reign, this hope is tempered by our own sinfulness. The church too often fails to live according to the vision of God's reign and falls short of justice in both its internal and external relations. Recognition of our fallenness must lead Christians to accept that the goal of "bringing about some kind of new and perfect society under God's governance" can lead neither to "Christianizing" society nor to a simplistic translation of ecclesiastical practices into civil society.[25] God's reign comes ultimately through God's will. Nevertheless, the work of challenging injustice in the world depends on the belief that, despite the sinfulness of the church, God's grace is present in the church's public service of consecrating the world *ex opere operato*. Liturgical and sacramental ethics explore how liturgy and sacraments ought to form and inform Christian individuals and communities through God's grace as they confront injustice in their own times and places.

While liturgical and sacramental ethics ought not to be imposed upon those outside the church, they ought not to require uniformity of worship that stifles pluralism within the church either. Ramsey recommends that the

---

24. Cavanaugh, *Torture and Eucharist*, 12. Emphasis in the original.
25. Everett, "Liturgy and Ethics," 208.

unity of Christian worship admit "extraordinary variety."[26] He suggests that the measure of Christian unity ought not to be the synchronicity of our liturgical practices—a silent meeting of the Society of Friends or an Evangelical revival is liturgy as much as a Roman Catholic mass is liturgy. Rather the measure of our public service consecrating the world is whether it emulates the work of Jesus Christ through the Holy Spirit: "[I]n all cases the rule of faith and life and worship alike is some common understanding of God's presence with us and His action for us in Jesus Christ, and the triumph of that action."[27] With this rule of faith, life, and worship, our concern ought to be less whether a particular form of worship meets our personal spiritual needs and more whether it helps us to perceive God's work in the world, to participate in the body of Christ, and to explore the deeper social, cultural, political, economic, and moral implications of the triumph of God's reign. This concern should also lead Christians to critique the dynamics of injustice in their own churches as much as, if not more than, those dynamics outside of the church. Liturgical and sacramental practices that fail to embody justice for all persons regardless of race, ethnicity, socioeconomic status, gender, or sexuality do not live up to the rule of faith, life, and worship.

Finally, liturgical and sacramental ethics must allow that the formative power of liturgy and sacraments may be limited by our own weaknesses in terms of participation. Sometimes we go through the motions. We may not always be open to the grace extended to us. Liturgy and sacraments cannot magically transform our characters. Where liturgical and sacramental practices do not conform to the rule of God's presence and Christ's action, liturgy and sacrament may actually dull our capacities to be just. Nevertheless, liturgy and sacraments—properly understood as the work of the church in the service of God and neighbor, emulating the servanthood of Jesus Christ in disclosing the hidden reality of God's reign in the world—do extend grace to us. Of course, we must be properly disposed to receive that grace and extend that grace to others. Saliers comments,

> The prayer of Christian liturgy faces the world's ambiguity and evil. But it is precisely in the world that God is to be glorified by doing the works of Christ. Worship ascribes glory to God alone; but unless glorification is shown in works of justice, mercy, and love faithful to God's commands, Christ's liturgy is not fully enacted.[28]

26. Ramsey, "Liturgy and Ethics," 141.
27. Ibid., 142.
28. Saliers, "Liturgy and Ethics," 181.

Saliers admits that this link between liturgy and ethics is "easily neglected."[29] The link to work for justice, however, lies within the fundamental meaning and practice of Christian liturgy and sacraments.

This more expansive interpretation of liturgy and sacraments suggests that liturgical and sacramental ethics are possible for Christians today despite the challenges of privatization, politicization, and pluralism as well as of injustice within the church and of failures to receive God's grace offered in worship. The central insight of theologians drawing the connection between liturgy, sacraments, ethics, and justice is that our ritual lives in church communities ought to shape Christians to become just people in response to the vision of God's reign conveyed in worship. These theologians draw upon the work of virtue ethicists over the last century who have argued that the moral life cannot be reduced to important moments of decision about what is good and right, but also includes the time between those moments in which our consciousness is formed to make these determinations. Our moral character depends in part upon "the quality of our consciousness," to borrow philosopher Iris Murdoch's terminology. How we see the world and how we understand our place in it shapes what we decide is the right and good action in moments of decision. From this perspective, ethics ought to move beyond consideration of rules and consequences to account for how character and perception influence our interpretations of rules and consequences in particular situations. Ethics also ought to explore how moral character and accurate perception are cultivated, especially in the context of religious belief and practice. Murdoch asks, "How can we make ourselves better?" To which she answers, not through mere force of will, but through altering the quality of our consciousness, and one key way to alter consciousness is through religion:

> Religion normally emphasizes states of mind as well as actions, and regards states of mind as the genetic background of action: pureness of heart, meekness of spirit. Religion provides devices [for example, prayer or meditation] for the purification of states of mind. . . . And if quality of consciousness matters, then anything which alters consciousness in the direction of unselfishness, objectivity, and realism is to be connected with virtue.[30]

Among the religious devices that alter the quality of our consciousness are liturgy and sacraments, through which participants may come to view the

29. Ibid., 176.

30. Iris Murdoch, *The Sovereignty of Good* (New York: Routledge, 1970), 83–84.

world and their work in it in light of the vision of justice under the reign of God. While Christians may bristle at Murdoch's reduction of liturgy and sacraments to devices for moral transformation rather than as modes for worship of God, her insight that religious practices can foster this transformation remains important for linking liturgy and sacraments to ethics and work for justice.

Liturgy and sacraments alter the quality of our consciousness by guiding us through a particular vision that grounds "an actual reorientation of sensibility and intentional acts . . . a new self-understanding and 'world-picture.'"[31] This self-understanding and world-picture uphold certain norms and behaviors as meaningful. Liturgy maintains this vision through "the continuing exercise of recalling, sustaining, and reentering that picture of the cosmos."[32] As we rehearse this vision in liturgy, we practice seeing the world from a different perspective than our own, which too often is encumbered by human limitation. Rather we are asked in liturgy to adopt a world-picture from God's perspective. Liturgy thus "provides a guiding horizon that both reframes our questions and guides our thinking in certain directions."[33] By entering this vision, we become "de-centered." Susan Ross describes this de-centering as a humiliating experience, in that we become aware "of our place in our own world and in the universe."[34] She continues, "This kind of humility means that we are aware of the needs of others, not so much as needs that precede our own . . . but as needs that may have as much priority as our own."[35] With greater appreciation of the needs of others, especially in light of God's outpouring of grace, participants in liturgy also may find their own wills decentered by God's will for "life, freedom, justice, peace, love, humanity, and all the other marks of God's kingdom."[36] When we become decentered in liturgy, the quality of our consciousness becomes transformed so that "God is present in such a way that our lives, hearts, and minds have the possibility of being shaped into the patterns of the kingdom of Christ."[37] The task of liturgical and sacramental ethics is to discern those patterns as revealed in our worship practices and to examine how they shape Christians to envision the world according to the hidden reality of salvation and to work for justice in accordance with God's

31. Saliers, "Liturgy and Ethics," 180.

32. Ibid., 174.

33. Stubbs, "Liturgy and Ethics," 7.

34. Ross, *Extravagant Affections*, 77.

35. Ibid.

36. Geoffrey Wainwright, "Eucharist and/as Ethics," *Worship* 62, no. 2 (1988): 131.

37. Stubbs, "Liturgy and Ethics," 2.

reign. The sacramentality of liturgy calls us to seek these patterns in all of our experiences, including our experiences outside of worship practices.

The actual content of the vision or world-picture conveyed depends upon the lived practice of liturgy and sacrament. The discernment of the patterns of God's reign in liturgy and sacrament requires examining how Christians enact liturgy and sacrament. When examining the lived practice, the world-picture upheld by liturgy and sacrament may become more apparent. Others' needs and God's will for establishing love, peace, freedom, justice, humanity, and life in response to those needs may also become more apparent. With these revelations, liturgy and sacrament can uphold particular norms and behaviors for Christians, shaping them to bear virtues consonant with the coming of God's reign in fullness. Through the formation of Christians in this way, liturgy and sacraments can accomplish through God's grace the public service of consecrating the world. The following sections examine the moral vision upheld by two sacraments, Eucharist and Reconciliation, in order to better discern what the needs of others may be in the wake of crime and social injustice and what God's will might be for a just Christian response.

THE MORAL VISION OF THE EUCHARIST

At the center of the sacramental and liturgical life lies the Eucharist. While Catholic tradition maintains the importance of all sacraments, the Eucharist holds a special place as "the perfection of the spiritual life and the end to which all the sacraments tend."[38] As the Eucharist perfects the spiritual lives of participants, it also shapes our moral lives as "the primary and indispensible source from which the faithful are to derive the true Christian spirit" and "the summit toward which the activity of the church is directed."[39] Among the effects of the Eucharist, the *Catechism of the Catholic Church* describes how the proclamation of the forgiveness of sins in the celebration of the Eucharist draws us away from future sins. "The Eucharist strengthens our charity" as Jesus Christ gives himself to us, embodying the perfection of charity.[40] When we share more deeply in the life of Christ through the Eucharist, we find it more difficult to turn away from Christ and his moral guidance. The Eucharist thus commits us to love of neighbor, especially to love of neighbors who are poor, oppressed, and marginalized as we recognize Christ in their midst.[41] The moral

---

38. Thomas Aquinas, *Summa Theologica* III.73.3c. Quoted in *Catechism of the Catholic Church*, ¶1211. See also ¶1324 and 1374.

39. Second Vatican Council, *Sacrosanctum Concilium*, ¶10 and ¶14.

40. Aquinas, quoted by *Catechism of the Catholic Church*, ¶1394.

transformation brought about by the Eucharist not only occurs on an individual level, but also affects the whole community of the church, which is united as the body of Christ through the Eucharist.[42] Within Catholic tradition, the Eucharist is the pinnacle of liturgy and sacrament, the perfection of the work of the church in consecrating the world through public service in emulation of Jesus Christ.

Although the Catholic Church recognizes the ways in which the Eucharist forms the moral as well as the spiritual lives of Christians, it has not always drawn on the richness of the sacraments, especially the Eucharist in its reflections upon and work toward justice, whether social justice or justice in response to individual wrongdoing. In *Responsibility, Rehabilitation, and Restoration*, the U.S. bishops mention the Eucharist in passing as a "real encounter with the Saving Lord and central Catholic sign of justice and mercy,"[43] but they do not explain the relevance of the Eucharist to crime, punishment, or justice in detail. With respect to broader issues of social justice, Himes notes that the church has often failed to link the Eucharist with its mission in society. He writes, "Even Vatican II was disappointing on this matter of connecting liturgy and social justice. Several authors have noted that the two crucial relevant documents of the Council, the Pastoral Constitution on the Church in the Modern World and the Decree on Liturgy, 'either understated or ignored' the linkage."[44] Notwithstanding this oversight in official documents of the church, many Catholic (as well as non-Catholic) theologians in recent decades have highlighted the significance of the Eucharist for Christian responses to injustice in the world.[45]

41. Ibid., ¶1397.

42. Ibid., ¶1396.

43. United States Conference of Catholic Bishops, *Responsibility, Rehabilitation, and Restoration: A Catholic Perspective on Crime and Criminal Justice* (Washington, DC: United States Conference of Catholic Bishops, 2000). Available online at http://www.nccbuscc.org/sdwp/criminal.shtml.

44. Himes, "Eucharist and Justice," 213. Himes is quoting R. Kevin Seasoltz, "Justice and the Eucharist," *Worship* 58 (1984): 508.

45. Some examples include Cavanaugh, *Torture and Eucharist*; Himes, "Eucharist and Justice"; Seasoltz, "Justice and the Eucharist"; Mahoney, "The Eucharist and Social Justice"; and Geoffrey Wainwright, "Eucharist and/as Ethics." See also E. Byron Anderson, "A Body in the Spirit for the World: Eucharist, Epiclesis, and Ethics," *Worship* 85, no. 2 (2011): 98–116; Andrea Bieler and Luise Schottroff, *The Eucharist: Bodies, Bread, and Resurrection* (Minneapolis: Fortress Press, 2007); Monika K. Hellwig, *The Eucharist and the Hunger of the World*, 2nd ed. (Kansas City, MO: Sheed & Ward, 1992); John P. Hogan, "The Eucharist and Social Justice," in *Romero's Legacy: The Call to Peace and Justice*, ed. Pilar Hogan Closkey and John P. Hogan (Lanham, MD: Sheed & Ward, 2007), 25–34; Anne Y. Koester, ed., *Liturgy and Justice: To Worship God in Spirit and Truth* (Collegeville, MN: Liturgical, 2002); Judith A. Merkle,

The New Testament texts that describe the institution of this sacrament by Jesus Christ and its celebration in early Christian communities validate these theologians' work to connect the Eucharist and justice. During the Last Supper, Jesus drew his disciples together and offered to them bread and wine, his body and blood, telling them of his death and resurrection for the forgiveness of sins.[46] His celebration of the Last Supper fulfills the covenant established with Israel for the reconciliation of all creation with God and provides a foretaste of the reign of God in its fullness. It also brings to mind the numerous other meals described in the Gospels, in which Jesus ate with prostitutes and tax collectors; he included at his table people who were excluded from society and whom he would welcome in God's kingdom. In Luke's account of the Last Supper, Jesus responds to a dispute among the disciples by instructing them that those who became servants of others and stood with him in his trials would receive the kingdom of God.[47] Gospel accounts of the Last Supper and other meals with Jesus emphasize the importance of covenantal relationships as the mark of life in Christian community and ultimately in God's reign. They also uphold visions of inclusiveness and servanthood as markers of the morality of these relationships.

Following Jesus' death and resurrection, the early Christian community endeavored to "do this in remembrance" of him through the celebration of the Eucharist as a communal meal. Acts of the Apostles 2:42-47 conveys the importance of the breaking of bread among members of these communities

"The Eucharist and Justice," *Liturgical Ministry* 17 (2008): 133–38; Thomas W. Porter, ed., *Conflict and Communion: Reconciliation and Restorative Justice at Christ's Table* (Nashville: Discipleship Resources, 2006); Margaret Scott, *The Eucharist and Social Justice* (New York: Paulist, 2008); Kevin Seasoltz, *A Virtuous Church: Catholic Theology, Ethics, and Liturgy for the Twenty-First Century* (Maryknoll, NY: Orbis, 2012); and Paul Wadell, "What Do All Those Masses Do for Us?: Reflections on the Christian Moral Life and the Eucharist," in *Living No Longer for Ourselves*, ed. Hughes and Francis, 153–69.In addition to these authors, many Catholic feminists have discussed the relationship between sacraments, especially the Eucharist, and justice, particularly in light of the denial of ordination to women and the cultural, social, and religious subordination of women. Notable among these authors is Susan Ross. In addition to *Extravagant Affections,* see her "Salvation in and for the World: Church and Sacraments," in *The Praxis of Christian Experience: An Introduction to the Theology of Edward Schillebeeckx*, ed. Robert J. Schreiter and Mary Catherine Hilkert (San Francisco: Harper & Row, 1989), 101–15; "God's Embodiment and Women: Sacraments," in *Freeing Theology: The Essentials of Theology in Feminist Perspective*, ed. Catherine Mowry LaCugna (San Francisco: HarperSanFrancisco, 1993), 185–209; and "Liturgy and Ethics: Feminist Perspectives," *Annual of the Society of Christian Ethics* 20 (2000): 263–74. For discussions of the Eucharist in relationship to racial justice, especially in the church, see Copeland, *Enfleshing Freedom*, 107–28; Hayes, *Standing in the Shoes My Mother Made*, 35–50; and Massingale, *Racial Justice and the Catholic Church*, 120–25.

46. See Mark 14:12-26; Matt. 26:17-30; and Luke 22:7-38. Also, John 6:52-58 and John 13.

47. Luke 22:24-30.

who lived together, shared their belongings in common, and gave all their possessions to those in need. As they re-created supper with Jesus, their communal meal memorializing Jesus' life and death became "a sacramental meal which evoked not only the memory of those sacred events but also the experience of the risen messiah."[48] The text of Acts links the breaking of bread within the early Christian community to its public service to others, especially to the poor.

The earliest account of the Eucharist in early Christian communities comes from Paul's First Letter to the Corinthians, in which Paul explains that by taking the bread and wine, participants in the Eucharist share in the body and blood of Christ and so are made one body with one another.[49] Some community members in Corinth overate and got drunk during the Lord's Supper, while others went with nothing. For Paul, this behavior desecrates the body of Christ in all of its senses. First, the Corinthians failed to memorialize appropriately the night when Jesus sacrificed his actual body. They also failed to recognize the presence of Jesus' body in the bread. Finally, disunity in the community breaks the body of Christ represented in the church. Paul asks the members of the Corinthian church to examine themselves, "For all who eat and drink without discerning the body, eat and drink judgment against themselves."[50] These instructions suggest both that each member of the church must examine her individual conscience before partaking of the Eucharist and that the community as a whole must discern the ways in which its members have become divided from each other. Without this moral discernment, the community is not appropriately disposed to the eucharistic celebration.

Several themes relevant to the moral formation of Christians arise from New Testament descriptions of the Eucharist, particularly with respect to the vision of justice. Eucharistic celebration occurs within the context of a covenant that binds God to human beings and upholds the importance of maintaining relationship for the well-being of humanity. The inclusiveness of the eucharistic table suggests the inclusiveness of the covenant and ultimately of God's reign. The demands placed upon participants in the meal are not only spiritual and otherworldly. Rather participation in the Eucharist requires moral transformation as we become servants to others, especially to those who are in need and excluded from relationship. Without this transformation, we defile the

48. Joseph Martos, *Doors to the Sacred: A Historical Introduction to Sacraments in the Catholic Church,* revised edition (Liguori, MO: Liguori/Triumph, 2001), 214.

49. 1 Cor. 10:16-17.

50. 1 Cor. 11:29.

Eucharist. By celebrating the Eucharist, a new community is created that should endeavor to seek reconciliation among its members and with the wider world.

The New Testament accounts of the Last Supper and early celebrations of the Eucharist indicate that through the ongoing practice of this sacrament, Christians remember Jesus' victory over the principalities and powers of this world through his death and resurrection, not only by sharing the bread and wine, but also by coming together as a community and "reaching out to all those who are excluded and sharing with them all that one has,"[51] thus embodying God's justice. The inclusiveness and servanthood upheld within the covenantal relationships of the church stand in contrast to the standards of justice in the wider world, especially among the privileged and powerful. New Testament texts describing early eucharistic celebrations thus offer an alternative vision of justice in accordance with the reign of God that ought to reorient Christians' approaches to both individual wrongdoing and social injustice.

The description of the Eucharist in New Testament texts also highlights a tension within its celebration today. As we partake in the Eucharist in the present moment, we are called to remember Jesus Christ's death and resurrection in the past and to anticipate the coming of the reign of God in its fullness in the future. The Eucharist collapses time so that its participants experience God's past, present, and future simultaneously. Cavanaugh describes this experience of the Eucharist as producing a desire for what is "not yet" even amidst what has "already" come with Jesus Christ. He writes, "If the Eucharist is indeed a memorial of the whole Christ . . . then it recalls more than the past events of Jesus' life, death, and resurrection, but also expresses an ardent longing for the completion of the Kingdom Christ inaugurated."[52] Through participation in the Eucharist, Christians glimpse God's reign in which life overcomes death, peace conquers violence, sin is forgiven, all of creation is reconciled, the covenant is fulfilled, and God's love and justice reign. We find hope in the body of Christ, experienced in both the elements of the Eucharist and the community gathered at the table. The Eucharist awakens what Andrea Bieler and Luise Schottroff call our "eschatological imagination," which enables us to see our world as it could become fully in the reign of God as well as to recognize the extent to which our world remains fallen. They write, "This is exactly what the eschatological imagination holds: the reality of brokenness and a hope for wholeness."[53] The tension between the "already" and the "not yet" in

51. Seasoltz, "Justice and the Eucharist," 13.
52. Cavanaugh, *Torture and Eucharist*, 226.
53. Bieler and Schottroff, *The Eucharist*, 7.

eschatological imagination awoken in the Eucharist is the source of the ardent longing described by Cavanaugh for God's life, peace, forgiveness, love, and justice.

This longing rooted in the eschatological imagination of the Eucharist is not other-worldly, not an individualistic escape from our troubles in the spiritual sustenance offered by a distant God. Rather the Eucharist is bodily, communal, and political; thus, well-considered celebration of the Eucharist ought to draw Christians more deeply into confrontation with the injustices of the world. Kevin Seasoltz writes, "It implies deep confrontation with human alienation."[54] He continues,

> In our contemporary world there are many who are lowered by society; those who are thought to be unworthy or inferior are pushed lower and lower in the community until their own sense of dignity and worth is decimated too. . . . Christian ministry to these people must be ministry and service after the manner of Jesus. That means the very ones who are pushed or kept down by society are the ones to be raised up so they achieve that sense of dignity and worth essential to the redeemed human condition.[55]

As the Eucharist fosters visions of God's justice, which sometimes contrasts sharply with justice interpreted in human terms, Christians ought to become increasingly aware of injustices in our midst that demean and degrade our neighbors. Brokenness within our communities, violations of the bodies of human persons, exclusions from the political life of our society ought to inspire Christians to work for redemption, healing, and inclusion of all people.

The tension within the celebration of the Eucharist ought to provide deep motivational force for Christians to pursue the moral vision of this sacrament, especially in response to social injustice. Indeed, we ought to hear the call to seek social justice most loudly and clearly in our celebration of the Eucharist. It offers a foretaste of God's reign in which everyone is welcomed to Christ's table, especially those who are excluded from society. As we celebrate this sacrament, we remember and protest the death of Jesus *as a convicted criminal* at the hands of the Roman Empire. We are made into one body while we are also confronted with the brokenness of the body of Christ and the pervasive dynamics of exclusion and division in our churches, communities, and society. Paul calls us to discern the body, to recognize the sources of brokenness, exclusion, and

54. Seasoltz, "Justice and the Eucharist," 511.
55. Ibid., 522.

division amongst us and to work toward redemption, healing, and inclusion. When we fail to do so, we eat and drink judgment against ourselves, as we walk in the ways of the principalities and powers of this world. The eschatological imagination awoken in the Eucharist ought to indict our consciences about the ongoing reality of social injustice and our failures to live up to the vision of God's reign. It ought to lead us to recognize that people who commit crime are not the only people who need social reintegration and internal reform; the Eucharist reminds us that we are all called to these tasks, especially through the endeavor for social justice. Through this effort, Catholics should strive to counter the racial, ethnic, class, gender, and sexual discrepancies and disparities that remain significant factors in our society.

The pursuit of social justice, however, ought not to be rooted solely in a sense of conviction for our failures as church, community, and society. For Catholics, we must also base this work in the hope for the in-breaking of God's reign disclosed in the Eucharist. We celebrate Christ's resurrection and anticipate the coming of God's life, peace, forgiveness, love, and justice in fullness. The eschatological imagination nourished by the Eucharist, which makes known both the brokenness and redemption of the world, ought to create a yearning to confront the alienation that degrades and demeans our neighbors on the basis of race, ethnicity, gender, sexuality, and class. Susan Ross reminds us, "The Eucharist is about something much larger—human reconciliation with God and with each other."[56] She continues, "Participation in the Eucharist ought always to push one 'outward' to live the liturgy's eschatological vision, and at the same time, push 'inward' so that liturgical expressions can—as much as possible, in their limited and imperfect context—approximate an expression of that eschatological vision."[57] This "tension" within the celebration of the Eucharist ought to impel its participants into the pursuit of social justice in the world as an aspect of living within God's reign already in our midst. Catholics specifically, but also Christians in general, who find hope in the celebration of the Eucharist, may be fed for the work for social justice.

Paul's recommendation to the Corinthian community that they discern the body before eating and drinking the eucharistic meal concerns not only injustices on the communal and social level. He is also concerned that individual wrongdoing may be a barrier to full communion. The majority of Paul's First Letter to the Corinthians discusses personal decisions that could be stumbling blocks to others or that could break down the community. Paul's argument

56. Ross, "Liturgy and Ethics," 264.
57. Ibid., 264–65.

about needing to attend to individual wrongdoing for the well-being of the community suggests that the Eucharist provides the context for Christian pursuit of justice on the individual level as well the communal and social level. Placing the Eucharist at the center of our response to our social and criminal justice crises would suggest that another sacrament—Penance and Reconciliation—might provide additional resources for dealing with injustice on individual, communal, and social levels.

THE MORAL VISION OF PENANCE AND RECONCILIATION

An appeal to the sacrament of Penance and Reconciliation in response to individual wrongdoing and social injustice may seem misguided on several counts. First, Protestants generally do not recognize this sacrament (even though they do often emphasize practices of confession and forgiveness in connection to eucharistic liturgy), and since the Second Vatican Council, relatively few Catholics participate in it.[58] Compared to the Eucharist, the sacrament of Penance is more marginally practiced in Western Christianity. The reason for its marginal status is related to a second issue: the perception of its practice as a legalistic rendering of a list of one's sins in order to restore one's ultimate place in heaven. Seen in this way, Penance would seem to offer little to our spiritual and moral lives. Such a practice would not be terribly helpful in bringing us into right relationship with God or neighbor. Rather it seems to involve a sort of metaphorical self-flagellation for the sake of alleviating unhealthy guilt instead of an effort to restore the wholeness of the wrongdoer for full communion with the body of Christ, resulting in reconciliation. Thirdly, the sacrament of Penance may seem to involve dysfunctional power relationships between the church hierarchy and the laity. This sense may be heightened in the wake of sexual abuse scandals involving clergy who exploited their power against vulnerable laity, especially children. Describing Friedrich Nietzsche's classic critique of Penance, liturgical theologian Bruno Hidber writes (in a critique of Nietzsche's perspective), "The priest . . . professionally cultivates anguish using a strategy of inculpation, with a sophisticated system of sins and guilt, of pardon and punishments, with which to make persons suffer and render them dependent upon himself."[59] If Nietzsche is correct, then Penance would be a poor resource for dealing

58. Thanks to Elizabeth Bounds for her reminder about the importance of confession and forgiveness within the liturgical life of many Protestants.

59. Bruno Hidber, "From Anguish to Refound Freedom: Penance in the Tension between Sacraments and Ethics," *Worship* 68, no. 2 (1994): 103.

with wrongdoing. Finally, it would be a mistake to recommend Penance straightforwardly as a model for our criminal justice systems. As moral theologian John Berkman observes, we cannot simply translate this practice into civil society, and we ought not try to "Christianize" penality.[60] In light of these difficulties, it would seem that this sacrament would not guide us well in responding to injustice in our context. Despite these difficulties, Penance and Reconciliation—not prison—has been the normative means in Catholicism for responding to wrongdoing in the community. Examining the history and theology of this sacrament reveals that it is more complex than the problems described suggest and that its practice may offer some resources for responding to individual wrongdoing and social injustice.

Catholics trace the practice of Penance and Reconciliation to scripture and early Christian communities. Jesus describes a process for addressing wrongdoing in the community in the Gospel of Matthew.[61] He recommends first privately confronting members of the church who have sinned. If a private conversation does not return a sinning member to the fold, the conversation progressively includes more members of the community, beginning with two or three others and eventually with the whole church. If the offender still refuses to listen, then the church as a whole may exclude him from the community. The following passage, however, suggests that the church ought to maintain forgiveness as the guiding principle for responding to sin and conflict, as Jesus tells Peter that he ought to forgive someone who has sinned against him, "Not seven times, but, I tell you, seventy-seven times."[62] The figure of seventy-seven does not represent a limitation upon how often Jesus' followers ought to forgive. Rather it signals an abundance of forgiveness, beyond a number so large that most people would find it unreasonable or ridiculous. Jesus' disciples are called to "forgive [their] brothers and sisters from [their] hearts," and they should endeavor to forgive others, even when they continue to make mistakes, based on the hope of eventually restoring right relationship.[63]

Paul's letters also provide some indications of how early Christians responded to sinners in their midst. As previously discussed, Paul chastises the Corinthian community for divisions in its celebration of the Eucharist. Drawing on the analogy of the body of Christ in 1 Corinthians 11, he calls for

60. John Berkman, "Being Reconciled: Penitence, Punishment, and Worship," in *The Blackwell Companion to Christian Ethics*, ed. Stanley Hauerwas and Samuel Wells (Malden, MA: Blackwell, 2006), 95–109.

61. See Matt. 18:15-20.

62. See Matt. 18:21-35.

63. Matt. 18:35.

the irreproachable behavior of community members and asks that they "discern the body" before eating and drinking the Lord's Supper. Without addressing individual culpability and communal disunity, members of the Corinthian community risk eating the bread and drinking the wine unworthily, and so to break Christ's body. Participation in the Eucharist thus requires some sort of reconciliation of individuals and community to one another so that the church may fully exemplify the body of Christ. Earlier in this letter, Paul warns of the need to "clean out the old yeast" from the community "so that [it] may be a new batch, as [it really is] unleavened."[64] Based upon the call for the community to become the "unleavened bread of sincerity and truth," Paul endorses the expulsion of a man engaged in sexual immorality (he is living with his stepmother) from the community.[65] He seems to recommend this judgment for the good of the man as Paul suggests that the Corinthians are "to hand this man over to Satan for the destruction of his flesh, so that his spirit may be saved in the day of the Lord."[66] Paul hopes that the man's exclusion will result in his deliverance from forces that led him to sinful behavior and his preparation for the Lord's coming. Rather than emphasizing forgiveness, Paul stresses the necessity of discipline and judgment in building up the church community. He continues by suggesting that the community ought to respond to conflicts internally, rather than appealing to courts of law. Paul exhorts the Corinthians to avoid conflict in the community by living lives with one another that are beyond reproach.

For Paul, the body of Christ is a reconciled community that also continues to seek and deepen reconciliation. Following his initial encounters with the Corinthians, Paul had a conflict of some unknown sort with them, and his Second Letter to the Corinthians (which is probably a conglomeration of several letters) captures his effort for reconciliation. He writes that reconciliation within the church is based upon God's reconciliatory work through Jesus Christ: "All this is from God, who reconciled us to himself through Christ, and has given us the ministry of reconciliation."[67] Judgment and discipline ought not be extended indefinitely; forgiveness ought to arise eventually in a reconciled and reconciling church.

From Jesus and Paul, we may discern some important insights about responding to wrongdoing. Any response, first, ought to occur within a communal context. We are each accountable to our other community members

64. 1 Cor. 5:7.
65. 1 Cor. 5:8.
66. 1 Cor. 5:5.
67. 2 Cor. 2:7.

for being responsible ourselves and for holding them responsible for their actions. The community must be disciplined, which requires judgment about what benefits or harms the community and its members. It may be appropriate to punish members who harm others, for example, by excluding them from the community for a time, but such punishment must be directed toward the ultimate good of the offenders. Moreover, the community must prefer forgiveness and reconciliation as the ultimate outcome. This preference is based upon the forgiveness and reconciliation already extended by God. Failure to embody this forgiveness and reconciliation harms the body of Christ. All of these responses to wrongdoing occur in a eucharistic context in which we remember the reconciling work of Christ on the cross through the bread and wine and so participate in the body of Christ as the church.

Christians in the generations after Jesus and Paul based their practices of Penance and Reconciliation upon these insights, especially in developing practices in response to serious and public sins. While the procedures described by Jesus may be appropriate for private sins that directly affect only a few community members, they could not necessarily address sins that affected the whole community in a serious and public manner, such as apostasy during one of the Roman persecutions. Early Christian communities confronted the question of what to do with baptized believers who continued to sin perhaps even in ways that suggested their rejection of the gospel. The answer of many of these communities was an elaborate and demanding process of "recatechizing" the wrongdoer, which developed into what is known as "canonical penance" with the Christianizing of the Roman Empire.

While the early forms of these practices varied from community to community, over time some common features developed. Sinners would confess to a bishop, who would assign penitential works such as fasting, praying, or almsgiving, and they would be enrolled in the order of the penitents.[68] The repentant sinner would be excluded from the Eucharist, but not necessarily excluded from the community. Church members would pray for them weekly and would serve as mentors to them. During their period of penitence, sinners would progress through several stages that drew them back into the community over time. Initially, as "weepers," they remained outside of the church and asked for prayers of the faithful. "Hearers" could enter the back of the church for the Liturgy of the Word, and "kneelers" could come into the church to receive the bishop's blessing, but were dismissed with the

68. For discussion of the early practices of Penance and Reconciliation, see Martos, *Doors to the Sacred*, 278–91. Also, Monika K. Hellwig, *Sign of Reconciliation and Conversion: The Sacrament of Penance for Our Times* (Wilmington, DE: Michael Glazier, 1984), 27–44.

catechumens before the Eucharist. Finally, "standers" could stay for the entire liturgy without receiving communion. Progression through these stages could take months, years, or even decades depending on the severity of the sin and the recalcitrance of the offender. When the community was convinced that the sinner had completely reconverted, the bishop would lay hands upon him to reincorporate him fully into the body of Christ.

The practice of canonical penance has several flaws, but it may still offer some insight into how to respond to individual wrongdoing. The practice went out of use after Christianity became the predominant religion of the Roman Empire because it was perceived as too demanding, especially as many people were less dedicated Christians than in previous generations. The tightknit communities of the early church became diluted, breaking down the strength of the communal context of canonical penance. Because someone could go through the penitential process only once in a lifetime, most Christians waited to go through the process until the ends of their lives, sometimes even waiting until they were on their deathbeds to repent and seek reconciliation. After the fifth century, the practice no longer emphasized the reconversion of the sinner through moral and spiritual formation in a communal context and instead seemed to mete out penalties for violating the law in a legalistic fashion. An additional barrier to canonical penance was the breakdown of the strong communal ties that came with high standards of membership in Christian communities prior to Constantine and that were the basis for providing support to penitents endeavoring to rejoin the church in fullness. Penitents became increasingly stigmatized as the goal of reintegration into the community received less attention and as a "questionably sharp distinction" between sinners and saints developed in the church.[69] Ultimately, canonical penance fell into disuse. Historian Joseph Martos remarks,

> Penitence, as it was experienced and conceived in patristic times, was a path of discipline that led to the eradication of morally destructive and socially disruptive behavior to a life of love of God and service to others. . . . At least it was meant to be that. In practice, however, it did not always look that way to ordinary Christians. To them penitence, especially canonical penitence, often looked more like something to be avoided at all costs.[70]

69. Hellwig, *Sign of Reconciliation*, 41.
70. Martos, *Doors to the Sacred*, 286.

The ideal of Penance and Reconciliation during this time period set out the possibility of reforming one's life in the context of a supportive and loving community through works that improved one's character and relationships. Too often the practice involved shaming and exclusion, which led to its eventual abandonment in the life of the church.

Despite many shortcomings, the sacrament of Penance and Reconciliation during the patristic period still has much to recommend it for our understanding of how to respond to people who cause harm in our communities. First, it was closely linked with eucharistic practices, providing continuity within the spiritual and moral life of the church. Reconciliation offered powerful rituals signaling the exile and return of the sinner to the community. At times, these rituals helped express the solidarity of the church in sinfulness, which would help to reduce the isolation and stigmatization of people in the order of the penitents. Theologian Monika Hellwig describes one such ceremony in which bishops, clergy, and congregations would meet and prostrate themselves weeping before penitents.[71] The church was united in sinfulness, but also in the work of redemption. The community remained involved in the life of the sinner through prayer and guidance. Everyone was responsible for reconciliation and the transformation of sinful lives.

During the Middle Ages, practices of private confession or "tariff penance" developed first around Irish monasteries and then spread throughout Europe.[72] These practices became the predominant practices of Western Christianity for over a millennium, replacing practices of canonical penance. With the move of this sacrament to the private confessional, the emphasis on responding to sin communally was typically lost. The effort to transform the lives of sinners was also generally lost. With some exceptions, such as Thomas Aquinas, medieval Christians viewed the works of satisfaction assigned in Penance as penalties for legal violations rather than actions undertaken to bring about conversion in their lives. They completed the penalties to restore their status in the church and in heaven. The rituals of Penance became less closely tied to the Eucharist. Despite the withdrawal of Penance from the communal and ritual life of the church, and the shift away from an emphasis on reconversion, practices of private confession offered several benefits, especially with the loss of canonical penance. Sinners and "saints" became less distinguished from each other in the community. Christians would have more than one opportunity in their lifetimes to participate in the sacrament of Penance and Reconciliation, and

71. Hellwig, *Sign of Reconciliation*, 39–40.

72. For discussion of medieval developments, see Martos, *Doors to the Sacred*, 291–305 and Hellwig, *Sign of Reconciliation*, 45–61.

they would have access to ongoing guidance from religious leaders (not always priests) throughout their lives.

With Vatican II, the council worked to merge the patristic and medieval practices of Penance and Reconciliation. Twentieth-century theologians recovered the biblical and patristic notion that sin is less a violation of law (although it is often that) and more the wounding of relationships, particularly in a covenantal setting. They also emphasized that law is not an end in itself, but instead a tool that serves the end of right relationship. Reconciliation should then not aim toward meting out penalties for violating the law and rather work toward the reconversion of the sinner through moral and spiritual formation in a communal context. The influence of these theologians is apparent, for example, in *Gaudium et Spes*, the Pastoral Constitution on the Church in the Modern World, from the Second Vatican Council. About the nature of sin, the Fathers write, "Often refusing to acknowledge God as his source, man [*sic*] has also upset the relationship which should link him to his last end; and at the same time he has broken the right order that should reign within himself as well as between himself and other men and all creatures."[73]

Based on this insight, Rome revised its rituals of Reconciliation, making them "less individual and more communal, less legalistic and more liturgical, less concerned with the enumeration of sins and more concerned with conversion of the heart."[74] The result was three rites: one rite based upon private confession and tariff penance; one communal and public rite, which should be used only in cases of severe emergency; and one rite that combines the other two, beginning with a communal and public ceremony, followed by private confession. The last rite in particular provides an opportunity for communal examination of conscience prior to confession. Together these practices draw upon many of the strengths of ancient and medieval practices. The church has renewed its emphasis upon the Eucharist as the central locus of reconciliation within the church. The communal rites clarify the solidarity of the church in sinfulness and provide a context within the community to respond to wrongdoing with prayer and guidance. Christians could regularly participate in Reconciliation and benefit from the moral and spiritual formation provided by the sacrament.

While I do not want to recommend these practices straightforwardly as a model for our criminal justice systems and I do not want to "Christianize" penality, I do believe that the sacrament of Penance and Reconciliation can offer some guidance for discerning how to respond to individual wrongdoing

73. Vatican Council II, *Gaudium et Spes*, in *Vatican Council II: The Conciliar and Post Conciliar Documents*, study edition, ed. Austin Flannery (Northport, NY: Costello, 1975), ¶13.

74. Martos, *Doors to the Sacred*, 316.

and social injustice. The history of the sacrament suggests that it is best to understand individual wrongdoing not in legalistic terms as a violation of the law (again, which it sometimes is) but as a violation of relationships. Viewing sin as a violation of relationship leads to an effort to transform those relationships and the character of the offender, rather than an effort merely to compel the offender to comply with the law.[75] Practices of Penance and Reconciliation throughout the history of the church have emphasized that sin harms the whole community and so in some way requires a communal response. Even private confession suggests that one is accountable not only to God but also to the church community, represented by the confessor. People who commit wrongdoing must work to correct the harms they have done to community members. At the same time, community members ought to provide guidance and relationship in order to restore the wrongdoer to full communion. Some regimen of punishment may be necessary, such as the penitential works assigned in the patristic church, but the purpose of the regimen ought not be to inflict pain but to transform the character of the wrongdoer. Some level of separation from the community may be necessary for a time, as it was for the sinner mentioned in Paul's Second Letter to the Corinthians, but the primary goal is reintegration of the offender into the community. Some judgment and discipline are required for the health and wholeness of the community, but Christians are ultimately called to extend forgiveness to wrongdoers. The reason for the preeminence of forgiveness is that we recognize our solidarity in sinfulness and appreciate the forgiveness already extended to us through Jesus Christ. Based upon this experience of forgiveness, the church, the reconciled community, becomes a reconciling community. Hellwig writes, "Church . . . must be the reconciliation, the welcome home of the Father expressed by the family of God, which makes the repentance and conversion possible."[76] In response to individual wrongdoing, the example of this sacrament upholds the importance of seeking reconciliation above all else, even when some form of punishment or penitential works are necessary for the purposes of internal reform and social reintegration.

75. John Berkman argues that at times the sacrament of Penance and Reconciliation has been based on a theology of sin as rupture of communion with God caused by violation of divine law, while at other times, it has been based on a theology of sin as lack of spiritual and moral well-being or health. In the former case, the emphasis of the sacrament has been upon restoring our status before God and the church, putting a sinner on the right side of the law. In the latter case, the emphasis is upon transforming and healing the sinner's soul. My emphasis here is more upon the latter interpretations of sin and redemption. See Berkman, "Being Reconciled," especially 97.

76. Hellwig, *Sign of Reconciliation*, 24.

Underlying these insights into how to respond to individual wrongdoing is an assumption about the agency and status of wrongdoers. They remain part of the community even when they are excluded to some degree. Because the sacrament of Penance and Reconciliation is oriented toward reconversion and reintegration into community through moral and spiritual formation, those people undergoing Penance must have some capacity to turn themselves toward the good in response to God's grace. Hidber observes, "[I]n one's rapport with God the person must never be reduced to an object to be controlled, even when one presents oneself as a sinner who has betrayed freedom. Rather, one is to be treated as one disposed to conversion."[77] Wrongdoers ought to be viewed as possessing the agency necessary to reform their lives when provided the support of the broader community. Moreover, they ought not be seen as ontologically flawed. Hidber continues, "Sacramental grace does not permit the penitent in the confessional to be judged as a criminal. Instead the penitent must be received as a child of God who is returning to the Father's house and, in fact, the house of God is the house of reconciled sinners."[78] The practices of Reconciliation suggest that even wrongdoers ought to be treated as active moral agents who can be guided toward the good in relationship with their communities and that they ought to be treated as brothers and sisters within those communities.

The sacrament of Penance and Reconciliation also offers some resources for discerning how to respond to broader social injustices. If we narrow our understanding of sin to personal sins that could be listed in a private confession, then the links of this sacrament to social injustice will remain unclear. However, if we recognize social injustice as the product of social sin, then we may be pressed to discern how Reconciliation could help us seek redemption from the oppression in our midst. This sacrament could help us to take public responsibility for social injustice; it may lead us "to take a critical stance in relation to values and structures we take for granted, which make or mar the lives and happiness of great segments of the human population."[79] Hellwig suggests that in order for Reconciliation to address social injustices, we must recognize that this sacrament ought to address not only personal sins, but also social sins. She writes,

> Reconciliation as the total task of the church, synonymous with redemption, is concerned with worldly as well as personal

77. Hidber, "Being Reconciled," 111.
78. Ibid., 115.
79. Hellwig, *Sign of Reconciliation*, 146.

dimensions. It is concerned with the restoration of social structures in Christ because social structures are a dimension of human existence, and spirituality cannot be divorced from our responsibility for one another even in the large structures of the public realm.[80]

If sin extends beyond personal sin, then the reconciling work of the church ought also to extend beyond private confession, and in our private confessions, we ought to acknowledge the ways in which we each have been complicit in social sin. Hellwig recommends adaptation and expanded use of the combined communal and private rite of Reconciliation in order to encourage "a more communitarian style of examination of conscience" through the use of scripture reading and sermons for the instruction of the congregation about particular social injustices.[81] Theologian James Cross echoes Hellwig's suggestion and furthers it by recommending communal storytelling and dialogue in a process of "prophetic catechesis about social sin."[82] Hellwig notes,

> The challenge is to find a way of prophetic witness that is not compromised and invalidated from the outset by self-righteousness, judgmental attitudes, defensiveness against exposure to one's own weakness and sinfulness, blindspots of which one is not even aware while zealously preaching to others and exposing their false values.[83]

This process of recognizing our complicity in social sin and the ways in which we all fall short—not just those people who are deemed "criminal"—is the first step toward seeking forgiveness and responding to the call for conversion of ourselves as individuals and of our entire society. Of course, conversion requires that we turn away from our past lives, so in these practices of Penance and Reconciliation in response to social injustices, we might discern prophetic methods for changing these circumstances, altering our own character and that of wider society.

80. Ibid., 142.

81. Ibid., 146.

82. James T. Cross, "Communal Penance and Public Life: On the Church's Becoming a Sign of Conversion from Social Sin," in *Faith in Public Life*, ed. William J. Collinge (Maryknoll, NY: College Theology Society, 2007), 290.

83. Hellwig, *Sign of Reconciliation*, 151.

CONCLUSION

Any adequate response to mass incarceration in the United States must attend to problems of social justice as well as problems of criminal justice; the two are fundamentally intertwined. In addition, it must offer resources for responding to the individuals who commit crime, causing harm to their victims, communities, and even themselves. A response from a Catholic perspective also ought to draw upon the core of Catholic tradition and its resources for understanding the world. Sacramental and liturgical ethics that explore the contributions of the Eucharist and Penance for interpreting the call of Christians to work for justice satisfy these criteria.

The celebration of the sacraments through liturgy is the central religious practice of Catholics. In the sacraments, we find the hidden reality of salvation in the world. Through liturgy, we engage in the public service of consecrating the world in emulation of the servanthood of Jesus Christ. We become the church, the *ekklesia*, the scattered community of Christians across the world called together to witness to God's reign in our midst, particularly by striving for justice for the poor, oppressed, and marginalized. Liturgy and sacraments provide a vision of the world that shapes not only our spiritual lives, but also our moral lives. This vision draws us out of ourselves to appreciate the needs of others in light of God's will for all of us, and as we take the vision offered in liturgy and sacraments as our own, we are called to act in new ways for justice. As liturgy and sacraments are always communal rites, our celebration draws us into the community that is a foretaste of God's reign. In these ways, liturgy and sacraments are united with ethics and the work for justice. As we participate in them, we are drawn into a public, political, and pluralistic tradition that is called toward justice emulating God's reign for life in the community and in the world beyond.

Consideration of the Eucharist and Reconciliation unearths aspects of these sacraments in particular that can help us to respond both to individual wrongdoing and social injustice, enabling us to find resources to unwind the relationship between our criminal and social justice crises. The Eucharist conveys a vision of covenantal relationships in which all people are included and the needs of all people, especially the poor, oppressed, and marginalized, are met. We find in the Eucharist a foretaste of God's reign in which life, peace, forgiveness, love, and justice overcome death, violence, hatred, indifference, and sin. But we also remember the death of Jesus Christ as a convicted criminal and are reminded that he is present among those people who are most ostracized from relationship. The eschatological imagination awoken in the Eucharist exposes the ways in which we continue to fall short of the vision of justice in

God's reign, while also offering hope that the principalities and powers of this world that maintain injustice will not ultimately stand. The unification of the *ekklesia* brought about in the Eucharist requires that participants examine their individual consciences and communal relationships to ensure that the body of Christ is not broken by sin and injustice. In the Eucharist, we are reoriented toward justice in God's reign as we confront the injustices of our society.

This vision of ultimate justice found in the Eucharist grounds practices of Penance and Reconciliation in response to individual wrongdoing. The practice of this sacrament throughout the history of the church suggests that while we need discipline and judgment, forgiveness ought to guide our responses to people who cause harm to others. This insight is based upon the view that individual wrongdoing—sin—ought to be understood primarily as a wounding of relationships rather than only as a violation of law. Where discipline and judgment are necessary, even to the point where someone must be isolated from the community, the end of these actions should always be the eventual restoration of the wrongdoer to full relationship. Discipline and judgment also ought to occur as much as possible in the context of community, with members assuming responsibility for the social reintegration and internal reform of wrongdoers. The community should continually offer guidance and support even to exiles, and the responses of community members should be based on the acknowledgment that wrongdoers always remain children of God, brothers and sisters. Moreover, we must remember that we are all sinners needing the forgiveness of God and neighbor. We all participate in social sin that creates the broader context of individual wrongdoing and that fosters the injustices that lead to poverty, oppression, and marginalization. We must seek redemption from social sin as well as personal sin.

While the moral visions disclosed in the sacraments suggest alternative norms and values for responding to our criminal and social justice crises, it remains unclear what courses of action sacramental and liturgical ethics would suggest in our context. The next chapter provides some ideas, beginning with recommendations for responding to individual wrongdoing in our criminal justice systems today. The final chapter considers responses to social injustices that have helped to create and are exacerbated by mass incarceration. One measure of these courses of action will be whether they resemble the visions offered by liturgy and sacraments. Another measure will be whether they can work in practice. In light of the latter concern, the following chapters will engage in dialogue with the discipline of criminology.

4

A Model for Criminal Justice Reform

This chapter explores promising reforms to our criminal justice systems and relates the practices of those reforms to the practices of the sacraments. Based upon liturgical and sacramental ethics, Penance and Reconciliation has actually been the normative means within Catholic tradition for responding to wrongdoing. In the bishops' words, it is the fundamental Catholic model for "taking responsibility, making amends, and reintegrating into the community."[1] This sacrament has been closely linked to the Eucharist throughout the history of the church; Penance and Reconciliation arguably cannot be understood fully outside of the context of the eucharistic community. Moral theologian William Cavanaugh maintains that while the Eucharist is the locus of forgiveness and reconciliation in the church, its practice also requires judgment, or in Paul's words, discernment, within the community.[2] The Christian community seeks unity by evaluating when members conform to the powers of the world, rather than to the ways of discipleship. Ideally, in judging those who violate other individuals or the community, the church extends the opportunity to become reincorporated into the body of Christ through Reconciliation. While modern practices of this sacrament often seem individualistic and privatized, penitential practices in the early church were communal and public. Also, while Penance today is often perceived as metaphorical self-flagellation for the sake of alleviating unhealthy guilt, the purpose of these practices was seen as "medicinal," restoring the wholeness of the wrongdoer for full communion with the body of Christ and resulting in reconciliation. The sacrament of Penance and Reconciliation, not prison, has been the normative means in Catholicism for achieving the ends of social reintegration and internal reform of people who do wrong.[3] Many analogies

---

1. United States Conference of Catholic Bishops, *Responsibility, Rehabilitation, and Restoration: A Catholic Perspective on Crime and Criminal Justice* (Washington, DC: United States Conference of Catholic Bishops, 2000). Available online at http://www.nccbuscc.org/sdwp/criminal.shtml.

2. William T. Cavanaugh, *Torture and Eucharist* (Malden, MA: Blackwell, 1998), 234–52.

can be found between practices of Penance and Reconciliation, in particular, and practices of restorative justice and rehabilitation found by criminologists to be effective for reducing reoffending. This chapter considers the possibilities of these means for effectively responding to crime and individual wrongdoing, ultimately proposing a model for our criminal justice systems based fundamentally on restorative justice and secondarily on rehabilitation, resorting to incarceration only when these courses of action fail.

model for criminal justice

Before proceeding to this argument, I want to remind readers that this chapter addresses only some of the criteria for an adequate response to our criminal and social justice crises. Criminal justice reform is necessary in an effort to address our crisis of criminal justice; the proposals of this chapter aim to provide direction for such reform. The need to assure skeptical readers of not only the morality but also the effectiveness of criminal justice reform has motivated my interdisciplinary engagement with criminology here. I seek to demonstrate that restorative justice and rehabilitation can reduce reoffending, lead to social reintegration of offenders, maintain public safety, and establish justice for all people affected by crime. But reform is not sufficient; the proposals of the next chapter aim to provide direction for changing the broader context of social injustice that our criminal justice systems reflect and sustain.

On Restorative Justice

Of course, the sacrament of Penance and Reconciliation cannot be instituted as the central practice of a modern Western penal system. The discussion of the previous chapter reveals how this sacrament is rooted in ecclesial community. We cannot simply translate Penance and Reconciliation into a pluralistic society that does not maintain the same religious and communal commitments that ground this sacrament. Nevertheless, similarities between early Christian penitential practices and modern restorative justice practices may provide theological support for the latter among Catholics. In *Responsibility, Rehabilitation, and Restoration,* the U.S. bishops seem to recognize the analogy between the sacrament of Penance and Reconciliation and practices of restorative justice, but they do not elaborate upon these connections or offer significant justification of restorative justice from a theological perspective.

3. For discussions of the development of the sacrament of Penance and its relationship to Eucharist, see Joseph Martos, *Doors to the Sacred: A Historical Introduction to Sacraments in the Catholic Church,* revised edition (Liguori, MO: Liguori/Triumph, 2001); Monika K. Hellwig, *Sign of Reconciliation and Conversion: The Sacrament of Penance for Our Times* (Wilmington, DE: Michael Glazier, 1982); and Bernhard Poschmann, *Penance and the Anointing of the Sick* (New York: Herder & Herder, 1964).

Restorative justice has been a growing movement in criminal justice reform since the 1970s. Advocates have defined restorative justice in a variety of ways, and several issues arise when trying to come up with a satisfactory definition.[4] First, the term has been used to describe an assortment of practices that do not necessarily bear much resemblance to each other. Among the practices called "restorative justice" are victim-offender mediation and dialogue (also commonly known as victim-offender reconciliation), family-group conferencing, citizen- and neighborhood-accountability boards, truth and reconciliation commissions, community conferencing, and numerous hybrids of each of these. Despite the differences among these practices, they tend to share "a wide array of face-to-face non-adversarial decision-making dialogue encounters between victim, offender, and community members in response to specific crimes and/or incidents of harm."[5] Second, because of lack of clarity about the meaning of "restorative justice," the term has frequently been used to describe practices that seem neither restorative nor just. Although many states have adopted restorative justice language in their juvenile justice legislation, for example, it is worth noting that "in some states . . . [it] was passed as part of the same juvenile justice legislation that contained more punitive provisions mandating expanded transfer to criminal court."[6] In some instances, "restorative justice" seems to have been used as a moniker for nonrestorative practices. Finally, a movement for restorative justice has arisen at the same time as several other alternative conceptions of justice that sometimes overlap and sometimes conflict with restorative justice, especially "community justice" and "transformative justice."

While some restorative justice advocates would disagree, for the purposes here, the definition of restorative justice provided by criminologists Gordon Bazemore and Lode Walgrave will suffice. They have formulated a definition of restorative justice as "every action that is primarily oriented to doing justice by repairing the harm that has been caused by crime."[7] Each term within this definition requires elaboration. Bazemore and Walgrave, like most restorative

4. The debates about defining restorative justice are often intricate and heated. For a review of relevant literature, see my *Restorative Justice: Theories and Practices of Moral Imagination* (El Paso, TX: LFB Scholarly Publishing, 2012), especially pages 97–107.

5. Gordon Bazemore and Mara Schiff, *Juvenile Justice Reform and Restorative Justice: Building Theory and Policy from Practice* (Portland, OR: Willan, 2005), 35.

6. Ibid., 6.

7. Gordon Bazemore and Lode Walgrave, "Restorative Juvenile Justice: In Search of Fundamentals and an Outline for Systemic Reform," in *Restorative Juvenile Justice: Repairing the Harm of Youth Crime*, ed. Gordon Bazemore and Lode Walgrave (Monsey, NY: Criminal Justice Press, 1999), 48.

justice advocates, view crime principally not as a violation of the law, but as a violation of relationships by offenders when they cause harm to others. The harm caused may include "material losses, physical injuries, psychological consequences, relational problems, and social dysfunctions."[8] The people affected by criminal harm are, foremost, the direct victims of crime, but also members of the community in which the crime occurred. In many circumstances, the people who committed the crime are also seen as suffering harm caused by their own actions. "Doing justice" requires at least three things: first, protecting the procedural rights of victims, offenders, and community members as citizens of a particular jurisdiction; second, attaining satisfaction of all stakeholders that justice has been done; and finally, establishing a "feeling of equity" in that like cases have been treated alike. In light of the elaboration of these terms, restorative justice can be described as every action that is primarily oriented to achieving satisfaction and equity for people affected by crime, including victims, offenders, and community members, while upholding their legal rights. Satisfaction and equity are achieved by "repairing the harm" caused by crime; by providing victims, community members, and offenders an opportunity to participate in the response to crime; and by working toward and maintaining justice and peace within the community.

Although many different practices fall under this definition, restorative justice practices in U.S. jurisdictions share some common features. Typically police or court officials will refer a case to a restorative justice agency or practitioner who will prepare the stakeholders in an offense for a meeting. Depending on the circumstances of the offense and the needs of the stakeholders, either the meeting will be held face-to-face or a mediator may shuttle between victims, offenders, and community members. In addition to these stakeholders, family and friends may also attend to offer support to victims and offenders. The first step in the encounter among stakeholders is to identify the harms that have resulted from the offender's crime, which is usually done as each stakeholder has an opportunity to tell his or her story of the offense and its effects. Victims and community members also may often be able to ask offenders what motivated them to commit the crime, why they chose a particular victim, what they were thinking about while committing the crime, and other questions that help to understand the circumstances of the offense. Offenders may become more aware of the extent of the pain and suffering they have caused through this process. After delineating the harms suffered by victims, community members, and even offenders, the group works together to reach consensus about what is necessary to repair the harms. Most of the

8. Ibid., 49.

obligations to repair harms fall upon offenders, although in some circumstances, groups will recognize some responsibility of communities to support and guide offenders. After this meeting, the restorative justice program or practitioner monitors the progress of the offender in satisfying the terms of the agreement in a specified time period. In most jurisdictions, failure to meet the requirements of this process results in the offender's return to traditional criminal or juvenile justice procedures.

An example of a restorative justice case may clarify the process.[9] "Joaquin" is a fourteen-year-old boy who has been struggling since his parents' recent divorce. Difficulties in negotiating his parents' work and custody schedules left him with large blocks of unsupervised time, especially immediately after school. Joaquin ended up spending much of his time with an older friend, who suggested that they paint graffiti around their neighborhood. Joaquin and his friend tagged several locations, including a school, a store, and a private garage. After they were caught, Joaquin opted to participate in the local restorative justice program, while his friend chose to go through traditional juvenile court. The restorative justice coordinator, "Sarah," contacted the school principal, the storeowner, and the homeowner. Everyone agreed to participate, except the homeowner, who said that she did not want to spend her time in a restorative justice conference. On the day of the meeting, Sarah began with introductions and then asked Joaquin to explain what he had done. Visibly nervous, Joaquin quietly told the story of going out with his friend, while his mother silently held his hand. The storeowner and school principal then had the opportunity to explain the effects of Joaquin's actions. The storeowner complained that this was the fifth incident of his building being tagged and that his insurance premiums climbed with each incident. The school principal explained that he needed to pay a custodian overtime to paint over the graffiti as well as to pay for painting supplies. Although it may not seem like much money, he said that because of a tight school budget, this incident meant that the school could not afford new equipment for the soccer team. Ann also invited some community members to participate in the conference. A grandmother who lived alone in the neighborhood worried about feeling less safe because of signs of deterioration like graffiti. A parent with a child in the high school expressed frustration that school money was going to waste on paint when other students could have benefited from it.

Based on these contributions to the conference, the group identified the harms of the crime as not only the property damage caused by Joaquin, but also

9. The following is a composite based upon my experiences of participant-observation with five restorative justice programs in Colorado.

the secondary consequences of this damage—the loss of trust among neighbors, the increasing costs of being seen as a "bad" neighborhood, and the loss of opportunity to pursue other important goods for community members. They also recognized that Joaquin caused these harms not because he was a "bad kid," but because he lacked appropriate supervision and direction. To repair the harms, the group agreed that Joaquin should paint an exterior wall of the store and work a specified number of hours there to compensate the store owner for his extra expenses. He should also organize a fundraiser such as a car wash to reimburse the school. Members of the group hoped that the presence of this young man doing positive things would restore faith and trust in the neighborhood. The school principal agreed to find a mentor for Joaquin so that he would have better role models and supervision. Joaquin apologized for what he had done and admitted that he did not realize that he was causing so much trouble for everyone. After the meeting, Sarah remained in contact with Joaquin to ensure that he completed the terms of the agreement.

Several connections can be drawn between restorative justice and the sacrament of Penance and Reconciliation, suggesting that sacramental and liturgical ethics provide theological support for reforms of our criminal justice systems based in restorative justice. First, both restorative justice and Reconciliation emphasize the communal context of wrongdoing, whether such wrongdoing is viewed as crime or sin. For both, wrongdoing is seen not only as a violation of a rule or law, but as a harm done to other persons and to the communities in which we live. Both also aim toward restoration of all members of the community, both wrongdoers and those people who have been harmed, and toward the continuation of relationship in ways that enable all persons to flourish.[10] Restorative justice and Reconciliation build upon the recognition that wrongdoers need community support and guidance in order to bring about internal reform and reintegration into community. Neither allows retribution or punishment for the sake of punishment, but both insist that people who do wrong must take responsibility for their actions and making things right as much as is humanly possible. Both practices also begin with conversation

10. While Reconciliation is based on the ultimate hope that full relationship with God throughout all of creation will be restored, restorative justice advocates are typically more circumspect about the possibilities of reconciliation and forgiveness leading to restoration of full relationship. They appropriately recognize that reconciliation and forgiveness from victims cannot be required or expected at the outset of a restorative justice conference. The goal of restorative justice tends to be more modest with "repairing the harm." Reconciliation and forgiveness may be an outcome of restorative justice; relationships may be mended. But a successful restorative justice conference could result in a complete severing of relationship between victim and offender, provided that the offender and victim are not also cut off from their communities.

about the wrongs done and dialogue about what led the wrongdoer to act in a harmful way and what is necessary to respond adequately to those actions. Finally, both maintain that everyone must be treated as community members, as human beings, as people with fundamental worth who need to be brought back into full relationship with others. In short, Reconciliation and restorative justice, at least in their ideal forms, endeavor to hold people accountable while challenging them to change their lives, reject vengeance, reach out to victims, and restore a sense of community.

In addition to their similar values, the penitential practices of the early church bear resemblance to contemporary restorative justice practices. As restorative justice provides a procedure for responding to crime outside of the traditional channels of our criminal justice systems, the procedures developed by early Christian communities for dealing with sinful behavior through canonical penance offered an alternative to resorting to the Roman legal system. These procedures began when penitents confessed their sins and asked the community for an ascetical regimen that would retrain them in the ways of Christ. Often penitents were "excommunicated," although they continued to participate in worship and other community activities while not partaking of the Eucharist. While penitents were sometimes segregated within the community, they undertook their ascetical regimen in continual relationship with the community, which oversaw and monitored penitents, offering guidance and support. Upon completion of their disciplinary sentences, penitents would be forgiven and restored to full communion. Historical practices of Penance and Reconciliation are in many ways analogous to practices of restorative justice today. Recognizing the connections between these practices should encourage Catholics and other Christians to support efforts to implement restorative justice in our criminal justice systems and perhaps even to get involved in restorative justice programs in their communities.

Restorative justice, however, has received some important critiques. One of the most significant challenges to restorative justice is that the meaning of "community" is unclear and that without a clear sense of what community is and who participates in it—and in modern societies, whether it continues to exist at all—the practices of restorative justice cannot achieve the end of social reintegration. The breakdown of community is perhaps analogous to the dilution of the early Christian church when the Roman Empire became nominally Christian following the reign of Constantine (and later, juridically Christian under Theodosius I). Practices of canonical penance depended upon communities in which members shared a core belief system, exhibited strong commitment to those beliefs in every aspect of their lives, and cared about the well-being of other members as they tried to live in accordance with their common beliefs. In these communities, members underwent years of instruction and guidance to become full participants in the church, and if their sinfulness led them away from full participation, the community offered strenuous means for reconversion. Canonical penance practices built upon this bedrock of community to offer support to members who had strayed from their way of life and who wanted to restore their communion. After Constantine, the lack of communal support and the increasing stigmatization of penitents led to greater unwillingness to participate in canonical penance because members of the church could no longer rely on the guidance and support of a committed community. The example of canonical penance suggests that if restorative justice practices depend upon community in similar ways, then clarity about community is necessary to ensure that restorative justice can foster social reintegration of people who have committed a crime. It also warns that without strong communities, restorative justice could devolve into punitive practices that could isolate, stigmatize, and harm wrongdoers.

Several problems surface in discussions about community among restorative justice advocates. The notion of "community" is often idealized, covering over significant conflicts both within and among communities. Often the same geographical area contains multiple, overlapping communities that differ socially, culturally, economically, and politically. Some communities are broken whether because of lack of material resources or because of communal norms that undermine relationship among neighbors, and these communities do not attend well to the needs of their members. The most broken communities are also often the communities most deeply affected by crime and mass incarceration. Punitive or stigmatizing norms in some communities can prevent members from participating well in restorative justice because these norms undermine support for the social reintegration of someone who has committed a crime. Through restorative justice, communities may also find the means to reach too far into offenders' and victims' lives, as "there can be a tendency to extend control efforts beyond behavior that is clearly harmful to others to attitudes and ways of being that have to do with who we are as persons."[11] The danger of overreach may be particularly onerous in areas where multiple communities uphold different communal norms or in communities where racial, ethnic, class, gender, and other biases contribute to the devaluation of some members. In such instances, offenders participating in restorative justice practices may find themselves judged and punished based upon factors other

---

11. M. Kay Harris, "Reflections of a Skeptical Dreamer: Some Dilemmas in Restorative Justice Theory and Practice," *Contemporary Justice Review* 1 (1998): 68.

than their actions. Another problem is that communities may come to dominate restorative justice practices. Community members may assert their interests over the needs of victims or offenders in the wake of crime, when the primary focus should stay upon the people most directly affected by the crime. Finally, if "community" is defined too vaguely and it can mean anyone who is not the victim or the offender of a crime, then the distinction between community and society at large can be lost. [This issue may result in restorative justice looking little different from traditional criminal justice processes that assert that the state prosecutes crime because the society as a whole has been harmed through the violation of law.] An abstract notion of community can cause the communal context of restorative justice to be lost; an idealized notion of community can cause the complexity of communal contexts to be ignored. [12]

These dangers of community will always linger behind restorative justice practices, and participants must always remain cognizant of the potential that abstracting away from actual communities or idealizing communities can cause real harm. Nevertheless, some efforts can help to mitigate these dangers, beginning with more concrete definitions of community. Restorative justice advocates Paul McCold and Benjamin Wachtel propose a definition based not upon geography, but on relationships. They argue that a community has less to do with a place than with "a feeling, a perception of connectedness—personal connectedness both to other individual human beings and to a group."[13] Communities may be tied to places, but they can also transcend places as people have connections as individuals and groups outside of their neighborhoods. Some places hold multiple communities, and some places lack any meaningful community because the people in those places do not share a feeling or perception of connectedness. [The lack of community in a place, however, need not be final; people in a place can work together to build relationships with one another and to recognize their ties to each other.] Multiple communities in the same place can negotiate conflicts among themselves by working across social, cultural, economic, or political barriers to acknowledge connections that transcend identification with any one community and to address ways in which these barriers may have contributed to the disadvantage of any particular community.[14] In restorative justice practices, community members could be

12. For more detailed discussion of these dangers, see Robert Weisberg, "Restorative Justice and the Danger of 'Community,'" *Utah Law Review* 343, no. 1 (2003): 343–74.

13. Paul McCold and Benjamin Wachtel, "Community Is Not a Place: A New Look at Community Justice Initiatives," *Contemporary Justice Review* 1 (1998): 71–86.

14. Restorative justice practices can offer a setting for negotiating these conflicts, especially drawing on the truth-and-reconciliation model of restorative justice, which works to uncover the truth of past

called upon to participate based upon their "personal networks of relationship" with victims or offenders. The task of identifying community should begin by identifying the individuals and groups to whom victims or offenders are personally connected. The connections may be related to the places from which they come, but because of the complexity of community in the modern world, they need not be place-based.

Some of the values and practices of restorative justice can also serve to mitigate the dangers of community. Restorative justice requires that decisions be made based upon consensus. If everyone who participates in a restorative justice practice must agree with the requirements placed upon an offender, then participants must negotiate disagreements about communal norms relevant to repairing the harm caused by crime. They may also protest any requirements that reach too far into victims' or offenders' lives or that are punitive or stigmatizing. Consensus decision-making processes alone, however, may not be sufficient in instances where a domineering presence in restorative justice practices can shut out dissenting perspectives. Restorative justice practitioner Kay Harris warns,

> I fear that we have not yet figured out how to avoid the introduction of paternalistic, discriminatory, and other attitudes and stances. . . . The use of consensus decisionmaking processes provides some protection, but pressures applied to acquiesce to a majority view may be difficult to withstand. This suggests that the importance of clarifying and repeatedly affirming the core values of a restorative justice orientation cannot be overemphasized.[15]

[Prior to and during restorative justice practices, the goals of repairing harm related to a crime should be reiterated, especially in contrast with any retributive or punitive aims.]In all interactions, the personhood, humanity, and worth of all participants—victims, offenders, and community members—must be honored. Justice must also be upheld by protecting the procedural rights of all participants; by working toward satisfaction that justice has been done for victims and offenders; and by promoting equity among similar cases so that responses to some offenders are not inordinately demanding, especially for

actions that harmed members of one community at the hand of members of another community and to provide resources to work toward reconciliation. These practices were used most famously to repair the harms of apartheid in South Africa, but have also been used in other settings, such as in the southern United States around racial conflicts.

15. Harris, "Skeptical Dreamer," 69.

reasons based on racial, ethnic, gender, class, or other biases. When the participants in restorative justice cannot uphold these core values, intervention by the state may be necessary. Judicial review of restorative justice agreements may help ensure that these values are maintained. While these correctives to the dangers of community in restorative justice are no guarantee against abuses, they can offer some important protections for all participants.

In addition to questions about the meaning of community, another critique of restorative justice comes from Andrew Skotnicki. He argues that the expectation that restorative justice practices could foster significant change in the behavior of wrongdoers is unrealistic, and that "the [prison] cell, the means of punishment, assists in the attainment of the end of punishment, whether the offender wills it or not."[16] He writes, "From the perspective of character ethics, the multiple levels of self and society affected by criminal transgression could not be addressed in any significant way as a result of a single encounter between victim and offender, no matter how sincerely structured."[17] For Skotnicki, the claims of restorative justice to bring about internal reform of criminal offenders are simply too ambitious. Restorative justice depends too much on the acquiescence of the offender, who is likely to be recalcitrant. Its practices demand too little. We need prisons to bring about a true change of heart, mind, and will.

In fairness, restorative justice does require offenders to admit their wrongdoing and to choose to repair the harm that they have caused; if someone willfully denies culpability, then other approaches to criminal justice are necessary. However, a large majority of felony defendants who reach the trial stage of criminal procedures plead guilty.[18] Of course, pleading guilty in a courtroom is different than accepting moral responsibility for one's actions. Many restorative justice advocates argue, nevertheless, that many offenders who refuse to accept moral responsibility do so because of the risk of facing serious harm in our criminal justice systems, which can contribute to a sense of victimization even among offenders.

16. Andrew Skotnicki, "Foundations Once Destroyed: The Catholic Church and Criminal Justice," *Theological Studies* 65 (2004): 805.

17. Skotnicki, "How Is Justice Restored?," *Studies in Christian Ethics* 19, no. 2 (2006): 197. Annalise Acorn presents a similar critique of restorative justice in *Compulsory Compassion: A Critique of Restorative Justice* (Seattle: University of Washington Press, 2005).

18. The proportion of offenders who do not admit wrongdoing is relatively small: about 85–90 percent of felony defendants who reach the trial stage of criminal procedures plead guilty. Brian Forst, "Prosecution," in *Crime: Public Policies for Crime Control*, ed. James Q. Wilson and Joan Petersilia (Oakland, CA: ICS, 2002), 509–36.

Beyond the issue of recalcitrant offenders, however, is Skotnicki's question about the effectiveness of restorative justice in reducing recidivism, our best criminological measure of whether an intervention with offenders contributes to significant change in their behavior.[19] Although much more work still needs to be done to address this question, the best data to date suggest that while previous evidence indicates that punitive responses to crime such as incarceration increase recidivism, restorative justice interventions on average significantly decrease recidivism, although the effect is small—about 7 percent. This effect is greatest on low-risk offenders.[20] Another important study on restorative justice indicates that "restorative justice may work better with more serious crimes than with less serious crimes, contrary to the conventional wisdom."[21] Evaluations of restorative justice used in response to violent offenses report success with significantly reducing, or at least not increasing, recidivism. The effects of restorative justice on reoffending among offenders who committed property crimes were smaller and less consistent. Nevertheless, restorative justice did as well or better than incarceration in reducing recidivism with property crime, indicating that restorative justice may be an effective alternative to incarceration with many offenses. Finally, although restorative justice is most commonly accepted for addressing relatively minor, nonvictim offenses, the evidence for restorative justice reducing recidivism among offenders who commit these crimes is the least convincing. As a whole, the best criminological data to date suggest that restorative justice may be most effective in reducing recidivism among low-risk offenders who commit serious, violent offenses, and to a lesser degree, among low-risk offenders who commit property crimes.[22] For these types of offenders, restorative justice practices, not

19. The evaluation of restorative justice practices is a complicated matter for many reasons. For more information, see my *Restorative Justice*, 142–56.

20. James Bonta et al., "Restorative Justice and Recidivism: Promises Made, Promises Kept?," in *Handbook of Restorative Justice: A Global Perspective,* ed. Dennis Sullivan and Larry Tifft (New York: Routledge, 2006). This study by Bonta and his colleagues is a meta-analysis of all published evaluations of restorative justice programs of all types in comparison with incarceration and rehabilitative alternatives. Note that the authors distinguish between high-risk offenders and offenders who commit serious crimes: "Those who have committed serious, violent crimes and those who are at high risk to re-offend . . . are not necessarily the same" (116). In this context, risk refers to the probability of reoffending, not to the severity of the offense. Someone may be a low-risk offender even though he may have committed a serious violence offense. Similarly, someone may be a high-risk offender who only commits petty crimes. The main concern is not with the severity of the offense but with the likelihood that a person will offend again.

21. Lawrence Sherman and Heather Strang, *Restorative Justice: The Evidence* (London: The Smith Institute, 2007), 69.

prison, are among the best means available to us today to achieve the purposes of punishment described by Skotnicki. Whether restorative justice leads to multilayered internal reform or social reintegration is difficult to prove through criminological methods; at least in terms of recidivism, it seems to be a better means than prison.

Restorative justice advocates argue that reducing recidivism is only one positive outcome of these practices. As the definition alone indicates, restorative justice tries to accomplish many different goals: achieving fairness and satisfaction for all parties affected by a crime; protecting participants' legal rights; repairing the material, physical, psychological, relational, and social harms caused by crime; including victims, offenders, and communities in responding to crime; providing a forum for victims to express anger and fear and to be heard, supported, and taken seriously; reestablishing the social efficacy and cohesion of communities; and finally, reintegrating both victims and offenders in a safe and secure environment. The success of restorative justice at achieving all of these goals, however, has not been fully evaluated. Nevertheless, some data indicate the promise of these practices. For example, participants in victim-offender mediation and dialogue and family-group conferences generally report high levels of satisfaction relative to their counterparts in other criminal or juvenile justice processes or to those who were referred to mediation but did not participate.[23] Victims, however, report slightly

22. Again, the distinction between risk and severity of offense needs to be maintained.

23. For summary, see John Braithwaite, *Restorative Justice and Responsive Regulation* (New York: Oxford University Press, 2002), 45–72; and Leena Kurki, "Evaluating Restorative Justice Practices," in *Restorative Justice and Criminal Justice*, ed. Andrew von Hirsch et al. (Portland, OR: Hart, 2003), 293–314. Also, Robert B. Coates and John Gehm, *Victim Meets Offender: An Evaluation of Victim-Offender Reconciliation Programs* (Valparaiso, IN: PACT Institute of Justice, 1985), and "An Empirical Assessment," in *Mediation and Criminal Justice: Victims, Offenders, and Community*, ed. Martin Wright and Burt Galaway (London: Sage, 1989), 251–63; Gabrielle M. Maxwell and Allison Morris, "Research on Family Group Conferences with Young Offenders in New Zealand," in *Family Group Conferences: Perspectives on Policy and Practice*, ed. Joe Hudson et al. (Monsey, NY: Criminal Justice Press, 1996), 88–110; Paul McCold and Benjamin Wachtel, *Restorative Policing Experiment: The Bethlehem Pennsylvania Police Family Group Conferencing Project* (Pipersville, PA: Community Service Foundation, 1998); Paul McCold and Ted Wachtel, *Restorative Justice Theory Validation*, paper presented at the Fourth International Conference on Restorative Justice for Juveniles, 2000, Tübingen, Germany; Edmund McGarrell et al., *Returning Justice to the Community: The Indianapolis Juvenile Restorative Justice Experiment* (Indianapolis: Hudson Institute, 2000); David B. Moore with L. Forsythe, *A New Approach to Juvenile Justice: An Evaluation of Family Conferencing in Wagga Wagga* (Wagga Wagga, Australia: Charles Sturt University Press, 1995); Heather Strang, *Victim Participation in a Restorative Justice Process* (New York: Oxford University Press, 2001); Mark S. Umbreit, "Mediating Victim-Offender Conflict: From Single-Site to Multi-Site Analysis in the U.S.," in *Restorative Justice on Trial: Pitfalls and Potentials of Victim-Offender Mediation—International*

lower levels of satisfaction than other participants, although their satisfaction is still higher than that of victims who experienced more common criminal or juvenile justice processes.[24] In a meta-analysis of studies that addressed participant satisfaction in restorative justice programs using a variety of practices, James Bonta and his colleagues found that on average about 88 percent of offenders expressed satisfaction with their experience; about 82 percent of victims likewise expressed satisfaction.[25] Victim-offender mediation and dialogue has also been found to reduce victims' anger, anxiety, fear of revictimization by the same offender, and fear of crime in general.[26] Both victims and offenders find the processes and outcomes associated with victim-offender mediation and dialogue to be fair, and at least nine out of ten participants would recommend victim-offender mediation and dialogue to a friend.[27] Agreements are reached in practically all cases using victim-offender mediation and dialogue, and the vast majority of plans are completed, indicating that victims and offenders who participate in victim-offender mediation usually experience restorative outcomes, including reparation, compensation, apology, and reintegration.[28] More extensive data regarding satisfaction is not yet

Perspectives, ed. Heinz Messmer and Hans-Uwe Otto (Dordrecht: Kluwer, 1992), 431–44; Mark S. Umbreit, Victim Meets Offender: The Impact of Restorative Justice and Mediation (Monsey, NY: Criminal Justice Press, 1994); Mark S. Umbreit, Mediation of Criminal Conflict: An Assessment of Programs in Four Canadian Provinces (St. Paul, MN: The Center for Restorative Justice and Mediation, University of Minnesota, 1995); Mark S. Umbreit and Ann Warner Roberts, Mediation of Criminal Conflict in England: An Assessment of Services in Coventry and Leeds (St. Paul, MN: The Center for Restorative Justice and Mediation, University of Minnesota, 1996); and Mark S. Umbreit, Robert B. Coates, and Betty Vos, "The Impact of Victim-Offender Mediation: Two Decades of Research," Federal Probation 65, no. 3 (2001): 29–35.

24. For summary, see Braithwaite, Restorative Justice and Responsive Regulation; and Kurki, "Evaluating Restorative Justice Practices." Also, Strang, Victim Participation in a Restorative Justice Process; Mark S. Umbreit and Robert B. Coates, "Cross-Site Analysis of Victim-Offender Mediation in Four States," Crime and Delinquency 39, no. 4 (1993): 565–85; Umbreit and Roberts, Mediation of Criminal Conduct in England; and Umbreit, Coates, and Vos, "The Impact of Victim-Offender Mediation."

25. James Bonta et al., "Restorative Justice and Recidivism: Promises Made, Promises Kept?," in Handbook of Restorative Justice, ed. Sullivan and Tifft, 114.

26. Umbreit and Coates, "Cross-Site Analysis." See also Strang, Victim Participation in a Restorative Justice Process; Heather Strang and Lawrence W. Sherman, The Victim's Perspective: RISE Working Paper 2 (Canberra: Law Program, RSSS, Australian National University, 1997); Umbreit, "Mediating Victim-Offender Conflict"; and Umbreit and Roberts, Mediation of Criminal Conduct in England.

27. Braithwaite, Restorative Justice and Responsive Regulation; Umbreit and Coates, "Cross-Site Analysis"; Umbreit and Roberts, Mediation of Criminal Conduct in England; and Umbreit, Coates, and Vos, "The Impact of Victim-Offender Mediation."

available for other types of restorative justice programs such as sentencing circles, or citizen- and neighborhood-accountability boards.

While one response to Skotnicki's critique of restorative justice is to cite criminological data supporting its effectiveness at achieving its various goals, another response from a Catholic perspective ought to be theological. Skotnicki maintains that encounters in which offenders sincerely seek to repair the harm that they inflicted on their victims and communities cannot bring about their internal reform without a sentence to prison to foster the transformation of character. People who commit crime have not only done wrong; their very characters are damaged. I wonder whether Skotnicki would similarly argue the participation in the sacrament of Penance and Reconciliation could not effect meaningful transformation of sinners. He might respond that the distinction between restorative justice and Penance is that Penance is a sacrament. It is therefore effective not because of anything done by the sinner in Penance, but because of the grace of the Holy Spirit. The penitent must be open to God's grace offered in the sacrament, but grace brings about internal reform. This caveat about the difference between restorative justice and Penance is important for Catholics to remember as we advocate for restorative justice. However, it does seem that our tradition supports the notion in ways that Skotnicki denies that practices in which people confront their wrongdoing in conversation with others and receive ongoing support from their communities as they repair the harm that they have caused can foster change of character.

Restorative justice makes several contributions as part of a proposal for criminal justice reform grounded in a Catholic perspective. Its practices provide means for responding to crime and individual wrongdoing in ways that reduce reoffending, foster the social reintegration of offenders, contribute to public

28. Braithwaite, *Restorative Justice and Responsive Regulation*; Burt Galaway, "The New Zealand Experience Implementing the Reparation Sentence," in *Restorative Justice on Trial*, ed. Messmer and Otto, 55–80; John Haley, "Victim-Offender Mediations: Japanese and American Comparison," in *Restorative Justice on Trial*, ed. Messmer and Otto, 105–30; Tony Marshall, "Restorative Justice on Trial in Britain," in *Restorative Justice on Trial*, ed. Messmer and Otto, 15–28; McCold and Wachtel, *Restorative Policing Experiment*; Edmund McGarrell, *Restorative Justice Conferences as an Early Response to Young Offenders* (Washington, DC: Office of Juvenile Justice and Delinquency Prevention, U.S. Department of Justice, 2001); Kim Pate, "Victim-Offender Restitution Programs in Canada," in *Criminal Justice, Restitution, and Reconciliation*, ed. Burt Galaway and Joe Hudson (Monsey, NY: Willow, 1990), 135–44; Thomas Trenzcek, "A Review and Assessment of Victim-Offender Reconciliation Programming in West Germany," in *Criminal Justice, Restitution, and Reconciliation*, ed. Burt Galaway and Joe Hudson (Monsey, NY: Willow, 1990), 109–24; Umbreit and Coates, "Cross-Site Analysis"; Umbreit and Roberts, *Mediation of Criminal Conduct in England*; and Umbreit, Coates, and Vos, "The Impact of Victim-Offender Mediation."

safety, and establish justice for all people affected by crime, especially victims. Restorative justice also maintains the importance of treating all stakeholders in a crime, including offenders, as fully human persons. The analogies between restorative justice and penitential practices suggest that Catholics can view restorative justice as aligning with the norms and values of liturgical and sacramental ethics. However, restorative justice is not an appropriate or complete response to all crimes and all offenders. Its practices are best suited to low-risk offenders who commit property crimes or serious, violent offenses. We will need additional resources for offenders who are more prone to reoffending and whose crimes are drug related. When considering adequate means for the internal reform and social reintegration of high-risk offenders, other efforts will also be needed for offenders for whom the relatively brief and contained experience of restorative justice will be insufficient or who do not take responsibility for their crime.

ON REHABILITATION

The "medicinal" understanding of Penance and Reconciliation may serve as a basis for supporting rehabilitative efforts within criminal justice systems. Again, we must remember that the purpose of Penance and Reconciliation is not metaphorical self-flagellation, but the restoration of wrongdoers to healthy and whole communion with the body of Christ. This sacrament is the normative means by which wrongdoers in Catholic tradition are reformed internally and reintegrated into community. Furthermore, the acts of satisfaction in Penance, which are "the external sign of one's desire to amend one's life,"[29] are not to be understood as punishments for the sake of punishment, but as regimens for retraining oneself in the ways of Christ. This interpretation of punishment as having "medicinal value" rather than serving purely punitive purposes is echoed today in *Catechism of the Catholic Church*, which states that "as far as possible [punishment] should contribute to the correction of the offender."[30] In many ways, penitential regimens may be thought of as analogous to rehabilitative efforts to encourage and facilitate healthful change in the behaviors and attitudes of criminal offenders. Rehabilitative practices that serve these purposes can then be supported within a Catholic sacramental framework.

29. United States Conference of Catholic Bishops, *Responsibility, Rehabilitation, and Restoration: A Catholic Perspective on Crime and Criminal Justice* (Washington, DC: United States Conference of Catholic Bishops, 2000). Available online at http://www.nccbuscc.org/sdwp/criminal.shtml.

30. *Catechism of the Catholic Church* (Vatican City: Libreria Editrice Vaticana, 1994), ¶2266.

In many circles, both progressive and conservative, "rehabilitation" has become a "dirty word."[31] One side has latched onto Robert Martinson's conclusion that "nothing works" to rehabilitate offenders. Therefore, the only legitimate justifications of punishment are either to deter or to incapacitate offenders—or in the case of some advocates, to harm them. It is too much to hope that offenders could change their lives for the better. The other side recognizes that the implementation of rehabilitation over the past two centuries has too often focused on risk management rather than true rehabilitation. Advocacy of rehabilitation has historically depended on the argument that "treatment" (whatever that word might entail) is a "'means' to the 'end' of community safety."[32] Unfortunately, the result frequently has been that offenders themselves have been treated as means rather than ends, as patients to be manipulated rather than human persons with moral agency. Offenders, who often recognize this tendency, then come to resist rehabilitation. Restorative justice advocate and practitioner Kay Harris observes, "In general, the distaste for such programs is linked to a sense that these interventions involve things being 'done to' or 'prescribed for' passive recipients who are characterized as deficient, ineffectual, misguided, untrustworthy, possibly dangerous, and almost certain to get into trouble again."[33] No one wants to be manipulated, particularly by social scientists or therapists who think they know what is best for one. Criminologists Tony Ward and Shadd Maruna observe that as a result of this somewhat warranted distrust of rehabilitation among offenders, "[offenders] will happily talk about going straight, self-change, recovery, or redemption, [but] . . . almost none will tell you that they need to be 'rehabilitated.'"[34] The suspicion of rehabilitation from almost all quarters has led to the use of a variety of words other than "rehabilitation" (for example, reentry, resettlement, reintegration, recovery, desistance, etc.) that purport to do the same things as rehabilitation, but under a different guise.[35]

One must be cautious in recommending rehabilitative reforms for our criminal justice systems—our history with these ideals and practices in the United States is not sterling, as evidenced by multiple failures since the

31. See Tony Ward and Shadd Maruna on the history of skepticism about "rehabilitation," in *Rehabilitation: Beyond the Risk Paradigm* (New York: Routledge, 2007), especially chapter 1.

32. Ibid., 172.

33. M. Kay Harris, "In Search of Common Ground: The Importance of Theoretical Orientations in Criminology and Criminal Justice," *Criminology and Public Policy* 4 (2005): 311–28. Quoted in Ward and Maruna, *Rehabilitation*, 16.

34. Ward and Maruna, *Rehabilitation*, 15.

35. Ibid., 1–7.

invention of the penitentiary. These failures can be attributed to at least two overlapping issues: poor implementation and lack of understanding of effective treatments. The first issue will in all likelihood continue to be a problem; we will inevitably make mistakes in developing and using even the best procedures available and we must beware of repeating past mistakes. Criminologists, however, have made great strides since the 1970s in understanding and describing evidence-based rehabilitative practices that decrease recidivism. Rehabilitative practices that attend to risk, needs, and responsivity of offenders prove most effective. The factor of risk indicates that "the intensity of human service intervention should be proportional to the offender's risk to re-offend."[36] While this conclusion may seem obvious, too often rehabilitative programs have focused on low-risk offenders because they seem "safe," while high-risk offenders have gone to jail or prison where they have little access to rehabilitation. "Treating low-risk offenders," observes criminologist James Bonta, "has minimal impact on recidivism."[37] Rehabilitative programs ought to concentrate on offenders who are frequently written off as untreatable; such offenders actually are the most likely candidates for reforming their lives in response to an intervention. These programs ought also to attend to the factor of need, which suggests that interventions should focus on criminogenic needs such as "substance abuse, cognitions supportive of crime, and social support of crime," versus noncriminogenic needs, such as low self-esteem or depression.[38]

36. James Bonta et al., "Restorative Justice and Recidivism: Promises Made, Promises Kept?," in *Handbook of Restorative Justice*, ed. Sullivan and Tifft, 111. For more information on the "Risk-Need-Responsivity Model" of rehabilitation, see Donald A. Andrews, "Enhancing Adherence to Risk-Need-Responsivity: Making Quality a Matter of Policy," *Criminology and Public Policy* 5, no. 3 (August 2006): 595–602; Donald A. Andrews and James Bonta, *The Psychology of Criminal Conduct*, 2nd ed. (Cincinnati: Anderson, 1998); Donald A. Andrews and James Bonta, *The Psychology of Criminal Conduct*, 3rd ed. (Cincinnati: Anderson, 2003); Donald A. Andrews, James Bonta, and R. D. Hoge, "Classification for Effective Rehabilitation: Rediscovering Psychology," *Criminal Justice and Behavior* 17 (1990): 19–52; Donald A. Andrews, James Bonta, and J. Stephen Wormith, "The Recent Past and Near Future of Risk and/or Need Assessment," *Crime and Delinquency* 52 (2006): 7–27; Donald A. Andrews and Craig Dowden, "Managing Correctional Treatment for Reduced Recidivism: A Meta-Analytic Review of Programme Integrity," *Legal and Criminological Psychology* 10 (2005): 173–87; Francis Cullen and Paul Gendreau, "Assessing Correctional Rehabilitation: Policy, Practice, and Prospects," *Criminal Justice* 3 (2000): 109–75; Francis Cullen, "Rehabilitation and Treatment Programs," in *Crime: Public Policies for Crime Control*, ed. Wilson and Petersilia, 253–90; Paul Gendreau and Donald A. Andres, "Tertiary Prevention: What a Meta-Analysis of the Offender Treatment Literature Tells Us About 'What Works,'" *Canadian Journal of Criminology* 32 (1990): 173–84; Doris Layton MacKenzie, *What Works in Corrections: Reducing the Recidivism of Offenders and Delinquents* (Cambridge: Cambridge University Press, 2006); and Christy A. Visher, "Effective Reentry Programs," *Criminology and Public Policy* 5 (2006): 299–304.

37. Bonta et al., "Restorative Justice and Recidivism," 111.

Finally, rehabilitative programs should be responsive to the particular capacities, learning styles, and motivations of offenders. Appropriate rehabilitative interventions with high-risk offenders show the highest rate of recidivism reduction when compared with both incarceration and restorative justice; they contribute to a decrease in reoffending of about 26 percent.[39] If rehabilitative treatment is delivered in the community rather than in prison or residential settings, recidivism is reduced even more—about 35 percent. Rehabilitation that is geared toward the risk and offense levels of offenders as well as to their responsiveness to treatment receives the strongest support of all interventions in contemporary criminological literature—contrary to the conclusions of Martinson as well as of advocates of deterrence, incapacitation, and harm as justifications for punishment.

Even if appropriate rehabilitative interventions are effective at reducing recidivism, we ought not to advocate for them on these grounds alone. The reasons for this caveat are both practical and moral. On one hand, rehabilitation cannot work unless offenders invest themselves in the process, and offenders are unlikely to invest themselves in rehabilitation if the only reason to do so is that it reduces the risk that they will reoffend, a reason based primarily on the well-being of the community and not on the well-being of the offender. Ward and Maruna argue,

> All forms of rehabilitation require the active acceptance and willing participation of intervention participants in order to work. Individuals can be forced to sit and listen, they can even be forced to participate in some talk therapy, but they cannot be forced to change. . . . Any rehabilitation option offered to prisoners and probationers needs to make sense to clients themselves and be clearly relevant to the possibility of their living a better life.[40]

The ends of rehabilitation must include better lives for offenders as well as community safety. Without offering the possibility that offenders' lives will be improved, rehabilitative programs have little to offer to encourage them to change their lives.

On the other hand, horrendous abuses can be justified if the only standard to judge rehabilitation is effectiveness at reducing recidivism.[41] For Catholics, however, the sacrament of Penance and Reconciliation provides some moral

38. Ibid.
39. Bonta et al., "Restorative Justice and Recidivism."
40. Ward and Maruna, *Rehabilitation*, 17–19.

guidance about values that should inform rehabilitation of offenders. As this sacrament is built upon a view of wrongdoing as a violation of relationships, the purpose of any rehabilitative effort must go beyond ensuring an offender's compliance with the law to strive for internal reform and reintegration in the community. With the relational context of wrongdoing, an offense cannot be viewed in isolation, but must be understood within the broader contexts of the offender's life story and his social and communal relationships. The sacrament of Reconciliation is not only concerned with particular incidents of wrongdoing, but also with the reality of the whole person who committed those actions. Offenders cannot achieve the ends of internal reform and social reintegration alone; they need relationship with others and guidance from their communities. With rehabilitative practices, offenders always ought to be understood as subjects rather than objects. Change in their lives requires their agency with the support of the community. Offenders remain children of God, always seeking what they view as good, although all too often in deeply flawed ways. These insights from the sacrament of Reconciliation suggest that rehabilitative practices must also be judged according to whether they bring about change in the lives of offenders that benefits the offenders themselves, whether they account for the role of communal and social relationships before and after crime, and whether they attend to offenders as whole persons and active agents in their reform. Rehabilitative practices ought never to reduce people who have committed crime to mere clients or patients. From the perspective of sacramental and liturgical ethics, even people who have committed crime always bear dignity as human persons and have the potential of finding healing necessary for internal reform and social reintegration.

41. An extreme, but informative, example can demonstrate the danger of using effectiveness as the only measure of rehabilitative practices. I could easily devise a response to theft that would prevent offenders from ever shoplifting again. Because they would not steal again, we could consider them rehabilitated and the treatment effective. Recidivism rates would be nil. This response is time-honored, practiced throughout history and around the globe: cutting off the hands of thieves. If our only standard to judge rehabilitation is effectiveness, then such a practice could be deemed acceptable. Numerous other examples can be found in the history of prisons that show how an emphasis on effectiveness without recognition of the inherent dignity of even the prisoner can lead to cruelty. One of the most harrowing was concocted at one of the first penitentiaries, the Eastern State Penitentiary in Philadelphia. The philosophy driving this penitentiary maintained that prisoners needed to practice monastery-like silence in order to reflect on their wrongdoing and allow God's inner light to arise within them. Prisoners who violated this silence were forced to wear "iron gags," five-inch strips of metal that lay over an inmate's tongue, held in place by a leather belt. The goal was effectiveness at reducing reoffending; the intention was not to inflict pain but to bring about inner change; the "rehabilitative" practice was monstrous. These examples suggest that while effectiveness is important, it can never be the only standard when evaluating rehabilitation.

While effective at reducing recidivism, the risk-need-responsivity model of rehabilitation encounters some challenges when confronted with these practical and moral concerns. With its strong emphasis on risk, this model provides little to motivate offenders. As Ward and Maruna observe,

> It is unclear how an approach *focused* on the prevention of harmful consequences to others can encourage offenders to change their own behavior in fundamental ways. . . . What is required at the clinical level is some attention to helping offenders build a better life (not just a less harmful one) in ways that are personally meaningful and satisfying, and socially acceptable.[42]

Another implication of this focus on risk is that the risk-need-responsivity model tends to rely upon a restricted and passive view of human nature. Offenders are reduced to descriptions of traits that can be used to assess their likelihood to reoffend, and treatment plans are devised to manipulate those traits. Any sense of an offender's life story or plans is lost. Offenders are seen as problems for community safety rather than as persons. This reduced assessment of offenders also fails to attend to the communal and social conditions that may contribute to crime. "Because the focus is on individuals and their potential for harmful behavior, little attention is paid to the interdependency of people."[43] If crime is the result of isolated individual choices, then the presumed response—and the response of the risk-need-responsivity model—is to isolate the individuals who make those choices. These difficulties with the risk-need-responsivity model suggest that this model ought to be reevaluated in normative terms. Ward and Maruna note that "[the risk-need-responsivity model] is justified on the grounds of 'what works.' Its empirical justification is its normative justification and vice versa."[44] The guidance of sacramental and liturgical ethics, however, indicates that a moral response to wrongdoing must be justified in terms more significant than effectiveness.

In light of these issues, revision of the risk-need-responsivity model of rehabilitation may be necessary for it to be acceptable in view of liturgical and sacramental ethics. Some criminologists have suggested an alternative model—the "good lives model"—that builds upon the strengths of the previous model in reducing recidivism while emphasizing the importance of offender agency in any rehabilitative program. In their discussion of this model, Ward

42. Ibid., 83. Emphasis in original.
43. Ibid., 83.
44. Ibid., 88.

and Maruna appeal to an Aristotelian anthropology that supposes that human beings are teleological creatures oriented toward the end of living good lives. Catholics could connect to this anthropology through Aquinas's appropriation of Aristotle. The good lives model "begins from the assumption that offenders are essentially human beings with similar needs and aspirations to nonoffending members of the community."[45] All offenders are subjects, not merely objects, and as human persons, they seek some fundamental goods (for example, life, friendship, community, knowledge, creativity, etc.) that shape the direction of their lives. Ward and Maruna describe these "primary human goods" as "states of affairs, states of mind, personal characteristics, activities, or experiences that are sought for their own sake and are likely to increase psychological well-being if achieved."[46] People commit crime when they do not have the external or internal resources necessary to achieve these goods. Crime becomes

---

45. Ibid., 24. For other discussions of the "good lives" model of rehabilitation, or strength-based rehabilitation, see Ros Burnett and Shadd Maruna, "The Kindness of Prisoners: Strength-Based Resettlement in Theory and in Action," *Criminology and Criminal Justice* 6 (2006): 83–106; Shadd Maruna and Thomas P. LeBel, "Welcome Home?: Examining the Reentry Court Concept from a Strengths-Based Perspective," *Western Criminology Review* 4, no. 2 (2003): 91–107; Mayumi Purvis, Tony Ward, and Gwenda Willis, "The Good Lives Model in Practice: Offence Pathway and Case Management," *European Journal of Probation* 3, no. 2 (2011): 4–28; Peter Raynor and Gwen Robinson, *Rehabilitation, Crime, and Justice* (New York: Palgrave, 2005); Joanne Thakker and Tony Ward, "The Good Lives Model and the Treatment of Substance Abusers," *Behavior Change* 27 (2010): 154–75; Tony Ward, "The Good Lives Model of Offender Rehabilitation: Basic Assumptions, Etiological Commitments, and Practice Implications," in *Offender Supervision: New Directions in Theory, Research, and Practice*, ed. Fergus McNeill, Peter Raynor, and Chris Trotter (Devon, UK: Willan, 2010), 41–64; Tony Ward and Theresa A. Gannon, "Rehabilitation, Etiology, and Self-Regulation: The Good Lives Model of Sexual Offender Treatment," *Aggression and Violent Behavior* 11 (2006): 77–94; Tony Ward and Mark Brown, "The Good Lives Model and Conceptual Issues in Offender Rehabilitation," *Psychology, Crime, and Law* 10 (2004): 243–57; Tony Ward and Claire Stewart, "Criminogenic Needs and Human Needs: A Theoretical Model," *Psychology, Crime, and Law* 9 (2003): 125–43; Tony Ward and W. L. Marshall, "Good Lives, Aetiology, and the Rehabilitation of Sex Offenders: A Bridging Theory," *Journal of Sexual Aggression: Special Issue: Treatment and Treatability* 10 (2004): 153–69; Tony Ward, Theresa M. Gannon, and Ruth E. Mann, "The Good Lives Model of Offender Rehabilitation: Clinical Implications," *Aggression and Violent Behavior* 12 (2007): 87–107; Robin J. Wilson and Pamela M. Yates, "Effective Interventions and the Good Lives Model," *Aggression and Violent Behavior* 14 (2009): 157–61; Pamela M. Yates and David S. Prescott, *Building a Better Life: A Good Lives and Self-Regulation Workbook* (Brandon, VT: Safer Society Press, 2011); and Pamela M. Yates and Tony Ward, "Good Lives, Self-Regulation, and Risk Management: An Integrated Model of Sexual Offender Assessment and Treatment," *Sexual Abuse in Australia and New Zealand: An Interdisciplinary Journal* 1 (2008): 3–20. See also www.goodlivesmodel.com for an abbreviated discussion of the model as well as other resources and an exhaustive bibliography.

46. Ward and Maruna, *Rehabilitation*, 113.

a means—either directly or indirectly, consciously or not—of achieving primary human goods.

Rehabilitation, according to the good lives model, ought to attend not only to risk, needs, and responsivity, but also to "priorities," which concern the primary human goods toward which offenders wish to direct their lives, their overall conceptions of the good, and their strengths and goals for achieving these goods.[47] By emphasizing priorities, proponents of this model believe that treatment can reduce the needs and risks of offenders by motivating them to find less destructive and more satisfying ways to achieve primary human goods. Rehabilitative treatment comes to focus on offenders' strengths, experiences, and expertise that can help them to achieve their ends, rather than concentrating on their deficits alone. Furthermore, based on the recognition that no one achieves primary human goods alone, the good life model also attends to the communal context to which offenders will return. Rehabilitation must account for how human beings are situated within their communities: "It is important that individuals convicted of crimes take responsibility and are accountable to their community, but it is equally imperative that the latter is receptive to these efforts and embrace offenders as fellow travelers not moral strangers."[48] Where weakened communities inhibit the capacities of offenders to pursue primary human goods and achieve good lives, rehabilitative programs must move beyond concern with the successes or failures of individual offenders to strengthen communities as well. Strong communities that can provide relationship and guidance are necessary for rehabilitation.

The good lives model answers many of the critiques of rehabilitation leveled by critics who worry that risk management has too often trumped true rehabilitation in practice, resulting in the objectification of offenders in "treatment." Drawing on Aquinas's ethics, Kathryn Getek Soltis, for example, writes, "In attempts to treat an individual's deficiency and distortion, the offender may not be fully engaged as a moral agent who must, to some extent, choose his or her own transformation through new habits of action. Rather, with minimal attention to moral agency, offenders may simply be held accountable to meeting certain external standards or benchmarks."[49] Because the good lives model accounts for priorities as well as risks, and asks offenders

---

47. Ibid., 132.

48. Tony Ward and Robyn Langlands, "Repairing the Rupture: Restorative Justice and the Rehabilitation of Offenders," *Aggression and Violent Behavior* 14 (2009): 205–14. See especially page 212 on the communal context of rehabilitation.

49. Kathryn Getek Soltis, "Just Punishment? A Virtue Ethics Approach to Prison Reform in the United States" (Ph.D. diss., Boston College, 2010), 33.

what their priorities are, its practices of rehabilitation are less prone to this critique. The standards and benchmarks to which offenders are held accountable are intrinsic to their prioritization of primary human goods and their conception of the good life. The offender's own strengths and goals are the main tools for achieving those goods, with the support of their communities. The primary reason for proposing this model is that the risk-need-responsivity model of rehabilitation failed to account for offenders' moral agency and the necessity of their motivation for bringing about their own transformation.

The similarities between the values upheld by the sacrament of Penance and Reconciliation and the good lives model of rehabilitation suggest that liturgical and sacramental ethics based in Catholic tradition could endorse this model as an appropriate starting place for rehabilitative reform of our criminal justice systems. Both this sacrament and the good lives model maintain that wrongdoers cannot be reduced to their offenses, but must be understood as human persons. Based on this recognition, both deny the validity of punishment for retributive ends or for the sake of punishment itself. Responses to people who do wrong must account for their ultimate ends as human persons and must never treat them as mere objects to be manipulated by either rehabilitative treatment or penitential regimens. Assuming that all people are teleological creatures, both Penance and the good lives model begin with discernment of what one's ends are, why one has turned away from or fallen short of them, and what is necessary to bring about reorientation to and achievement of them. Responses to people who do wrong should be medicinal, fostering healing and wholeness by encouraging and supporting new habits that are not harmful to oneself and one's neighbors. Neither Penance nor the good lives model takes an individualistic perspective on why people do wrong. While we must accept personal responsibility for our actions, both consider the communal and social contexts that may have contributed to individual wrongdoing and discern what sort of support from others may be necessary to enable the internal reform and social reintegration of wrongdoers. Because the good lives model of rehabilitation offers the means for people who commit crime to realize health and wholeness, because it upholds the human dignity and moral agency of wrongdoers, and because it connects individuals and communities, Catholics drawing upon liturgical and sacramental ethics could advocate for this form of rehabilitation in criminal justice reform.

While the good lives model has not been evaluated as extensively in terms of effectiveness because of its relative newness, its overlap with the risk-need-responsivity model implies that it may "work." Further evaluation of each model in the future is necessary. Because of its emphasis on "the individual's capacity to make decisions himself or herself," the good lives model may avoid some of the moral pitfalls of past attempts at rehabilitation.[50] It may also better motivate offenders to go straight, change themselves, and seek recovery and even redemption. Even with this recommendation, however, the history of rehabilitation in the United States indicates the need to continually reevaluate whether rehabilitative programs are well implemented and respect the inalienable and inviolable human dignity of offenders.

THE ONGOING, BUT LIMITED, NEED FOR PRISONS

Both restorative justice and rehabilitation require the active participation of offenders who admit their wrongdoing, take responsibility, and desire change in their lives. Of course, not every person who commits a crime will meet these criteria, so unfortunately we will continue to need prisons in our society. However, prisons are ineffective at reducing recidivism, and in some circumstances, they may contribute to reoffending. They have only a moderate effect on reducing crime rates overall. Prisons are expensive, and the money spent on them cannot be spent on other social goods such as education or public health or on criminal justice alternatives such as restorative justice and rehabilitation. Catholics must also acknowledge that prisons really are not the normative means of punishment in our tradition (*contra* Skotnicki), and we ought to admit that our use of prisons throughout our history reflects a tragic failure to achieve internal reform and social reintegration of people who do wrong through other means. The normative means of reintegration into the body of Christ and of ongoing internal reform in Catholicism are the sacraments, not prisons. Our calls for criminal justice reform must then be viewed through a sacramental lens that fosters restorative justice and rehabilitation while calling for a significantly reduced role for incarceration.

Prisons inherently contradict the norms and values upheld in liturgical and sacramental ethics. Whereas prisons erect walls and fences, the Eucharist is radically inclusive. Whereas prisons hide their inhabitants from the view of outsiders, the Eucharist summons its participants to see Christ in all others, including convicted criminals as he became one himself. Whereas prisons create division, the Eucharist conveys a world-picture of ultimate reconciliation and beckons us to serve others, especially those who are most degraded, in anticipation of God's reign. The sacrament of Penance and Reconciliation also stands in contrast with incarceration. Whereas prisons are based on retribution, Penance prefers forgiveness to punitiveness. Whereas prisons isolate people

---

50. Ward and Maruna, *Rehabilitation*, 119.

who commit crime, Reconciliation offers communal support to wrongdoers to bring about internal reform and social reintegration. Whereas prisons delineate a harsh line between criminals and the rest of us, the broader eucharistic context of Penance and Reconciliation reminds us that we all participate in the brokenness of the world through personal and social sin. Prisons break down the norms and values of forgiveness, humility, dialogue, healing, inclusiveness, and service upheld by liturgical and sacramental ethics. These contradictions indicate the necessity for Catholics to seek the end of our society's dependence on prisons.

Over the last decade, the growth of prison populations has slowed compared to the 1980s and 1990s. Addressing our criminal justice crisis will require reversing this growth, not merely slowing it. In a report for The Sentencing Project, Judith Greene and Marc Mauer write, "Even if there should be a leveling of population growth, that would still leave prison populations at historic highs that are unprecedented in American history or that of any other democratic nation."[51] We need to shrink the size of our prison populations if we are to bring an end to mass incarceration. Greene and Mauer describe policies in four states—Michigan, New York, New Jersey, and Kansas—that have downscaled their prison populations of the first decade of this century, even while state prison populations across the country grew 12 percent since 2000. These states conscientiously chose to downscale through multipronged reform efforts that would reduce prison populations and promote more cost-effective responses to crime. Each state used a different selection of policy changes, but together the sets of policies that they used provide a basis for policy recommendations for other states as well as for the federal government.

Among the most important initiatives in these states was to reform sentencing laws. Mandatory minimum sentences ought to be made less stringent or abolished entirely. The lengths of sentences, especially for nonviolent offenses, ought to be reduced significantly, and "three-strikes" laws and similar laws that lead to automatic life sentences without parole ought to be repealed. Judges ought to be given more discretion in sentencing, for example, by allowing "open pleas" in lower-level offenses so that judges, not prosecuting attorneys, decide on sentences. They also ought to be given more leeway to depart downward from the suggestions of sentencing guidelines.

Reforming sentencing laws does not necessarily mean that offenders will not have to confront the consequences of their wrongdoing. We need to invest in alternatives to incarceration that can prevent reoffending in more effective

51. Judith Greene and Marc Mauer, *Downscaling Prisons: Lessons from Four States* (Washington, DC: The Sentencing Project, 2010), 2.

and less expensive ways than prison. Many of these alternatives can draw on restorative justice and the good lives model of rehabilitation. With alternatives in place, judges have more flexibility in sentencing to divert offenders away from prison. States that decreased their prison populations often required offenders to participate in educational programs, vocational training, or substance abuse treatment depending on the particular circumstances of each case. These states also invested in better assessments of offender risk so that they could better determine who would be suited for these alternatives.

Another important reform has been to reintroduce parole in prison systems. Offenders can be offered "merit time" for participating successfully in educational, vocational, or treatment programs. "Reentry prisons" that offer more intensive programs and help prepare prisoners for release may ease their transition as parolees and decrease the likelihood that they will return to prison. Outside of prison, day reporting centers and other monitoring procedures can reduce the amount of time that someone needs to be supervised behind prison walls. Too often, parolees return to prison because of technical rule violations (for example, failing to pay court costs or failing to report a change of address or employment in a timely manner), not because of new criminal offenses. Intermediate sanctions could also be used more effectively instead of parole revocation for these sorts of violations. When paroled, ex-prisoners continue to need services for housing, employment, education, and substance abuse treatment to smooth their way into social reintegration.

Through similar efforts, these four states have made significant progress in downscaling their prison populations. New York, Michigan, New Jersey, and Kansas have all reduced the population of their state prisons by between 5 and 25 percent, saving taxpayers millions of dollars.[52] All four states saw declining crime rates following their downscaling efforts, indicating that reducing prison populations does not necessarily leave the general population in more danger. The models of these states can serve as examples to other states and the federal

---

52. For fuller discussion of these efforts and their effects, see Greene and Mauer, *Downscaling Prisons.* Another important resource on reducing prison and jail populations is Michael Jacobson's *Downsizing Prisons: How to Reduce Crime and End Mass Incarceration* (New York: New York University Press, 2005). New York's prison population dropped 20 percent between 1999 and 2009, and between 2007 and 2009, its department of corrections deactivated 2700 dormitory beds and closed three prisons as well as annexes at six other prisons, saving taxpayers an estimated $26.3 million in the 2010–2011 state budget alone. Michigan's prison population fell 12 percent between 2006 and 2009. That state closed eight prison facilities in 2009, saving taxpayers $118 million. New Jersey cut its prison population by 19 percent between 1999 and 2009, without increasing threats to public safety. In the same time period, violent crime fell in New Jersey by 21 percent and property crime by 23 percent. Finally, Kansas saw a 5 percent decline in prison population in just the six years between 2003 and 2009.

government in the effort to curb and reverse the growth of our criminal justice systems.

In cases where offenders present too great of a risk to public safety, we will still need prisons. From the perspective of sacramental and liturgical ethics, however, our practices of incarceration ought to change, especially in light of the vision of the Eucharist. Our celebration of the Eucharist ought to draw us more deeply into confrontation with human alienation in the world. God's presence in the Eucharist upholds the importance of divine-human relationship, and consequently, the importance of maintaining relationship for the well-being of humanity. The inclusiveness of Jesus Christ's table calls us to reach out to those who have been excluded from human relationship, and his service to the world demands that we become servants especially to people who have been downtrodden and despised. In remembrance of Christ's death as a convicted criminal and in anticipation of the coming of God's reign in fullness, we are summoned to become a reconciled and reconciling community, hoping and longing for life, peace, forgiveness, love, and justice. The eucharistic vision stands in sharp contrast to the prison, which is built upon broken relationship, exclusion, and retribution.

Reforming Prisons

While we may always need prisons on this side of God's reign in fullness, our use of prisons could be reformed to minimize the harm they cause both to the imprisoned and to those of us who are ultimately harmed by the loss of full relationship with all of our neighbors. Sacramental and liturgical ethics call upon Catholics and other Christians to advocate for reform of our prisons. In all penal practices of our prisons, prisoners must be treated as fully human persons and must be provided with the resources necessary to participate in the dignity, unity, and equality of all people. The ultimate ends of punishment—internal reform and social reintegration—ought to be upheld. While some prisoners may never be capable personally of internal reform, the possibility that they could bring about significant change in their lives must be maintained or else we risk treating them as merely caged animals. The community must strive to provide the guidance and support for prisoners to prepare themselves to return as fully reintegrated members, even if their full reintegration may never occur.

Unfortunately, our prisons rarely endeavor to achieve these ideals. Too often activities required of prisoners are designed to break them down rather than build them up. Such intentions are evident, for example, with the use of prison boot camps or the return of chain gangs in many states. The purpose of such practices is generally to punish prisoners for the sake of punishment, to cause them harm. Rather than activities aimed at harm and punishment, prisons should focus on activities that heal and restore prisoners. Prisons that instituted rehabilitation programs based on the good lives model would be a starting point for reform.

Another mechanism for building up prisoners is education. The majority of prisoners are functionally illiterate and need remedial and secondary education.[53] For prisoners with a GED or high school diploma, postsecondary education can help them enter the job market more successfully upon release. But education can do more than improve the marketability of ex-prisoners. It provides opportunities for reflection, effort, and accomplishment, which can contribute to a greater sense of self-worth. It can also help prisoners to situate their own experiences within the context of broader issues and realities, expanding the horizons of their understanding of the world. It can lead prisoners to gain a better sense of others' perspectives. As teachers come from outside, prisoners may build relationships with people from the wider community, and as teachers return to the outside, they may share their experiences with other people, helping to humanize prisoners. When prisoners succeed in their academic programs, they may be trained to become peer tutors and teachers, which can decrease the costs of educational programs and provide tutors and teachers an opportunity to help their fellow prisoners while furthering their own education. Given the large proportion of offenders who are functionally illiterate, the primary focus of educational programs in prisons ought to be remediating the failures of our elementary and secondary educational systems. However, many prisoners may also benefit from postsecondary education. Unfortunately, the abolition of Pell Grants for prisoners in 1994 has impeded greatly the ability of prisoners to gain access to higher education while behind bars.

A few programs, however, have continued to provide college-level courses for prisoners. University Beyond Bars (UBB), for example, provides postsecondary education in two prisons in Washington State.[54] Through the program, prisoners can take courses that fulfill the requirements for Ohio University's College for the Incarcerated. UBB pays tuition to Ohio University through donations, and volunteers teach the courses. Prisoners can earn an associates' degree or a noncredit-bearing certificate through UBB. Another program focused on higher education for prisoners is the Inside-Out Prison

53. "Literacy Behind Prison Walls," National Center for Education Statistics, U.S. Department of Education, http://nces.ed.gov/pubs94/94102.pdf. See also Megan Sweeney, *Reading Is My Window: Books and the Art of Reading in Women's Prisons* (Chapel Hill: University of North Carolina Press, 2010).

54. "University Beyond Bars," www.universitybeyondbars.org.

Exchange Program, which began at Temple University in Philadelphia in 1997.[55] Inside-Out builds partnerships between prisons and institutions of higher education in order to bring prisoners and college students together to study as peers. Courses are taught in prisons with an equal representation of prisoners and undergraduates. Through the dynamics of the courses, undergraduates are led to reconsider their assumptions about prisoners, crime, and justice in light of personal encounters in our criminal justice systems while prisoners are given the opportunity to reflect on their own experiences in light of a broader framework for understanding those systems. More than three hundred Inside-Out courses have been taught nationwide. Although the courses offered by Inside-Out cannot lead to a college degree for prisoners at this time, this program is currently developing Degrees of Freedom, which will offer prisoners opportunities to earn a bachelors' degree. Together UBB and Inside-Out demonstrate the possibilities for offering higher education to people in prison. These programs require creativity and persistence to navigate the complexities of correctional institutions and institutions of higher education. Nevertheless, postsecondary education need not be out of reach of prisoners if provided adequate financial, institutional, and personal support.

Vocational programs should complement educational programs in prisons. One of the main barriers to social reintegration upon release is the inaccessibility of work for ex-prisoners; appropriate job training can smooth a prisoner's way into employment. One program that offers vocational training for prisoners is Texas Second Chance.[56] For more than fifteen years, the Texas Department of Criminal Justice has partnered with Texas Food Banks to provide volunteers to work in warehouses and kitchens across the state. While volunteering, prisoners receive warehousing and inventory skills, certification on warehouse machinery, and professional culinary training. The program also includes mentorship from local business leaders as well as weekly class sessions where prisoners receive instruction. In addition to preparing food packages for hungry people in the community, participants in the program have also contributed to another program, Kids Kitchen, which prepares hundreds of meals per day for children in after-school programs. Through Texas Second

55. "The Inside-Out Prison Exchange Program," www.insideoutcenter.org.

56. Jessica Kwong, "Inmate Cooks Give Back at Food Bank," *San Antonio Express*, February 4, 2012, http://www.mysanantonio.com/news/local_news/article/Inmate-cooks-give-back-at-food-bank-3009175.php; "Texas Second Chance Program," San Antonio Food Bank, http://www.safoodbank.org/index.php/programs/more-programs/tx-second; "Texas Second Chance," Southeast Texas Food Bank, http://setxfoodbank.org/programs/texas-second-chance/; and "Programs," North Texas Food Bank, http://www.ntfb.org/au_programs-texas-second-chance.cfm.

Chance, prisoners directly benefit their communities while gaining highly marketable job skills.

Another set of vocational programs in many states involves dog training. These programs vary depending on local partnerships and resources. Some programs pair prisoners with shelter dogs up for adoption that need some training before finding a family. Other programs train dogs to become police dogs or assistance dogs for people with disabilities. One of the latter programs is built on a partnership between the Georgia Department of Corrections and the Middle Georgia Technical College. Through this program, prisoners complete a twelve- to fourteen-month Veterinary Assistant and Animal Caretaker course as they train dogs for the Guide Dog Foundation for the Blind in New York. Upon completion of the program, the dogs are sent to homes to complete their training before being placed with an owner with a disability, and the prisoners have a vocational certificate that can help them find stable employment upon release. The presence of dogs can dramatically change the prison environment as prisoners strive to qualify for the programs and interact positively with a vulnerable creature. As with the partnership between prisons and food banks, dog-training programs in prisons offer prisoners an opportunity to gain job skills while benefiting their communities. Other programs that enable prisoners to gain job skills while improving the prison environment and contributing to society ought to be developed.

While rehabilitative treatment, education, and vocational programs primarily aim at internal reform of prisoners, we ought also to reform prisons so that they can better bring about social reintegration. Doing so requires reimagining the possibilities of community both within prisons and between prisons and the world outside. Being integrated into society takes practice as one learns the skills, attitudes, and values necessary to be in appropriate relationships with others. Certain programs can provide the space for prisoners to practice being in community. The Alternatives to Violence Project, for example, promotes nonviolent problem solving in prisons.[57] AVP began in 1975 through the collaboration of prisoners in Green Haven Prison in New York with the Quaker Project on Community Conflict to create a workshop for youth coming into conflict with the law. The program has since spread worldwide, and workshops have been held in prisons, women's shelters, community centers, halfway houses, churches, and other locations. By participating in the workshops, prisoners learn new skills for engaging in community that they can then take out into the world upon release such as

---

57. "Alternatives to Violence Project—USA," http://www.avpusa.org/. Soltis also describes this program in her dissertation, 211–12.

conflict resolution and communication skills. They are also trained as facilitators of the program because their experiences help them to relate the workshops to the lives of other prisoners. One of the strengths of AVP is that it validates the contributions of prisoners in bringing about positive change in their communities both in prison and beyond prison walls.

Prisoners ought also to be in communal relationship with people outside of prison, which depends largely upon people outside of prisons venturing into them. Some of this can occur with facilitators and volunteers coming into prisons to work with rehabilitative, educational, or vocational programs. People outside of prisons can also volunteer to mentor prisoners, particularly as they prepare for release. Prisoner Visitation and Support, a program that facilitates volunteer visits with prisoners in federal and military prisons, can provide a model for encouraging relationships between prisoners and people who could provide them with support and guidance.[58] Religious groups have been especially important for providing people in prison the opportunity to participate in community. Kairos, a Christian program begun in 1976 in a Florida prison, offers an example of this community building.[59] This organization hosts weekend retreats inside of prisons led by volunteers from the outside. After the initial weekend, prisoners continue to participate in weekly support groups to which the outside volunteers return as mentors. This organization has also begun offering similar programming outside of prisons for the female partners of prisoners as well as specially designed programming for younger offenders. The emphasis of Kairos is upon Christians from outside of prisons bringing the light of the gospel into prisons. Unfortunately, this emphasis can minimize the extent to which the gospel can already exist in prisons and the ways in which outside volunteers could potentially learn about the gospel from prisoners. Despite these weaknesses in Kairos' theology, this organization provides a model of ways to build community in prisons and to connect prisoners to communities outside of prisons. It also offers an example of how people outside of prison can guide and support people inside.

One of the major challenges to social reintegration is a prisoner's return to his or her family. Although continuing and supporting family relationships can help to reduce reoffending, our prisons place many unnecessary barriers to maintaining these relationships.[60] Prisons are often located far from urban

58. See "Prisoner Visitation and Support," http://www.prisonervisitation.org/. Also, Soltis, "Just Punishment?," 214–15.

59. "Kairos Prison Ministry International, Inc.," http://www.kairosprisonministry.org/. For a fuller discussion of Kairos, see Byron Johnson, *More God, Less Crime: Why Faith Matters and How It Could Matter More* (Philadelphia: Templeton, 2012).

centers, where most prisoners' families live. Families often find it difficult to travel long distances to prisons, especially when they have to pay for transportation and perhaps a hotel stay. Prison overcrowding, which has led some states to outsource their prisoners to other states or to private prisons, has exacerbated this problem. When visits are possible, family members—including children—face a gauntlet of searches before a short visit, during which physical contact is typically prohibited. When visits are not possible, families may resort to collect telephone calls. Phone companies charge families exorbitant rates for calls from prisoners, while many states amass kickbacks from the calls as well. The high cost of collect telephone calls makes this option for maintaining relationship with a loved one in prison cost-prohibitive, especially for families that may have already lost the income from a family member in prison and that are living on an economic edge.

Whenever possible, prisons should work to maintain and even strengthen family relationships of prisoners, who should be housed as close to family as possible. This stipulation may require significant reorganization of prisons in many states, but if prison populations are downscaled, the possibilities for moving prisoners to locations closer to family expand. In some locales, religious congregations and community organizations have supported prisoners' families by offering free or low-cost transportation to prisons and by volunteering to house and feed families during visits. Assisting Families of Inmates (AFOI), for example, began in the late 1970s in Virginia when a group of Richmond churches pooled resources to provide transportation to families of prisoners for visits.[61] The organization also provides hot meals for families when they return from their trips. Using advances in technology, AFOI offers video visitation services as well. In addition to social services for prisoners' families, the organization hosts the Milk and Cookies Children's Program for children with parents in prison, which is a school-based support group. Other initiatives could work to make the visitation areas of prisons more hospitable by supplying toys or playground equipment. Girl Scouts of Central Maryland paired with the National Institute of Justice in 1992 to begin Girl Scouts Beyond Bars, which brings together girls and their incarcerated mothers for regular troop meetings.[62] Twenty-two states now have Girl Scouts Beyond Bars programs,

60. Creasie F. Hairston, "Prisoners and Families: Parenting Issues during Incarceration," paper presented at the Urban Institute's From Prison to Home conference, Washington, DC, January 30–31, 2002. See also "Prisoners and Their Families: Parenting Issues during Incarceration," in *Prisoners Once Removed: The Impact of Incarceration and Reentry on Children, Families, and Communities*, ed. Jeremy Travis and Michelle Waul (Washington, DC: Urban Institute Press, 2003), 259–82.

61. "Assisting Families of Inmates, Inc.," http://www.afoi.org/.

and Congress has appropriated $2 million to support their activities. In addition to efforts to make prison visits easier and more humane, collect telephone calls should become more affordable, especially by removing the possibility that states could legally profit from them. Because of the value of community, especially of the familial community, everything possible that could contribute to the social reintegration of prisoners while they are in prison ought to be done.

Prisons will continue to be necessary in any contemporary criminal justice system. We must, however, try to use them less frequently and begin to draw upon other important resources for responding to crime and individual offenders. Some people will refuse to take responsibility for their crimes. Some people need to be confined for purposes of public safety until they can make enough changes in their lives to be reintegrated into society. Sadly, some people may never be capable of reintegration. Despite our ongoing need of prisons, our reliance upon them should be limited by the recognition that they are generally ineffective at bringing about internal reform and social reintegration. From a Catholic perspective, the contradictions that prisons present to liturgical and sacramental ethics should lead us to end our society's dependence on prisons. We must acknowledge that the existence of prisons reflects not only the existence of people who are dangerous in our midst, but also the realities of social injustice. Prisons inherently make it difficult to treat prisoners as fully human persons, and they break down the norms and values of forgiveness, community, dialogue, and inclusion lifted up by the sacraments of the Eucharist and of Penance and Reconciliation. In light of the failures of prisons, we must work for policies that can downscale our prison populations, such as those implemented by Michigan, New York, New Jersey, and Kansas. With the people who remain behind bars, we must maintain the hope that they can one day be free by providing guidance and support through the good lives model of rehabilitative treatment, educational and vocational programming, and prisoner visitation, especially with families, but also with the wider community.

Conclusion: A Comprehensive Model for Criminal Justice

Drawing on contemporary criminology, I suggest an ideal for criminal justice systems that would rely on the strengths of both rehabilitation and restorative justice in reducing recidivism as well as in achieving other goals distinctive to each model. Each set of practices should focus primarily on those populations

---

62. "Girl Scouts Beyond Bars," Girl Scouts, http://www.girlscouts.org/who_we_are/our_partners/government_grants/community/gsbb.asp.

with which they are most effective at reducing recidivism. One way to accomplish this goal is to screen offenders for rehabilitative services through restorative justice programs. Criminologist and restorative justice advocate John Braithwaite offers a model for such a process in his pairing of restorative justice with "responsive regulation" to determine when *not* to use restorative justice, although I would adapt his model so that regulations beyond restorative justice aim at rehabilitation and incapacitation, rather than at deterrence and retribution (see figure 1).[63]

Figure 1. Pyramid of Restorative Justice, Rehabilitation, and Incapacitation

This model supposes that we should always offer restorative justice as the first response to offenders, regardless of the seriousness of their offenses. Only when offenders fail to respond to restorative justice (for example, if they deny responsibility, if they refuse participation, or if they display aggressive behaviors) should other interventions be employed. In this way, low-risk offenders would only be required to complete the terms of the agreement reached in their conferences. But high-risk offenders could be referred through restorative justice programs to appropriate rehabilitative services that would address their criminogenic needs (such as substance abuse and mental illness)

63. Braithwaite, *Restorative Justice and Responsive Regulation.*

in ways that respond to their capacities and motivations. These services would preferably be offered in community settings in all cases where concerns for public safety did not require the use of commitment or incarceration to incapacitate offenders. By responding to all offenders with restorative justice practices first and progressively requiring rehabilitation and incapacitation only as needed, the sanctions placed on all offenders could respond more appropriately to their levels of risk, need, responsiveness to treatment, and personal priorities, in accordance with the good lives model. Drawing on Thomistic ethics, Soltis suggests three criteria for evaluating whether prison is the most appropriate response to someone who has committed a crime. She suggests reserving incarceration only for people who commit crimes that harm the good of the community (versus "self-regarding vices" such as drug use), who have made a habit of injustice, and who demonstrate a willful rejection of the common good.[64] Based on these criteria, the numbers of people that we incapacitate in our prisons and jails could be greatly reduced as more people are diverted to restorative justice programs to create agreements to repair the harm caused by their crime or are enrolled in rehabilitative programs suited to them.

The discussion thus far has focused on how rehabilitation and restorative justice can be related to Catholic interpretations of the sacraments of Eucharist and Penance as well as supported by contemporary criminology. Criminal justice reform in the United States, however, cannot remain so narrowly focused given the broader context of the crisis in these systems in social injustice. Any adequate response to our criminal justice crisis must attend also to how it is fundamentally intertwined with a crisis of social justice. It must move beyond consideration of the means for responding to crime and individual wrongdoing, to consideration of how the United States became and continues to be the first genuine prison society. Without accounting for the broader context of our criminal justice crisis, we will not be able to create a society in which all members are treated as fully human persons empowered to participate in the dignity, unity, and equality of all people. Given the data describing our criminal justice systems, we must admit that this crisis is largely the result of a more significant failure to realize social justice throughout our communities. A sacramental response to criminal justice must entail work for social justice beyond criminal justice systems as well. The stark realities of racial, ethnic, and class disparities within criminal justice systems ought to alert us to factors other than crime rates that have contributed to the unprecedented numbers of people in U.S. jails and prisons. The call to reduce crime and reintegrate offenders is insufficient in any proposal to fix these systems; any responsible effort to address

64. Soltis, "Just Punishment," 133–37.

our criminal justice crisis must also respond to the call to work for social justice as well.

5

A Movement for Justice

The proposals of the previous chapter are important for responding to crime and individual wrongdoing in ways that reduce reoffending, lead to social reintegration of offenders, maintain public safety, and establish justice for all people affected by crime, especially victims. They provide direction for effective criminal justice reform. These proposals alone, however, will not end mass incarceration in the United States. The first genuine prison society was not created because of high crime rates, but because of social, cultural, economic, and political factors that coalesced into a willingness in our country to imprison more people for longer periods of time, especially young black men from socioeconomically disadvantaged backgrounds. Our crisis of criminal justice reflects a crisis of social justice in our society. The effects of mass incarceration in the United States, in turn, have helped sustain, and even worsen, this social justice crisis in ways that further marginalize, disempower, and endanger members of our society. Because of the ways in which criminal and social justice are fundamentally intertwined, an adequate response to these crises cannot stop with implementing restorative justice and rehabilitation as alternatives to incarceration or with downscaling prison populations. We must also attend to the ways in which social injustices fostered our criminal justice crisis and the ways in which our criminal justice policies and practices help perpetuate social injustices.

This criterion for an adequate response to our circumstances suggests that we must move beyond the questions of chapter 4 regarding how to respond effectively to crime and individual wrongdoing. It indicates that our concerns cannot be limited to crime control, guilt or punishment, costs or benefits, deterrence, retribution, or incapacitation. If we wish no longer to be the first genuine prison society, we must engage in more thoughtful reflection on our character, beliefs, and actions as individuals, as communities, and as a society as a whole. What kind of people do we want to be? What do we want our communities to be like? What holds us together, and what breaks us apart?

What barriers prevent us from achieving a common good in which everyone is treated as a fully human person? If not a genuine prison society, then what type of society do we wish to create? Director of The Sentencing Project Marc Mauer argues that answering these sorts of questions and acting upon our answers are necessary for ending mass incarceration. He writes, "The first step [in addressing mass incarceration] involves expanding the discussion of crime policy beyond the day-to-day debates on the relationship between prison and crime to more fundamental concerns about the type of society we wish to create."[1]

Catholics have a rich heritage of social teaching that informs our answers to these questions. This heritage ultimately finds its ground in our liturgical and sacramental life, particularly our participation in the Eucharist. Through liturgy, we engage in the public service of prayer, but also the public service rendered by the *ekklesia* unto others, especially the poor, oppressed, and marginalized. As sacramental, our service consecrates human life, disclosing the hidden reality of salvation and drawing us more deeply into the world in anticipation of the ultimate mystery of God's reign. Our hope in God's reign enlivens us as we work for justice by serving God and neighbors, particularly victims of injustice. The Eucharist, as the pinnacle of liturgy and sacrament, is the perfection of the church in the consecration of the world through public service in emulation of Jesus Christ. In this sacrament, Catholics and many other Christians are reoriented in light of a new vision or world-picture that upholds certain norms and behaviors as meaningful. Others' needs and God's will for establishing love, peace, freedom, justice, humanity, and life in response to those needs are disclosed. We are formed morally to a eucharistic vision, and this vision inspires our understanding of just individuals, communities, and societies. To answer the fundamental concerns about the type of society we wish to create and to find direction about how we should individually and collectively respond to our social justice crisis, Catholics must begin with our eucharistic life.

THE EUCHARISTIC VISION AND SOCIAL JUSTICE

Our ritual lives shape us morally. In our individual and communal worship practices, reiterated from week to week, we encounter a vision of God's reign. Liturgical theologian Don Saliers writes that liturgy is a "continuing exercise of recalling, sustaining, and reentering [a] picture of the cosmos," and that as

---

1. Marc Mauer, "The Causes and Consequences of Prison Growth in the United States," in *Mass Imprisonment: Social Causes and Consequences*, ed. David Garland (Thousand Oaks, CA: Sage, 2001), 10.

we become reoriented through this picture, we are "characterized."[2] As the Eucharist offers a vision of God's reign, our participation in this sacrament forms our consciousness, enabling us to view the world and our work in it in view of justice under God. In liturgy, we traverse through this vision, a world-picture that transforms our ways of being, perceiving, and acting in the world. We adopt views of the world from God's perspective. We become de-centered, aware of others' needs as they too are people loved by God. God's will becomes our own will. We become shaped by the patterns of God's reign. Through the grace conveyed in the Eucharist, this sacrament accomplishes the public service of consecrating the world as we engage in it as persons and communities united to the eucharistic vision.

The moral vision of the Eucharist directs us to justice. This world-picture of justice, however, is particular to God's reign and opposes the reign of the principalities and powers of this world and their understanding of justice. Justice in God's reign is rooted in covenant, an abiding and sacred agreement to maintain relationship for the well-being of all humanity. This covenant is inclusive, welcoming everyone to the table, especially people who have experienced the exclusion of poverty, oppression, and marginalization. Jesus Christ provides an example for us in our celebration of the Eucharist through his table fellowship, which offered seats even for moral outcasts—sinners, prostitutes, and tax collectors. We are also asked to emulate Christ at the eucharistic gathering by becoming servants to all others, particularly to those who are in need and who are excluded from relationship. The Eucharist invites us, the reconciled community, to strive for reconciliation among our members and within the wider world.

Together we remember in the Eucharist Christ's victory over the principalities and powers through his death and resurrection by embodying God's justice. We especially recall his condemnation as a criminal, which reminds us that this extension of justice, reconciliation, relationship, and inclusion reaches those people who are the most despised and degraded. We also anticipate the coming of God's reign in fullness. Our anticipation undergirds our hope that justice under God will ultimately triumph and feeds our longing for its realization. This eucharistic vision reorients Christians to communion, and when we are morally formed by this vision, we "find [ourselves] in many unexpected ways being a voice for those without a voice, speaking the truth when it is both awkward and unpopular, appearing to be . . . nonconformist."[3]

2. Don E. Saliers, "Liturgy and Ethics: Some New Beginnings," *The Journal of Religious Ethics* 7, no. 2 (1979): 174–75.

3. R. Kevin Seasoltz, "Justice and the Eucharist," *Worship* 58 (1984): 517.

As the eucharistic vision awakens our eschatological imaginations in remembrance of Christ's death and resurrection and in anticipation of God's reign, Christians are called to confront social injustice in our midst here and now. The Eucharist—the heart of our liturgical and sacramental lives—is radically this-worldly. William Cavanaugh describes the implications of the communion brought about by this sacrament:

> The church becomes visible, obeying the Eucharistic demand that true unity be achieved, that people overcome alienation from each other and become reconciled, caring for each other, especially the weak, in community and solidarity. The church, as in the Eucharist, thus becomes a present foretaste of the future eschatological feast. The poor can wait no longer; the church must witness to the Kingdom in the present.[4]

Living in the tension between our memories of Christ and our hopes for God's reign, we live in the present as followers united in the body of Christ, the church, who endeavor to embody the world-picture of the Eucharist, and we do so by working for social justice. Discussing themes similar to those lifted up by Cavanaugh, Kevin Seasoltz writes,

> [T]hose who celebrate the Eucharist in memory of Jesus, who follow his command to "do this," must feed the same sort of people and involve themselves with the same sort of dinner guests as Christ had at table. . . . Christ became incarnate primarily to free his people from slavery to sin and then from other forms of slavery which find their roots in slavery to sin. If the Eucharist is to be celebrated with integrity, the church must be about the same sort of liberation.[5]

Without confronting social injustice, we do not live into the eucharistic vision; we fall short of the moral transformation that this sacrament demands of us.

This description of the transformation of our consciousness in the Eucharist is of course idealistic. Sacramental and liturgical ethics must always account for the challenges of privatization and politicization of worship, of pluralism, of injustice within the church, and of problems with the meaning of participation in liturgy and sacraments. Nevertheless, social injustice raises

---

4. William T. Cavanaugh, *Torture and Eucharist: Theology, Politics, and the Body of Christ* (Oxford: Blackwell, 1998), 268.

5. Seasoltz, "Justice and the Eucharist," 519–20.

perhaps a more devastating challenge to us: our own indifference and lack of awareness about poverty, oppression, and marginalization. An important aspect of the power of the eucharistic vision is its potential to pique our consciences about the exclusion of some people. Kenneth Himes argues, "The vast majority of Catholics do not read magisterial statements, even the most important conciliar decrees. It is not the intellectual appeal of theological documents which moves people at the level of the daily life of the church. For Roman Catholics it is the Sunday eucharist [sic] that continues to be the important ecclesial experience."[6] Despite the challenges to liturgical and sacramental ethics, the Eucharist is the most likely medium through which Catholics will come to embrace the demands of social justice upon them. Himes continues, "Unless and until the concern for justice is integrated with the central spiritual exercise of the gathered community there will remain a sense that the social ministry of the church is an adjunct not a constitutive dimension of gospel life."[7] As Catholics, we must shed our indifference and lack of attention to social injustice in response to the call toward justice, relationship, inclusion, reconciliation, and hope found in the moral vision of the Eucharist.

This vision undergirds Catholic teaching about the kinds of people we ought to become and the type of society we ought to create. As Jesus Christ welcomed all people to his table, so we recognize that all people are equal before God. We share in a basic equality as we all bear God's image, the source of our dignity. Recognition of the dignity of all human persons is the basis for our pursuit of the common good and of humane and just conditions of life for every person. Without exception, every person must have access to everything necessary to enable her to realize herself fully. These conditions include not only material goods such as food, clothing, water, shelter, and healthcare, but also spiritual, intellectual, social, cultural, and political resources that mark our existence as human. We require these conditions because without them we cannot participate fully in the dignity, unity, and equality of all people. Just as social justice demands that we create a society that treats every person as fully human, it also compels us to oppose anything that marginalizes, disempowers, or endangers anyone. We must reject deliberate acts that dehumanize our neighbors. But because oppression is often much more insidious than any overt action, we must strive to identify and dismantle structures that directly or indirectly limit the capacities of some individuals and groups to achieve a life that rises to their dignity as human persons. In response to the eucharistic vision,

6. Kenneth R. Himes, "Eucharist and Justice: Assessing the Legacy of Virgil Michel," *Worship* 62, no. 3 (1988): 214.

7. Ibid.

we need to create "a new social, economic, and political order, founded on the dignity and freedom of every human person, to be brought about in peace, justice, and solidarity."[8] We must become people who "seek the good of others as though it were one's own good"[9] and who embody "a firm and persevering determination to commit oneself to the common good."[10]

If we wish to express fully our sacramental lives, if we want to exist, perceive, and act as if we have in reality been morally transformed by the eucharistic vision, if our liturgy is to become public service that consecrates the world in its fullest sense, then we need to work for social justice. With respect to our criminal justice crisis in the United States, we must attend to the ways in which mass incarceration both reflects and helps sustain a social justice crisis that marginalizes, disempowers, and endangers many members of our communities. We may begin our efforts by mitigating the deleterious effects of our criminal justice systems on the individuals, families, and communities most directly affected by their policies and practices.

RESPONSES TO EFFECTS OF MASS INCARCERATION ON SOCIAL JUSTICE

While our criminal justice systems reflect a crisis of social justice, they also help sustain, and even exacerbate, conditions in which many members of our society—not only prisoners—are not treated as fully human persons and are not vested with the resources necessary to participate in the dignity, unity, and equality of all people. Some of these conditions can be addressed through criminal justice reforms based on a model of restorative justice and rehabilitation, in which prisons are used only in exceptional cases where the incapacitation of an offender is necessary for public safety. But because the effects of our criminal justice systems extend beyond prison walls and reach ex-prisoners, families, and communities as well, we must also consider responses to the social injustices that these systems often worsen. In doing so, we must attend especially to the exclusion from the common good of people from racial or ethnic minority groups and from socioeconomically disadvantaged backgrounds, as these groups have been disproportionately affected by our criminal and social justice crises.

The following proposals offer a starting point for addressing the social injustices worsened by current criminal justice policies and practices. They

8. Pontifical Council for Justice and Peace, *Compendium of the Social Doctrine of the Church* (Washington, DC: USCCB Publishing, 2004), ¶19.

9. Ibid., ¶167

10. John Paul II, *Sollicitudo Rei Socialis* (1988), ¶38.

aim at mitigating the ways in which these systems marginalize, disempower, and endanger ex-prisoners, families, and communities. The proposals are not comprehensive; other actions can and should also be taken. The proposals are not final; we will need to reevaluate our courses of action as circumstances change. The purpose of describing these proposals is to demonstrate that concrete and specific actions now can ease the access of members of our society to just and humane conditions of life. Moreover, many groups are already making progress in achieving these conditions. Participation in furthering any of these proposals may help to express our desire to seek others' good as if it were our own, to advance the common good. These proposals help us to identify and dismantle structures associated with our criminal justice systems that threaten the conditions necessary to support the full human personhood of all members of society. Catholics and other Christians who feel called by a eucharistic vision to do something about our crises of justice can begin here.

ECONOMIC INCLUSION

Most people exiting our criminal justice systems face lives of poverty, not only immediately upon release, but for decades afterwards. Ex-prisoners find it difficult to enter the job market as their work skills have stagnated while locked up, they have lost contacts outside of prison that could help them find and hold jobs, and many employers are unwilling to hire former offenders. Some of these effects of incarceration could be lessened through increased rehabilitative, educational, and vocational programming both inside and outside of prisons. Other strategies outside of prisons should complement these efforts.

A few steps could encourage employers to hire ex-offenders. Since 1966, the Federal Bonding Program has provided security to employers who take a risk in hiring someone who is designated "not bondable" by insurance companies.[11] Employers seek Fidelity Bonds as guarantees against employee dishonesty, but commercial insurance companies will not bond certain categories of people deemed too risky, including anyone with a record of arrest, conviction, or incarceration. The U.S. Department of Labor, via state workforce agencies, offers Fidelity Bonds for these employees at no cost either to the employer or the job applicant. The bond covers the first six months of employment and reimburses employers for any loss due to employee theft without requiring payment of a deductible. The Federal Bonding Program reports remarkable success as only 1 percent of bonded employees have violated

11. "The Federal Bonding Program: A U.S. Department of Labor Initiative," Federal Bonding Program, http://www.bonds4jobs.com/.

the terms of the bond, resulting in a reimbursement to their employers. Since its start over four decades ago, however, only about 42,000 bonds have been issued, a relatively small number in comparison with the number of people released from jail or prison. Expansion of the Federal Bonding Program would provide more incentives to employers considering ex-offenders as employees.

A campaign to "Ban the Box" is another initiative aimed at opening employment doors for ex-offenders. Many job applications include a box to mark if the applicant has a criminal record. When applicants mark this box, employers can easily discard their applications even if applicants are well qualified for the job, their offenses are unrelated to the type of work for which they are applying, and they have changed their lives significantly since the time of their offense. Some of the questions on job applications seek information about any criminal history, even if years or decades have passed since the applicants' encounter with the criminal justice system. Applicants then face a dilemma: tell the truth and have their applications thrown out, or lie and hope that the lie will not result in their job termination in the future. As a result of efforts to ban the box, six states now prohibit employers from asking about criminal records on job applications and thirteen other states have cities or counties that have issued similar prohibitions.[12] In 2012, the Equal Employment Opportunity Commission recommended new best practices for considering criminal records in employment decisions: "that employers not ask about convictions on job applications and that, if and when they make such inquiries, the inquiries be limited to convictions for which exclusion would be job related for the position in question and consistent with business necessity."[13] With this policy, ex-offenders could get past initial screening for a job so that they may be considered more fully. Employers still can conduct criminal background checks later in the hiring process when a provisional job offer has been extended. Applicants could then discuss with employers whether their history would impede their work and explore the option of Fidelity Bonding to protect employers against any risk they may be taking. Banning the box could offer people trying to reestablish themselves after involvement in our criminal justice systems a greater chance of successfully finding employment and supporting themselves.

12. "Ban the Box Major U.S. Cities and Counties Adopt Fair Hiring Policies to Remove Unfair Barriers to Employment of People with Criminal Records," National Employment Law Program, http://www.nelp.org/page/-/SCLP/2011/CityandCountyHiringInitiatives.pdf?nocdn=1.

13. "Consideration of Arrest and Conviction Records in Employment Decisions Under Title VII of the Civil Rights Act of 1964," Equal Employment Opportunity Commission, http://www.eeoc.gov/laws/guidance/arrest_conviction.cfm#VIII. See ¶ V.B.3.

In addition to vocational and educational programs in prisons, other efforts should focus on ensuring that ex-prisoners have the resources and skills necessary to enter and remain in the employment market. One of the most direct ways of meeting this goal is by removing or decreasing bans against people with arrest, conviction, and sentencing records from receiving occupational licenses.[14] These bans vary from jurisdiction to jurisdiction so it is difficult to describe them comprehensively for all localities. Some states permanently prohibit government employment of people with felony records, while other states limit their bans to a number of years after conviction. Some bans from occupational licensure depend on offense type, while others apply to any person with a record of criminal arrest, conviction, or sentence. Some bans apply strictly to people with criminal records, while others apply to people who have in some way not shown "good moral behavior." Although all states can issue certificates of rehabilitation as a means of lifting these bans in individual cases, only six actually do so. In some cases, the barrier to licensure may have a reasonable justification with certain types of offenses when vulnerable populations may be at risk, for example, banning people with records of domestic violence or child abuse from childcare or home healthcare. Other bans lack clear justification, including bans against licensure as barbers, dentists, optometrists, plumbers, septic tank cleaners, embalmers, or beauticians. In some instances, applicants for licensure can seek an individual exception to a ban, but the processes to do so can be prohibitive. To better enable ex-offenders to find employment, states should reevaluate licensure requirements. When public safety does not require bans, states should lift them. Decisions about rejection from licensure should be made on an individual basis according to each applicant's capacity to do the work required without endangering others. The National Employment Law Project is a national organization that has led the way in reforming occupational licensure bans for people with criminal histories.[15]

---

14. For more information on occupational licensure bans, their effects, and strategies for lifting them, see Deborah N. Archer and Kele S. Williams, "Making America 'The Land of Second Chances': Restoring Socioeconomic Rights for Ex-Offenders," *New York University Review of Law & Social Change* 30 (2006): 527–84; Scott Davies and Julian Tanner, "The Long Arm of the Law: Effects of Labeling on Employment," *Sociological Quarterly* 44 (2003): 385–405; Byron Harrison and Robert C. Schehr, "Offenders and Post-Release Jobs: Variables Influencing Success and Failure," *Journal of Offender Rehabilitation* 39 (2004): 35–68; Karol Lucken and Lucille M. Ponte, "A Just Measure of Forgiveness: Reforming Occupational Licensing Regulations for Ex-Offenders Using BFOQ Analysis," *Law and Policy* 30, no. 1 (2008): 46–72; and Amy L. Solomon et al., *From Prison to Work: The Employment Dimensions of Prisoner Reentry* (Washington, DC: Urban Institute Press, 2004).

A strong social safety net can provide necessary support for people trying to find and keep employment. People convicted of felony drug crimes lost access to welfare benefits and food stamps with the 1996 Personal Responsibility and Work Opportunity Reconciliation Act. Laws passed in 1996 and 1998 further limit access to public housing for people with criminal records. The 1994 Violent Crime Control and Law Enforcement Act abolished prisoner access to Pell Grants, and people convicted of felony drug crimes can no longer receive federal financial aid for higher education after release from prison. These shortsighted policies deny people exiting our criminal justice systems access to useful resources for restarting their lives. Rather than promoting dependency, easier access to education, housing, food, and other basic resources can make the key difference in enabling someone to get a job and stay in it. Finding and keeping employment may then empower ex-offenders ultimately to escape poverty.[16]

INCORPORATION IN POLITICAL LIFE

Policies associated with our criminal justice systems also diminish the political power not only of people who have been in prison, but their communities too. Two specific initiatives could counteract their exclusion from public life, beginning with the enfranchisement of ex-prisoners. Currently about 5.3 million Americans do not have the right to vote. Disenfranchisement laws disproportionately affect African-American men, as three out of ten of the next generation of African-American men can expect to be disenfranchised at some point in their lives.[17] This prohibition from voting has likely affected the outcomes of at least seven Senate races and one presidential election, according to sociologists Christopher Uggen and Jeff Manza.[18] Disenfranchisement laws in the United States are unique among Western industrialized nations, and they

15. "Criminal Records and Employment," National Employment Law Project, http://www.nelp.org/site/issues/category/criminal_records_and_employment/.

16. For more on the role of the social programs in promoting employment among people leaving prison, see "Results-Based Public Policy Strategies for Promoting Workforce Strategies for Reintegrating Ex-Offenders," Center for the Study of Social Policy, http://www.cssp.org/policy/papers/Promoting-Workforce-Strategies-for-Reintegrating-Ex-Offenders.pdf, especially 12–14. See also Jeremy Travis, *But They All Come Back: Facing the Challenges of Prisoner Reentry* (Washington, DC: Urban Institute Press), 151–84; and Christopher Uggen, Sara Wakefield, and Bruce Western, "Work and Family Perspectives on Reentry," in *Prisoner Reentry and Crime in America*, ed. Jeremy Travis and Christy Visher (New York: Cambridge University Press, 2005), 209–43.

17. "Felony Disenfranchisement Laws in the United States," The Sentencing Project, http://www.sentencingproject.org/doc/publications/fd_bs_fdlawsinusMar11.pdf.

are a central component of the effects on social justice of our criminal justice systems, contributing to the creation of circumstances that civil rights attorney Michelle Alexander calls "the New Jim Crow." She writes, "If shackling former prisoners with a lifetime of debt and authorizing discrimination against them in employment, housing, education, and public benefits is not enough to send the message that they are not wanted and not even considered full citizens, then stripping voting rights from those labeled criminals surely gets the point across."[19]

Many states that have temporary or permanent disenfranchisement policies permit ex-prisoners to apply for the restoration of their voting rights. At the very least, these processes should be streamlined and made more transparent in order to facilitate more easily the restoration of rights for applicants. Community organizations can offer legal support to people working through these processes. Beyond these limited strategies, we should work toward the automatic restoration of voting rights upon release from prison. Some recent campaigns for these initiatives have been successful. In Virginia, one of the four states that permanently disenfranchises people with felony convictions, Republican Governor Bob McConnell has simplified the application process for the restoration of voting rights, and since his inauguration in 2010, he has granted the applications of more than 4,400 voters, more than any other governor in Virginia history. In early 2013, he endorsed the passage of a state constitutional amendment that would automatically restore the voting rights of people with nonviolent felony convictions. As a society, we should move toward the enfranchisement of all ex-prisoners upon release.[20] The actions

18. Christopher Uggen and Jeff Manza, "Lost Voices: The Civic and Political Views of Disenfranchised Felons," in *Imprisoning America: The Social Effects of Mass Imprisonment*, ed. Mary Pattillo, David Weiman, and Bruce Western (New York: Russell Sage Foundation, 2004), 165–204. See also Elizabeth A. Hull, *The Disenfranchisement of Ex-Felons* (Philadelphia: Temple University Press, 2006); Marc Mauer, "Mass Imprisonment and the Disappearing Voters," in *Invisible Punishment: The Collateral Consequences of Mass Imprisonment*, ed. Marc Mauer and Meda Chesney-Lind (New York: New Press, 2002), 50–58; Travis, *But They All Come Back*, 249–77; and Christopher Uggen and Jeff Manza, *Locked Out: Felon Disenfranchisement and American Democracy* (New York: Oxford University Press, 2008).

19. Michelle Alexander, *The New Jim Crow: Mass Incarceration in the Age of Colorblindness* (New York: New Press, 2012), 158.

20. Arguably, we should move toward full enfranchisement, including of people who are still in prison. Other industrialized Western democracies have made this move, including European Union member states and Canada. In 2004, the European Court of Human Rights found disenfranchisement laws in the United Kingdom to violate prisoners' human rights, declaring the ban from voting to be "arbitrary and disproportionate." Israel and South Africa also permit prisoners to vote. For an overview of various policies internationally, see Cormac Behan and Ian O'Donnell, "Prisoners, Politics, and the Polls:

of Governor McConnell, and of community organizations such as the Advancement Project, which has led the enfranchisement movement in Virginia, should serve as a model throughout the United States.

The political power of communities most deeply affected by the concentration of mass incarceration is also weakened by policies associated with our criminal justice systems. The U.S. Census counts prisoners where they are imprisoned, not where they last resided. As a result, the population of the communities where they come from (usually urban areas with high rates of poverty and large minority populations) is undercounted, whereas the population of communities that have prisons (usually rural, predominately white areas) is exaggerated. The latter areas house a large number of people who cannot vote and whose interests lie in other political jurisdictions. Prison-based gerrymandering dilutes the political power of *all* people who live in jurisdictions that do not have prisons, affecting municipal, county, state, and federal elections. The example of Anamosa, Iowa illustrates the problem.[21] One of the city wards includes the Anamosa State Penitentiary, which holds 96 percent of the ward's population. A man who lived near the prison won election to the city council with only two write-in votes—his wife's and next-door neighbor's. The residents of this ward had twenty-five times more voting power than residents of other wards in Anamosa. Prison-based gerrymandering affects the integrity of everyone's vote. However, because certain neighborhoods also lose representation because of the large number of their residents in prison, their citizens are more deeply impacted by this problem.

The most direct fix to prison-based gerrymandering is a change in U.S. Census Bureau policy.[22] With one action on the federal level, this problem could be repaired for all jurisdictions in the country. The Census would simply need to count prisoners according to their last-known addresses. In cases where prisoners do not have a previous address, they should be counted as "at-large residents of the state," just as military personnel are counted. Before this step

Enfranchisement and the Burden of Responsibility," *British Journal of Criminology* 48, no. 3 (2008): 319–36.

21. The story of Anamosa, IA is captured well in a short video on the Prison Policy Initiative website. "Prison Policy Initiative," Prison Policy Initiative, http://www.prisonpolicy.org/.

22. For discussion of policy proposals, see Eric Lotke and Peter Wagner, "Prisoners of the Census: Electoral and Financial Consequences of Counting Prisoners Where They Go, Not Where They Come From," *Pace Law Review* 24, no. 587 (2004): 587–607; and Peter Wagner, "Breaking the Census: Redistricting in an Era of Mass Incarceration," *William Mitchell Law Review* 38, no. 4 (2012): 1241–60. See also "Prisoners of the Census," Prison Policy Initiative, http://www.prisonersofthecensus.org/; and "Prisoners and the Census Count," Redrawing the Lines, http://www.redrawingthelines.org/prisonersthecensuscount.

is taken on the federal level, intermediate actions can be taken by municipal, county, and state authorities to correct their census data when mapping political jurisdictions. After the 2000 Census, over one hundred counties and municipalities chose to reject census counts that included prison populations when drawing districts. In the last few years, four states (New York, Maryland, Delaware, and California) outlawed prison-based gerrymandering. Efforts are underway in sixteen other states to pass similar legislation, and thirteen additional states include counties and municipalities that have rejected the practice. The Prison Policy Initiative is a national organization advocating for the end of prison-based gerrymandering. Relatively straightforward actions can—and have—been taken to reduce the effects of our criminal justice crisis on diminishing the political power not only of people who have been in prison, but also of their—our—communities.

REPAIRING FAMILIES

The effects of our criminal justice systems on social justice extend beyond people convicted of crimes to their families, especially to the children of incarcerated parents. While we must allow that the separation of abusive and neglectful parents from their children who may be endangered is necessary, most children experience the imprisonment of their mother or father as a traumatic event that can lead to lowered self-esteem, depression, emotional withdrawal, inappropriate or disruptive behaviors, or the inability to form attachment to others. The families of incarcerated people also often experience worsened poverty while their loved one is imprisoned and after release, as these families have lost a financial contributor and as ex-prisoners find it difficult to reenter the labor market. Families may face stigma and isolation from others as well as humiliation and shame about their situations. They confront numerous barriers to maintaining relationships with their family members in prison, including long distances to the prison, high collect phone call rates, letters marked "Inmate Correspondence" on the envelope, rigorous and embarrassing search procedures for visitation, and uncomfortable environments for seeing their loved ones, particularly for children. All of these factors contribute to the loss of financial, social, and emotional support for prisoners and their families both during and after incarceration.

Several efforts could lessen these effects on families and children. Where there is no evidence that ongoing relationships between parents, partners, and children are directly harmful to any family members, efforts should aim at supporting family relationships rather than replacing them. While parents are in prison, they should have access to parenting classes that help them build supportive relationships, learn positive supervision and discipline methods, develop skills for advocating for their children, and appreciate economic responsibilities to their children.[23] These classes ought to account for a variety of family structures and dynamics, including cultural differences, and should address parenting teenagers and young adults as well as infants and small children. Such classes also need to tackle the dangers of physical, mental, and sexual abuse. People with histories of family violence need especially to address these issues. Prisons ought also to facilitate relationships with family members through visitation, phone calls, letters, and other strategies such as having parents in prison record storybooks for their children. These encounters could be supported by offering counseling for all family members before and after visits, providing hospitality services during visits, making visiting rooms welcoming to children, and organizing low-cost transportation to and from prisons.[24] The exorbitant cost of collect telephone calls from prisons must be reduced. The Campaign to Promote Equitable Telephone Charges is leading this effort.[25]

Beyond the prison walls, the needs of families must be attended as well. The caregivers of children with parents in prison need additional support. Programs could help caregivers navigate criminal justice and other governmental systems such as child welfare and family services.[26] Legal assistance in obtaining the authority to make medical and educational decisions on behalf of children can help to smooth a child's transition to living apart from his or her parent. Caregivers also need additional financial assistance, for example, through subsidized guardianship. In instances in which the caregiver is a child's other parent, financial assistance could be enhanced through Temporary Aid for Needy Families, food stamps, Medicaid, and housing and childcare assistance. Children, caregivers, and other family members also need emotional and social support. Children could be provided resources through public libraries, schools, and mentoring and youth-development programs. The

23. "Children of Incarcerated Parents: An Action Plan for Federal Policymakers," Justice Center: The Council of State Governments, http://www.reentrypolicy.org/jc_publications/ federa_action_plan_/Children_Incarcerated_Parents_v8.pdf. See also Travis, *But They All Come Back*, 119–50.

24. "Reentry: Helping Former Prisoners Return to Communities," The Annie E. Casey Foundation, http://www.aecf.org/upload/publicationfiles/ir2980d32.pdf.

25. "The Campaign to Promote Equitable Telephone Charges," The Campaign to Promote Equitable Telephone Charges, http://www.etccampaign.com/.

26. On ways to assist caregivers of children with parents in prison, see Justice Center, "Children of Incarcerated Parents."

Family and Corrections Network provides a directory of national, state, and local programs for and about children with parents in prison, as well as an online library of resources for understanding and responding to their particular circumstances.[27] Many grassroots organizations offer forums for families of prisoners to engage with each other, including Families Against Mandatory Minimums, a national organization that advocates for criminal justice reform while providing space for discussing the effects of harsh sentencing on individual families.[28]

The responsibility of rebuilding and strengthening their relationships does not lie with prisoners, their children, or other family members alone. Broader communities ought to create safe places for families of incarcerated people to seek the assistance they need, including material, emotional, and social support. Religious congregations and organizations should work toward becoming what the Annie E. Casey Foundation (AECF) has called "Healing Communities" in which "loving, healthy relationships of support exist, and values of forgiveness and reconciliation, together with commitment to redemption, can be shared."[29] The AECF has partnered with numerous congregations and other religious organizations to enable them to become places that welcome "returning citizens" from prison and support their families. These communities actively seek to address the shame and stigma associated with the incarceration of a family member. They begin working with people who are incarcerated before their release and continue through the reentry process, including offering mentoring services. The AECF emphasizes the need both for pastoral vision, as ministers "create the vision necessary for their congregations to become healing communities," and for lay leadership, as congregants are necessary for implementing the vision in the life of the community.[30] The program for Healing Communities is built on the premise that "any church can and every church should" become "a community that embraces the returning citizen and his or her family."[31] It ought not matter whether a religious congregation or organization is large or small, rich or poor, white or black, Catholic or Protestant, Christian or not—it has some capacity to offer material, emotional,

27. "The Family and Corrections Network," The National Resource Center on Children and Families of the Incarcerated, http://fcnetwork.org/.

28. "Families Against Mandatory Minimums," Families Against Mandatory Minimums, www.famm.org.

29. "Healing Communities: A Framework for Congregations in Their Ministry to Families Affected by Incarceration," The Annie E. Casey Foundation, http://www.healingcommunitiesusa.org/Documents/aecfHealingCommunitiesrptfinal.pdf.

30. Ibid., 13.

31. Ibid., 13.

or social support to people who are incarcerated, returning citizens, and their families.

While all of these efforts for mitigating the effects of our criminal justice systems on families are important, we must also remember that the roots of these effects is mass incarceration. If we wish to have the greatest possible impact on reducing the social injustices faced by families of imprisoned people, we ought to advocate for reducing the number of people sent to prison and the length of prison sentences in the first place. We ought to pursue policies that downscale prison populations. We ought to transform our criminal justice systems to emphasize restorative justice and rehabilitation. We ought to use prisons only when necessary for public safety. Even in instances in which someone needs to be incarcerated, we must seek ways to minimize the harms of prison, especially to families of imprisoned people. Based on the hope that reconciliation is always a possibility, we must ensure that prisoners and members of their families are always provided with the resources necessary for persons bearing God's image.

MAKING COMMUNITIES SAFER

Communities also suffer from the effects of our criminal justice crisis. While crime occurs in every neighborhood, neighborhoods most deeply affected by concentrated poverty and mass incarceration experience crime of a different variety than other neighborhoods. Social disorganization enables the few people who would commit crime in these neighborhoods to do so more publicly, brazenly, and violently. The presence of people who can wantonly disregard the safety of others shuts down a community, leaving other community members trapped behind the doors of their homes, afraid to sit on their front steps or to let their children play outside.[32] We cannot simply ignore crime in vulnerable communities. Nothing else can be accomplished toward the achievement of social justice without first dealing with public safety. If people are not safe, they will not be able to participate in the common good, no matter how good our other programming and resources might be. Safety first. David Kennedy, criminologist and co-chair of the National Network for Safe Communities writes, "We cannot do economic development when people are afraid to go outside, can't fix education when the corner boys get all the girls

32. For discussion of the complex dynamics between law-abiding and law-breaking members of neighborhoods affected by the concentration of mass incarceration, see Elijah Anderson, *Code of the Street: Decency, Violence, and the Moral Life of the Inner City* (New York: Norton, 1999) and Mary Pattillo McCoy, *Black Picket Fences: Privilege and Peril Among the Black Middle Class* (Chicago: University of Chicago Press, 1999).

and face the other boys on the way to school, can't support families whose fathers are locked up, can't eradicate racism when the neighborhoods and world outside are both fulfilling each other's worst prejudices."[33] We can do almost nothing else for social justice without first ensuring safety.

Too often, however, efforts to make communities safer have led to the creation of what Andrew Skotnicki aptly calls "virtual penal colonies of racial and ethnic minorities" through practices such as "broken-windows" and "zero-tolerance" policing.[34] The goal of these models of law enforcement is to regulate and penalize even the smallest infractions as stringently as possible in order to deter people who would commit more serious crimes. The task of the police is to stop anyone in high crime areas for any minor offense, or even any inkling that he or she *might* commit a minor offense. This type of policing is ineffective at deterring people from committing serious offenses.[35] Moreover, zero-tolerance and broken-windows policing lead to alienation between law enforcement agencies and the law-abiding residents of these neighborhoods who endure often invasive and humiliating encounters with police. This alienation is laden with racial and ethnic tensions. These models of policing are "grinding and intrusive . . . the kind of policing that makes citizens in these neighborhoods think, at best, that the police are not on their side, and at worst, that they are a race enemy."[36]

While failing to prevent crime and leaving vulnerable community members feeling like they do not have viable partners in law enforcement agencies for creating public safety, zero-tolerance and broken-windows policing also feed our criminal justice crisis. Kennedy describes the perils of these practices,

> Neighborhoods churn as men go away, come back, move away again, as families lose their houses and move and splinter apart, as neighborhood bonds fray, people don't know each other as much, don't trust each other as much, don't look out for each other as much.

33. David Kennedy, *Don't Shoot: One Man, A Street Fellowship, and the End of Violence in Inner-City America* (New York: Bloomsbury, 2011), 22.

34. Andrew Skotnicki, "Foundations Once Destroyed: The Catholic Church and Criminal Justice," *Theological Studies* 65 (2004): 815.

35. On broken-windows policing, see Bernard E. Harcourt, *Illusion of Order: The False Promise of Broken Windows Policing* (Cambridge, MA: Harvard University Press, 2001); George E. Kelling and Catherine M. Coles, *Fixing Broken Windows: Restoring Order and Reducing Crime in Our Communities* (New York: Touchstone, 1996); and Gary Stewart, "Black Codes and Broken Windows: The Legacy of Racial Hegemony in Anti-Gang Civil Injunction," *The Yale Law Journal* 107 (1998): 2249–79.

36. Kennedy, *Don't Shoot*, 17.

. . . We have taken America's most vulnerable, most historically damaged, most economically deprived, most poorly educated, most stressed, most neglected, and most alienated neighborhoods and imposed on them an epidemic of imprisonment. We have given America's poor black communities an iatrogenic condition.[37]

The strategies we have used for making these neighborhoods safe have done not done so, in some cases potentially even creating conditions for even more crime.[38]

Safety first, but we cannot ensure safety by locking up all the criminals—we have tried that. Unsuccessfully. We need new models of policing that do not alienate already marginalized communities from the world outside, that offer protection for their residents, that draw upon and build up community resources, that do not result in high rates of incarceration in poor minority neighborhoods, and that stop crime, or at least, the variety of crimes that keep people from sitting on their front steps or from letting their kids play outside. Since the late 1990s, two overlapping models of policing, under the moniker of "pulling-levers policing," have been devised that seem to meet these ends.[39]

The first model focuses on stopping gun violence. Based on Operation Ceasefire, a project in Boston started in 1996, this model begins by identifying who is committing the violence. Studies found that a small number of young minority men involved in gangs were most often the perpetrators *and victims* of gun violence in Boston. Conversations with members of these gangs revealed that shootings usually arose not because of territory disputes or failed drug deals, but because of "beefs," petty disputes in the lives of young people. Gang

37. Ibid., 148.

38. See Dina R. Rose and Todd R. Clear, "Incarceration, Social Capital, and Crime: Examining the Unintended Consequences of Incarceration," *Criminology* 36, no. 3 (1998): 441–79; Dina R. Rose and Todd R. Clear, "Incarceration, Reentry, and Social Capital: Social Networks in the Balance," in *Prisoners Once Removed: The Impact of Incarceration and Reentry on Children, Families, and Communities*, ed. Jeremy Travis and Michelle Waul (Washington, DC: Urban Institute Press, 2003), 313–42; Todd R. Clear et al., "Coercive Mobility and Crime: A Preliminary Investigation of Concentrated Incarceration and Social Disorganization," *Justice Quarterly* 20, no. 1 (2003): 33–64; Todd R. Clear, *Imprisoning Communities: How Mass imprisonment Makes Disadvantaged Neighborhoods Worse* (New York: Oxford University Press, 2007); and Todd R. Clear, "The Effects of Higher Imprisonment Rates on Communities," *Crime and Justice* 37, no. 1 (2008): 97–132.

39. Both of these types of policing and how they originated are discussed in much more detail in Kennedy's *Don't Shoot*. See also the website for the National Network for Safe Communities, http://www.nnscommunities.org/, an organization that works to implement these policing strategies around the country.

members also conveyed their constant and often reasonable fear of becoming the next victim of gun violence, partly rooted in their belief that the police did nothing to protect them and that there were no legal consequences for illegal behavior. They consistently said that they hated the violence because of this fear, but that they felt that they had few options but to engage in it if they wanted to protect themselves and be safe.

The work of Operation Ceasefire and other similar efforts builds upon these insights about gang members' attitudes toward gun violence. Law enforcement agencies begin this policing strategy by targeting the gang that recently had proven the most volatile, the most likely to resort to gun violence when beefs got out of hand. After a short period in which every member of the gang is stopped for any minor offense, the agencies invite the gang members to a conversation. Along with community members and social service agencies, law enforcement professionals talk with representatives of the gang about the damage to the community caused by gang violence, and they offer alternative resources for anyone who might want to stop gang involvement. The gang members are told that unless the violence stops immediately, law enforcement will continue to target the gang. Every minor infraction committed by any member of the gang—not just the members who committed the violent act—will be prosecuted to the fullest extent of the law. If the violence stops, law enforcement will not pay any special attention to the gang. Gang members are also told that anyone outside of the gang who harms one of their members will also be prosecuted as if he had killed a police officer. Members of other gangs are then warned that the next gang to commit a violent act will have the spotlight turned on them.

This policing strategy directly addresses the realities of gun violence for gang members. On one hand, members of the targeted gang have a strong and specific reason to be deterred from violence and to tell their friends to put their guns away—"we will all keep getting in trouble if you do this thing." On the other hand, they have been guaranteed protection if anyone tries to harm them. This model is built upon the recognition that most boys and young men who engage in gun violence do not think that there will be legal consequences for their actions and are driven by fear instilled in them by living with violence every day of their lives. By answering these beliefs, programs like Operation Ceasefire offer gang members who might have chosen violence an "honorable exit" from responding to beefs. By bringing in community members and social services, these programs also offer gang members resources to start new lives. Where these programs have been implemented well, they have led to an immediate cooling effect among *all* of the gangs in a city, not just the targeted gang, and they have done so without the generalized law enforcement efforts of zero-tolerance and broken-windows policing.[40]

The second policing model applies some of the ideas behind Operation Ceasefire to close overt drug markets, places in which dealers can sell drugs in public while people come from outside the neighborhood to purchase them. This model also uses the resources of both law enforcement agencies and communities in partnership, and it draws upon research about drug markets to strategize an effective response. This research has found that relatively few people are typically involved in these markets as drug dealers—maybe a couple of dozen even in the busiest markets. The process begins by identifying who is dealing drugs and building up a strong legal case against them. Law enforcement agencies then invite them to a conversation. The invitation says that the agencies have evidence that the invitee has been selling drugs, that he

---

40. For a meta-analysis of evaluations of this policing strategy, see Anthony A. Braga and David L. Weisburd, "The Effects of 'Pulling Levers' Focused Deterrence Strategies on Crime," *Campbell Systematic Reviews* 6 (2012). Available at http://www.nnscommunities.org/Braga_Pulling_Levers_Review_CAMPBELL_RECORD.pdf. See also Greg Berman and Aubrey Fox, *Trial and Error in Criminal Justice Reform: Learning from Failure* (Washington, DC: Urban Institute Press, 2010), 45–60; Anthony A. Braga, "Pulling Levers Focused Deterrence Strategies and the Prevention of Gun Homicide," *Journal of Criminal Justice* 36, no. 4 (2008): 332–43; Anthony A. Braga et al., "Problem-Oriented Policing, Deterrence, and Youth Violence: An Evaluation of Boston's Operation Ceasefire," *Journal of Research in Crime and Delinquency* 38, no. 3 (2001): 195–225; Anthony A. Braga et al., "The Strategic Prevention of Gun Violence Among Gang-Involved Offenders," *Justice Quarterly* 25, no. 1 (2008): 132–62; Edward McGarrell et al., "Reducing Homicide through a 'Lever-Pulling' Strategy," *Justice Quarterly* 23 (2006): 214–29; Andrew Papachristos, Tracey Meares, and Jeffrey Fagan, "Attention Felons: Evaluating Project Safe Neighborhoods in Chicago," *Journal of Empirical Legal Studies* 4 (2007): 223–72; George Tita et al., *Reducing Gun Violence: Results from an Intervention in East Los Angeles* (Santa Monica, CA: RAND Corporation, 2004); Anthony Braga and Glenn L. Pierce, "Disrupting Illegal Firearms Markets in Boston: The Effects of Operation Ceasefire on the Supply of New Handguns to Criminals," *Criminology & Public Policy* 4 (2005): 717–48; Nicholas Corsaro and Edmund McGarrell, "Testing a Promising Homicide Reduction Strategy: Re-assessing the Impact of the Indianapolis 'Pulling Levers' Intervention," *Journal of Experimental Criminology* 5 (2009): 63–82; David M. Kennedy, Anne M. Piehl, and Anthony A. Braga, "Youth Violence in Boston: Gun Markets, Serious Youth Offenders, and a Use-Reduction Strategy," *Law and Contemporary Problems* 59 (1996): 147–96; Edmund F. McGarrell and Steven Chermak, "Problem Solving to Reduce Gang and Drug-Related Violence in Indianapolis," in *Policing Gangs and Youth Violence*, ed. Scott H. Decker (Belmont, CA: Wadsworth, 2003), 77–101; Anne M. Piehl, David M. Kennedy, and Anthony A. Braga, "Youth Violence and Problem Solving: An Evaluation of the Boston Gun Project," *American Law and Economics Review* 2, no. 1 (2000): 68–106; Richard Rosenfeld, Robert Fornango, and Eric Baumer, "Did Ceasefire, Compstat, and Exile Reduce Homicide?" *Criminology & Public Policy* 4 (2005): 419–50; and Wesley Skogan et al., *Evaluation of CeaseFire-Chicago* (Evanston, IL: Northwestern University, Institute for Policy Research, 2008).

will not be arrested at the meeting, that he may bring a friend or relative for support, that he will have an opportunity to see the evidence against him, that he will have the option to stop selling drugs, and that if he does not come to the meeting, the police will be in contact with him again in another setting. Most people who receive this invitation show up, usually with their mothers or grandmothers.

Meetings begin with community members and social service agencies talking about the effects of the drug market on the neighborhood and its residents. They also convey their hope that the people dealing drugs will stop and rejoin the community, and they offer any assistance they can to help drug dealers start on a new path. Law enforcement agencies then send in representatives, who describe each individual legal case to the invitees and show them all of the evidence against them, including videos and photos of them selling drugs. These representatives explain that they will not pursue these cases as long as the drug market disappears. If someone chooses to sell drugs again, the case against him will proceed. The law enforcement agencies give a deadline for when the market will close, usually within a few days. When this process has been used, drug markets have closed overnight, stayed closed, and not moved elsewhere, enabling residents of the neighborhood to retake the previously blighted area. In cities where this process has been used more than once, drug markets have closed *before* the meeting with drug dealers, law enforcement agencies, and community members.[41]

These two models of policing, both within the realm of pulling-levers policing, address the major threats to public safety in our most marginalized, disempowered, and endangered communities, and when well implemented, they do so immediately, effectively, and enduringly. Moreover, they do so with very few police stops or arrests, with relatively little police intrusion, and with the guidance, input, and cooperation of law-abiding community members. They do so without a lot of people cycling in and out of prison. In contrast with zero-tolerance and broken-windows policing, "They're not about locking people up. They're about *not* locking people up. They bend over backward not to lock people up. They're motivated by an understanding of the damage locking people up does to them, their families, their communities."[42] These changes in policing also build allegiances between community members and

---

41. See Braga and Weisburd, "The Effects of 'Pulling Levers.'" Also, Nicholas Corsaro and Edmund McGarrell, *An Evaluation of the Nashville Drug Market Initiative (DMI) Pulling Levers Strategy* (East Lansing: Michigan State University, School of Criminal Justice, 2010); and Erin Dalton, "Targeted Crime Reduction Efforts in Ten Communities: Lessons for the Project Safe Neighborhoods Initiative," *U.S. Attorney's Bulletin* 50 (2002): 16–25.

the world outside, especially with law enforcement agencies. Residents of these neighborhoods come to see that the world outside is not, at best, indifferent and uncaring, or at worst, actively working for their demise. Law enforcement professionals come to see that these residents really do not like drugs and guns and that they really do want a safe place to live and raise their kids. These groups become effective partners for safe communities, which then become the basis for addressing other failures of social justice.

With pulling-levers policing, the community is built up not by excluding or demeaning its most dangerous members, but by calling them to something different. In one gathering, a minister said to the boys and young men, "There's a word that you've heard . . . *redemption*. Redemption is a word that means your life is worth something, and your life is worth something to God. And so we're saying, you're worth something, that's why you're here tonight. Otherwise all this wouldn't be done for you."[43] This message is a lot different than any message sent by handcuffs, strip searches, and prison bars. It is a message that is a lot different than any message sent by clearing a corner with police cars and arresting anyone in sight. It is a message that is a lot different than any message sent by stopping and frisking every black boy and man in struggling neighborhoods. And it is a message that, if conveyed through the right kind of policing processes in conversation with members of vulnerable communities, makes us all safer.

REBUILDING COMMUNITIES

When safety can be more certain, other social injustices in communities most deeply affected by mass incarceration can begin to be addressed as well. Because concentrated incarceration results in disproportionately small populations of men in these neighborhoods, women become more vulnerable to inappropriate and even harmful relationships with the few men who remain, contributing to higher rates of sexually transmitted infections, unplanned pregnancies, and domestic violence. Women and their children also become more vulnerable to the loss of financial and emotional support from partners and fathers. Men find it difficult to build their lives as criminal histories accumulated under years of zero-tolerance and broken-windows policing haunt them as they seek education, work, and housing. The decreased economic viability of these neighborhoods means that residents have few routes that lead out of these

42. Kennedy, *Don't Shoot*, 218. Emphasis in original. On the relationship between crime reduction and decreased use of imprisonment through these models of policing see, Steven Durlauf and Daniel Nagin, "Imprisonment and Crime: Can Both Be Reduced?" *Criminology & Public Policy* 10, no. 1 (2011): 13–54.

43. Quoted in Kennedy, *Don't Shoot*, 176.

circumstances. Children in these neighborhoods are increasingly endangered as they navigate situations involving poor educational systems, struggling families, inadequate physical and mental healthcare, and crumbling communities. Too often these children are viewed as potential criminals, so they are tracked in a "cradle-to-prison pipeline" from a young age that leads them from school suspension to expulsion, from juvenile detention to incarceration, ultimately building a cycle of intergenerational involvement in our criminal justice systems that plagues these neighborhoods and their residents.[44]

The Children's Defense Fund (CDF) began a campaign to dismantle the cradle-to-prison pipeline in 2007 at Howard University in Washington, DC. Since this initial meeting, the CDF has hosted summits in cities throughout the United States in order to explore and promote best practices that prevent children from being funneled into criminal justice systems and that foster the well-being of children so they can become fully flourishing adults. These summits also aim at building communities that can address the struggles of their young people and confront local policies that contribute to the cradle-to-prison pipeline. The CDF recognizes that our criminal justice crisis affects not only people shifting in and out of prison; it also endangers children in our communities who are left without adequate conditions for realizing their inherent dignity as human persons. To counter these conditions, we must address not only the direct needs of these children, but also the needs of the adults in their lives and of their communities.

The CDF highlights several strategies in four areas for improving the conditions in communities whose residents are caught in the cradle-to-prison pipeline.[45] The first area is prenatal care and early childhood development. The CDF recommends providing support for parents, including culturally competent in-home visitation programs administered by nurses or counselors, which can help to prevent child abuse and domestic violence and improve parenting skills. These programs can also improve the health of mothers and children. Improved parenting skills, such as reading to children or using verbal discipline instead of corporal punishment, can help reduce stress in families that are in precarious economic, social, and emotional situations and provide conditions for children to develop behaviors that can help them succeed in school. Another support to parents is affordable childcare, which can enable

44. "Cradle-to-prison pipeline" is a phrase coined and trademarked by the Children's Defense Fund, http://www.childrensdefense.org/programs-campaigns/cradle-to-prison-pipeline/.

45. These strategies are discussed in detail in "Dismantling the Cradle-to-Prison Pipeline in Houston and Texas: A Study of Solutions," American Leadership Forum Class XXV, http://rehak.com/alf/90084 ALF Report 14.pdf.

parents to seek education and find adequate employment. Greater self-sufficiency through employment among women can make them less vulnerable to the loss of emotional and financial support of absent partners, as well as to other effects of the loss of men in the community, such as sexually transmitted infections, unplanned pregnancies, and domestic violence. Addressing some of the challenges that arise early in children's lives can help to put them on a path other than the cradle-to-prison pipeline.

The CDF also highlights education as an area for interrupting this pipeline. They describe four practices of schools that effectively guide students toward college and away from prison. One practice is to encourage intensive parent involvement in the school and a child's education. The use of parental liaisons who can facilitate communication between parents and school officials is one mechanism for enabling parents to understand better what is happening with their children and to advocate more effectively for their children's needs. Another practice is the requirement of intensive student commitment through long school hours. The majority of juvenile delinquency occurs in the hours between the times when school lets out and when parents get home. Longer school hours decrease this unsupervised time period while increasing the demands on students for full participation in their education. The CDF further recommends incorporating community activities into the curriculum. This practice can strengthen young people's ties to their neighborhood. Internships can expose them to professional work environments and help them build the informal social networks and soft skills that can lead to employment opportunities. Finally, schools that provide active mentorship opportunities can enable young people to find positive role models. Together these practices can keep students active and engaged in school and on a path toward college and work.

The third area for dismantling the cradle-to-prison pipeline is healthcare, including mental healthcare. Access to healthcare can help provide evaluation of problems that may lead children to be seen as troublesome, which then can contribute to introduction to juvenile and criminal justice systems through school disciplinary measures. When children's difficulties are identified early, interventions may be implemented when they might be most effective and least intrusive. Comprehensive healthcare can also help identify challenges in families and provide referrals to programs and services that could alleviate these challenges. Free prenatal and pediatric healthcare can bring children into the healthcare system so that preventative care becomes a regular practice of families, and they, in turn, become accustomed to seeking assistance through healthcare professionals. Collaboration among families, schools, and healthcare systems can help assure comprehensive responses to children's needs. Healthcare can be made more accessible through smaller neighborhood clinics in schools or storefronts, especially for teenagers. While an emphasis on healthcare for women and children is important, attention to the needs of young men as well can help them access medical attention and social services such as case management, job training, and counseling. Providing testing and treatment of sexually transmitted infections, mental health screening, and treatment of minor illnesses can improve the health not only of young men, but also of their partners and children. Healthcare can help young people prevent unplanned pregnancies, which can contribute to dropping out of school and being unable to find adequate employment, thereby perpetuating patterns of intergenerational poverty.

Finally, the CDF recommends strategies in the area of juvenile justice. Too often young people enter the cradle-to-prison pipeline through school disciplinary measures that too easily cross over into juvenile, and eventually criminal, justice systems. Channels away from juvenile justice systems for children in tenuous circumstances must be found. Nonjuridical alternatives to status offenses—actions that are not considered crimes when committed by adults but can result in referral to juvenile justice systems when committed by minors—can redirect children without putting them in juvenile justice systems. For example, letters from district attorneys' offices can effectively curb truancy before any other juvenile justice response is necessary. The Annie E. Casey Foundation's Juvenile Detention Alternatives Initiative (JDAI) has led the way nationally in developing alternatives to juvenile detention.[46] It has collaborated with juvenile justice agencies, other governmental entities, and community organizations to establish objective admissions criteria for youth in juvenile detention, to expedite release of young people who do not need to be detained, to reduce the amount of time it takes to process cases and the amount of time children spend in custody, and to shrink racial and ethnic disparities in juvenile justice systems. The JDAI also works to develop and strengthen alternatives to incarceration that work with families, schools, and communities to ensure children's needs are met. Some alternatives include using discipline practices modeled on restorative justice in schools, home- or community-based detention, and day or evening reporting centers for struggling young people.

The Harlem Children's Zone (HCZ) has implemented many of the strategies advocated by the CDF in a nearly one-hundred-block neighborhood of New York City. Adapting the language of the CDF, this organization

---

46. "Juvenile Detention Alternatives Initiative," The Annie E. Casey Foundation, http://www.aecf.org/MajorInitiatives/JuvenileDetentionAlternativesInitiative.aspx.

aims at building a "cradle-through-college-to-community pipeline" that can counter the cradle-to-prison pipeline.[47] The HCZ serves as an example of how to address comprehensively the areas highlighted by the CDF for improving conditions in struggling communities to ensure that all of their residents can experience the dignity, unity, and equality due to every human person.[48] The cradle-through-college pipeline begins with prenatal care and continues through a child's college career, based on a foundation of family, social service, healthcare, and community building programs. Since its inception in the early 1990s, the HCZ has pursued the goal of creating "a 'tipping point' in the neighborhood so that children are surrounded by an enriching environment of college-oriented peers and supportive adults, a counterweight to 'the street' and a toxic culture that glorifies misogyny and anti-social behavior."[49] This organization has built two tracks in its pipeline in order to achieve this goal.

Both tracks begin with prenatal care and early childhood development. Baby College provides parenting classes to young parents with children up to age three. Among the skills that parents learn are how to read to their children and how to use verbal discipline. Children can then enter a lottery to be admitted to the first track, which takes them into Promise Academy Charter Schools. If children gain admittance to the charter schools, their families proceed through Three-Year-Old Journey, a program that provides ongoing parenting classes; Get Ready for Pre-K, a six-week summer program for children to prepare for pre-kindergarten; and Harlem Gems, an all-day pre-kindergarten program. Upon completion of pre-kindergarten, children enter Promise Academy, which now provides education through high school. Its three schools operate ten hours per day and have an extended school year. Promise Academy also offers extensive after-school programming and an on-site clinic that provides free physical and mental healthcare and dental care.

The second track focuses on children in the neighborhood who attend regular public schools. In 1991, the HCZ opened its first Beacon Center. Taking advantage of school buildings that are empty after school, on weekends, and during summers, the organization created community centers that offer afternoon, evening, and weekend programs and all-day summer camps. Through Americorps, the HCZ also trains and employs "Peacemakers" in the schools who work as teaching assistants, emphasizing teaching literacy

47. "Harlem Children's Zone," Harlem Children's Zone, www.hcz.org.

48. For a detailed description of the inner-workings of the HCZ, see Paul Tough, *Whatever It Takes: Geoffrey Canada's Quest to Change Harlem and America* (New York: Houghton Mifflin, 2008).

49. "The HCZ Project," The Harlem Children's Zone, http://hcz.org/index.php/about-us/the-hcz-project.

and conflict resolution skills. The Peacemakers also started and run the Fifth-Grade Institute, an after-school program that helps children transition to middle school. During middle school, children get one-on-one attention through Academic Case Management that tracks their progress and helps them deal with any challenges in succeeding at school. Boys to Men and Girl Power are groups that offer gender-specific social development programming for middle school students, while A Cut Above provides academic help and leadership development as well as advocacy for students. The TRUCE (The Renaissance University for Community Education) Fitness and Nutrition Center addresses the health needs of students in middle school.

Academic Case Management continues through high school. Several programs draw high school students into their communities and help them stay involved in school. The Employment and Technology Center teaches students computer and job-related skills. Learn to Earn is an after-school program that prepares high school juniors and seniors for college and the job market through job-readiness training and life-skills workshops during the school year and employment during the summer. The College Preparatory Program offers year-round academic enrichment, and TRUCE Arts and Media cultivates artistic talent and media literacy while promoting academic growth. When high school students graduate to college, they can find continued support at the College Success Office, which helps students navigate the demands of university-level education.

Several family, social service, healthcare, and community building programs serve as a foundation for HCZ's pipeline from cradle through college. Community Pride organizes tenant and block organizations with the goal of converting properties from city-owned housing projects to tenant-owned cooperatives. Single Stop centralizes social services within one location for easier access to neighborhood residents. The Asthma Initiative and The Obesity Initiative help families manage these health challenges. The Family Development Program offers counseling and mental health treatment for families, while the Family Support Center offers crisis intervention. Project CLASS (Clean Living and Staying Sober) provides substance abuse treatment. Together these programs help address numerous factors that can contribute to the difficulties children face as they try to go to school. HCZ looks beyond the classroom to attend to challenges in families and neighborhoods that can keep children from escaping the cradle-to-prison pipeline.

The success of HCZ in helping children get through college despite growing up in neighborhoods affected by the concentration of mass incarceration has made this organization a model for similar efforts throughout the United States. The HCZ offers the Practitioners Institute, which trains community delegations from around the world about how to implement its practices. The U.S. Department of Education launched Promise Neighborhoods in 2010 to support models similar to HCZ in impoverished communities across the country. As of the end of 2012, the Department of Education has given nearly $100 million in grants to "local-led efforts to improve educational opportunities and provide comprehensive health, safety, and support services in high-poverty neighborhoods."[50] The grants have benefited about a thousand organizations that partner with Promise Neighborhood sites.[51]

Rebuilding communities through efforts such as HCZ and Promise Neighborhoods is necessary to dismantle the cradle-to-prison pipeline that shuttles children in impoverished neighborhoods into our criminal justice systems. Building a cradle-through-college-to-community pipeline requires a network of interrelated resources and programs that provide the conditions necessary for healthy families, successful schools, and safe neighborhoods. We are called morally to foster these conditions as part of our call to social justice.

Contributions of Catholics to Realizing Social Justice Proposals

These proposals for mitigating the effects of mass incarceration on social justice are only a starting point for working toward the inclusion in the common good of all people in our society. Many other courses of action can and should accompany these efforts to improve the conditions faced by ex-prisoners, families, and communities. We will also need to reevaluate these proposals over time to ensure that they are well implemented and effective at achieving their goals. Each of these proposals is now currently being used in some location in our nation, which should provide advocates for justice hope that change is possible.

Catholics ought to participate in furthering these proposals as part of their call to seek others' good as if it were our own and to advance the common good. Our participation should flow forth from our sacramental and liturgical lives. As our consciousness of injustice is transformed by the eucharistic vision, the world-picture of justice in God's reign summons us to tend to the needs of

50. "Secretary Duncan Announces Seventeen 2012 Promise Neighborhoods Winners in School Safety Address at Neval Thomas Elementary School," U.S. Department of Education, http://www.ed.gov/news/press-releases/secretary-duncan-announces-seventeen-2012-promise-neighborhoods-winners-school-s.

51. Evaluation of the effectiveness of Promise Neighborhoods is still in its infancy. For plans on how to evaluate these programs, see Kristin Anderson Moore et al., *Results and Indicators for Children: An Analysis to Inform Discussions about Promise Neighborhoods* (Washington, DC: ChildTrends, 2009).

people who have been excluded and degraded in our society. We must work to dismantle any structures that interfere with the capacity of anyone to achieve a life in accord with the dignity and equality of human persons. Furthermore, we must participate in the creation of conditions that support the well-being of every member of our society.

As Catholics look for ways to contribute to the work of the above proposals, we should begin by considering the resources for social justice that we have already created as a church. One of the strengths of Catholic community in the United States is that we have built not only churches, but also hospitals and clinics, schools and universities, and nonprofit organizations. In response to liturgical and sacramental ethics, the leaders of these institutions should more conscientiously examine how they could alleviate some of the social injustices that mass incarceration helps sustain.

One avenue for leadership among Catholics, for example, could come from Catholic business and legal professionals who gather regularly in local congregations as parishioners. Parishes could become centers for advocating campaigns to expand government-bonding programs for ex-offenders, to ban the criminal history box on job applications, and to reform employment licensure restrictions. Business professionals in parish communities, in partnership with organizations such as Catholic Charities, could also provide mentorship and training to ex-prisoners who are seeking employment. Legal professionals could provide assistance to people working through the application processes for reenfranchisement. Such efforts could also lead to parish-wide advocacy of counteracting disenfranchisement laws and reforming the U.S. Census to correct for prison-based gerrymandering. Churches can offer resources for learning about one's voting rights and how to get them restored. As these leaders build relationships with ex-prisoners, they may become stronger supporters for change in their wider communities.

While parish-based efforts may often be small at first, they can grow substantially to have a major impact on their surrounding communities. For example, in 1988, the Dolores Mission parish in the Boyle Heights area of Los Angeles began a program called "Jobs for a Future" to provide opportunities for young men involved in gangs and leaving prison to enter the employment market. Under the guidance of Father Greg Boyle, a Jesuit priest, this program expanded when it opened a bakery and a tortilla stand in order to employ the young men for whom it was most difficult to find a job placement. From this parish-based program, Homeboy Industries was born.[52] This nonprofit

---

52. "Homeboy Industries," Homeboy Industries, www.homeboyindustries.org. See also Gregory Boyle, *Tattoos on the Heart: The Power of Boundless Compassion* (New York: Free Press, 2010) and Celeste

organization supports itself largely from social enterprises, including a café and diner, a catering company, farmers' markets, a bakery, a grocery store, and a silkscreen and embroidery company. Homeboy Industries offers tattoo removal; employment and legal services; mental health, domestic violence, and substance abuse services; and case management. In addition, it has developed educational programs that include assistance with getting a GED and a training and certificate program for solar panel installation. Each month, Homeboy Industries serves over one thousand men and women who are former gang members or who were recently incarcerated. From a parish-based program, this organization has grown into a national model for providing assistance to people who want to leave gangs and who want to rejoin their communities after serving time in prison. While not all parishes will aspire to do this sort of work for social justice, the example of Father Boyle, the Dolores Mission parish, and Homeboy Industries suggests that leadership within parishes to help ex-prisoners with employment and legal challenges can lead to significant contributions to bringing about change.

Parishes might also consider how they might support families of people who are in prison. In addition to becoming Healing Communities, Catholic congregations could facilitate stronger relationships between prisoners and their families by offering funds to pay for collect phone calls, organizing van or bus trips to prisons for visitation, or donating toys and playground equipment to improve prison visits with children. One nun that I worked with collected children's storybooks and helped women in prison read the books on audiotape. She then sent the books and tapes to the women's children. Parishes could organize similar programs on a larger scale throughout our country. Churches should also offer emotional and social support to the partners and children of people in prison to mitigate the isolation and stigmatization often suffered by families.

Participation of community members is necessary in efforts to make neighborhoods safer through pulling-levers policing. Churches can facilitate conversation between law enforcement agencies and other community members, especially in circumstances where years of zero-tolerance and broken-windows policing have broken down these relationships. Leaders of congregations should be among the community members who attend meetings with people caught up in gun violence and drug markets. They should communicate the need to stop illegal behavior, but also offer support and resources for offenders who choose to change their lives. Their credibility

Fremon, *G-Dog and the Homeboys: Father Greg Boyle and the Gangs of East Los Angeles*, revised edition (Albuquerque: University of New Mexico Press, 2008).

in these conversations will be strengthened if they are engaged in their communities by offering some of the services associated with organizations like Homeboy Industries or Healing Communities.

Schools and universities can offer more in terms of rebuilding communities most deeply affected by the concentration of mass incarceration. Catholic parishes often still stand in these neighborhoods, which in many past generations were often populated with immigrant Catholics. Rather than looking to relocate to suburbs, these parishes should examine how they can deepen their ministries where they are. Catholic parish schools, which now often struggle to find enough students, might examine how they could serve their communities by emulating the models of schools highlighted by the Children's Defense Fund and the Harlem Children's Zone. The Cristo Rey Network is one example of a group of Catholic schools that have already begun this work.[53] The first Cristo Rey high school opened in Chicago in 1996 under the leadership of Father John Foley, a Jesuit priest. Since then, funding from a variety of private sources including the Bill and Melinda Gates Foundation and the Walton Family Foundation has enabled the opening of twenty-five more schools around the country. The focus of these schools is on serving socioeconomically disadvantaged students who live in the urban centers of our cities. Another source of funding for Cristo Rey high schools comes from corporate partners that hire students in entry-level jobs for five days per month and send the money for their work to the schools to underwrite tuition costs. Students gain work experience while contributing to a high-quality, college-preparatory education. Cristo Rey schools also partner with Catholic colleges and universities to empower their students to succeed in postsecondary education. These relationships can be expanded as high schools feed their students into these colleges and universities, which then should offer additional support to students from disadvantaged backgrounds to ensure their ability to return to their communities with a college degree.

Clinics and hospitals can also serve an important role in rebuilding communities affected by mass incarceration. The guidance of the Children's Defense Fund suggests that adequate physical and mental healthcare is necessary to break down the cradle-to-prison pipeline. Through their vast networks throughout the United States, Catholic clinics and hospitals can help provide necessary healthcare that can often identify or prevent issues that can lead young people into disciplinary measures beginning with school suspensions, but ending up eventually in juvenile justice systems, and ultimately, in prisons.

---

53. "Cristo Rey Network," Cristo Rey Network, www.cristoreynetwork.org.

While social injustices connected to our criminal justice crisis can be daunting, Catholics ought to begin their engagement with these problems by recognizing that we have at hand many resources for working for social justice. Acknowledging what we already do and then considering how we might improve or expand our engagement can provide hope despite the seeming hopelessness of our current circumstances. As we begin this work, we also should find hope within the liturgy and sacraments. The Eucharist awakens our eschatological imaginations, which leads us to see that God's vision of justice will triumph. The vision of the future promised to us that we find in the Eucharist should feed our hope that we can advance the cause of social justice in our present situation, despite the apparent intransigence of our criminal and social justice crises.

AFFORDING A NEW SOCIETY

The proposals described here for alleviating the effects of our criminal justice systems on social justice are not inexpensive. Doing everything suggested here will cost billions of dollars, which raises the fair question of whether we as a country can afford to realize these proposals fully.

Before assuming that everything described here will cost a lot of money, it is important to recognize that many of these proposals actually do not require much investment. Some of the proposals merely require a change in governmental or business practices that will necessitate nominal expenditures. It costs us nothing to restore to ex-prisoners the right to vote; it costs us little to count prisoners at their last known address rather than at their prison in the U.S. Census. Banning the criminal history box on hiring forms may cost businesses a small amount in terms of time spent reading and fairly evaluating job applications and getting criminal background checks later in the hiring process. Enabling ex-prisoners to get occupational licenses also costs little. The Federal Bonding Program could potentially get expensive, but its history of having claims on only 1 percent of its bonds suggests that this proposal is unlikely to be very expensive. The overall benefits to society with lower poverty rates and higher tax revenues may mitigate the costs of these proposals.

Many of the other proposals probably will not cost much more than other policies and practices that we are currently funding and that we would stop using if the new proposals were instituted. In some instances, new policies may both cost less and prove more effective at achieving their ends. For example, the practices of pulling-levers policing require the investment of months of work for numerous professionals in a large number of law enforcement agencies; they are not cheap practices. However, if we choose to implement these models, we will not be drawing on the work of these professionals to engage in zero-tolerance or broken-windows policing. Each of these policing practices requires a large investment in terms of moving cases through courts, incarcerating offenders, and providing probation and parole services. It may be an even trade in terms of funds for pulling-levers policing versus broken-windows or zero-tolerance policing, but it may also be the case that this new model is less expensive and more effective at actually making communities safer in the long run.

Some money for these proposals can also become available as we downscale our prison populations. In a single year, Michigan saved over $100 million by closing prison facilities. In two years, New York saved $25 million. If we choose not to incarcerate as many people, we can afford to provide a variety of resources that are more effective at reducing recidivism, bringing about internal reform, and facilitating social reintegration. Restorative justice and rehabilitation are expensive. Treatment for substance abuse and mental illness is expensive. Education and vocational training are expensive. But so is prison. Choosing not to rely so much on incarceration can free us to choose to invest in these alternatives.

We also ought to consider the expense of some of these proposals to be investments that can ultimately save us money in the future. The HCZ reports that it costs about $5000 per child per year on the cradle-through-college pipeline.[54] On average, states spend more than $28,000 per prisoner per year.[55] For the cost of incarcerating one person for one year, five children could participate in the HCZ. Those children will be much more likely to complete college, get a job that pays more than poverty wages, and contribute positively to their communities. Some of these proposals do cost a lot of money. We must ask ourselves whether we would rather spend this money to maintain the first genuine prison society, or invest it in a society in which all children have access to the conditions necessary to becoming fully flourishing adults.

Some people may experience direct financial losses if we choose to become the latter type of society. Marc Mauer reports that more than 700,000 people in the United States are employed in prisons and jails, and Michelle Alexander suggests that about two million people work in the bureaucracies tied to our criminal justice systems.[56] Workers in these systems have organized in powerful

54. "The HCZ Project," Harlem Children's Zone, http://www.hcz.org/about-us/the-hcz-project.

55. Tracey Kyckelhahn, "State Corrections Expenditures, FY1982-2010," Bureau of Justice Statistics, http://bjs.ojp.usdoj.gov/content/pub/pdf/scefy8210.pdf.

56. Marc Mauer, *Race to Incarcerate*, 2nd ed. (New York: New Press, 2006), 11; Alexander, *The New Jim Crow*, 230–32.

unions that tend to resist changes in penal policies and practices that oppose mass incarceration.[57] Many rural communities throughout the country depend on prisons as the main local industry based on the belief that prisons bring more jobs and economic activity—a belief that has been shown repeatedly to be mistaken.[58] Prison profiteers and private prison corporations can maintain their profitability only if we have large prison and jail populations. Individuals and groups that have become dependent on mass incarceration could raise significant opposition to criminal justice reform and efforts to alleviate social injustices exacerbated by our dependence on prisons. People who profit from prisons depend on incarceration being a growth industry. Aside from groups and individuals whose income and wealth draw upon putting people behind bars, many other people do not see criminal justice reform as a matter of social justice. They do not acknowledge the ways in which criminal and social justice are fundamentally intertwined. These challenges suggest that in order to bring about the proposals of this and the previous chapter, we will also have to deal with the social injustices from which our criminal justice systems arose.

A Movement for Justice

Mass incarceration not only helps sustain social injustice; it also reflects social injustice. Our criminal justice crisis arose from several social, cultural, economic, and political factors that contributed to the marginalization, disempowerment, and endangerment of many members of our society. Fear of increasing social disorder, often tied to changing racial dynamics in the late 1960s and early 1970s, fueled a desire in our culture to "restore proper respect for law and order," to "get tough on crime," to "wage a war on

57. Joshua Page, "Prison Officer Unions and the Perpetuation of the Penal Status Quo," *Criminology and Public Policy* 10, no. 3 (2011): 735–70; and *The Toughest Beat: Politics, Punishment, and the Prison Officers Union in California* (New York: Oxford University Press, 2011).

58. On the limitations of this economic strategy for rural communities, see Terry Besser and Margaret Hanson, "The Development of Last Resort: The Impact of New Prisons on Small Town Economies," *Journal of the Community Development Society* 35 (2004): 1–16; Susan Blankenship and Ernest Yanarella, "Prison Recruitment as a Policy Tool of Local Economic Development: A Critical Evaluation," *Contemporary Justice Review* 7 (2004): 183–98; Gregory Hooks et al., "Revisiting the Impact of Prison Building on Job Growth: Education, Incarceration, and County-Level Employment," *Social Science Quarterly* 91, no. 1 (2010): 228–44; Tracy Huling, "Building a Prison Economy in Rural America," in *Invisible Punishment*, ed. Mauer and Chesney-Lind, 197–214; Ryan King, Marc Mauer, and Tracy Huling, "An Analysis of Economics of Prison Sitings in Rural Communities," *Criminal Public Policy* 3 (2004): 453–80; and Clayton Mosher, Gregory Hooks, and Peter B. Wood, "Don't Build It Here: The Hype Versus the Reality of Prisons and Local Employment," in *Prison Profiteers: Who Makes Money from Mass Incarceration*, ed. Tara Herivel and Paul Wright (New York: New Press, 2007), 90–97.

drugs." At the same time, economic shifts contributed to growing inequality and the concentration of poverty in "jobless ghettos." Residents of these "hyper-ghettos," who were disproportionately African American, had little access to educational resources or training for high-skilled jobs. The economy shifted to low-paying service jobs in suburban areas, and the real value of wages declined in comparison with increased economic productivity, especially for workers at the bottom of the employment hierarchy. The expansion of jobless ghettos and the deepening of poverty within them contributed to increasing social disorganization in our most vulnerable communities. Law-abiding residents of these neighborhoods had less capacity to control the expansion of overt drug markets and the explosion of gun violence, while people outside of these neighborhoods could too easily label all of the residents within them as lazy, retrograde, ungovernable, and vicious—labels that often draw on racial and ethnic stereotypes. Jobless ghettos came to be seen as the core of the breakdown of law and order in the United States, and many people in our society viewed their poor black residents as irredeemably bad—all potential criminals, if not criminals in fact. The demonization of young, poor black male inner-city residents fed political rhetoric that drove criminal justice policies since the late 1960s. Politicians and policymakers who feared being outflanked on the right on crime issues rejected rehabilitation and became ever-more punitive. As a society we became more willing to throw people in prison for longer periods of time than we used to be. We especially became more willing to throw more young, poor black men in prison for longer periods of time than we used to be. The prison became the primary means of pushing these men to the edges of our society, replacing our historical practices of slavery and segregation.

If we wish no more to be the first genuine prison society, no more to be a society aptly described as "the New Jim Crow," no more to be a society marked by mass incarceration, then we need to become aware of how our criminal justice crisis reflects this history steeped in social injustice and to work toward a change in our consciousness surrounding issues of race, ethnicity, poverty, and crime in the United States. This change of consciousness should undergird our answers to questions about the types of individuals, communities, and society we want to become. Civil rights attorney Michelle Alexander warns that "tinkering" with the criminal justice system alone will ultimately fail to address our justice crises adequately. Even if we achieved all of the proposals enumerated thus far, we would not have necessarily attended to the factors that led to mass incarceration in the first place. Furthermore, it is doubtful that we could achieve these proposals without first recognizing the roots of our criminal justice crisis in social injustice and feeling convicted about the need to do better at ensuring that everyone in our society has access to conditions that enable them to experience the unity, equality, and dignity of human personhood. Alexander writes,

> The notion that all of these reforms can be accomplished piecemeal—one at a time, through disconnected advocacy strategies—seems deeply misguided. All of the needed reforms have less to do with failed policies than a deeply flawed public consensus, one that is indifferent, at best, to the experience of poor people of color.[59]

We need to begin to care deeply about the ways in which many people in our society are subordinated and degraded, and we need to care deeply across lines of race, ethnicity, and class. Alexander continues,

> Those who believe that advocacy challenging mass incarceration can be successful without overturning the public consensus that gave rise to it are engaging in fanciful thinking, a form of denial. Isolated victories can be won—even a string of victories—but in the absence of a fundamental shift in public consciousness, the system as a whole will remain intact.[60]

Dismantling the first genuine prison society, the New Jim Crow, and mass incarceration requires not only policy reform, but more fundamentally, reform of our consciousness about what makes a good person, a good community, a good society amidst racial, ethnic, and class differences.

To bring about this change of consciousness, Alexander argues that we need to build multiracial coalitions in a movement to address the social injustices that created our criminal justice crisis in the first place. The civil rights movement can serve as a model for this new movement in that it worked for policy reform at the same time that it built a movement for transforming racial, ethnic, and class consciousness in the United States. Part of this new movement will involve talking about the ways in which mass incarceration came about principally not to control crime, but because of the perpetuation of the social, cultural, economic, and political factors rooted in the denial of the full human personhood of certain members of our society, especially of people from racial and ethnic minorities and from socioeconomically disadvantaged backgrounds.

59. Alexander, *The New Jim Crow*, 233.
60. Ibid., 234.

Alexander contends, "We must admit, out loud, that it was *because of* race that we didn't care much what happened to 'those people' and imagined the worst possible things about them. The fact that our lack of care and concern may have been, at times, unintentional or unconscious does not mitigate our crime—if we refuse, when given the chance, to make amends."[61]

Beyond recognition of our failures of social justice, this movement will have to offer a vision of the type of society we wish to create. We must move toward something. Alexander describes one vision to draw a new movement forward:

> a society in which all human beings of all races are treated with dignity, and have the right to food, shelter, health care, education, and security. This expansive vision could open the door to meaningful alliances between poor and working-class people of all colors, who could begin to see their interests as aligned, rather than in conflict—no longer in competition for scarce resources in a zero-sum game.[62]

In this vision, poverty, oppression, and marginalization have given way to equality, empowerment, and unity based on the dignity of every human person. Everyone is welcomed to full participation in society, and everyone has access to the conditions necessary to enable her to realize herself fully. This vision of society leaves no room for mass incarceration.

For Catholics and many other Christians, we enter into a vision that holds these ideals before us every time we come to the eucharistic table. In communion with one another, we experience a transformation of consciousness like that which Alexander evokes in her call to recognize the dignity of all human beings and to care across lines of race, ethnicity, and class. This sacrament leads us through a world-picture in which God's reign of justice triumphs over the principalities and powers of this world and their compromised understanding of justice. We are invited to justice rooted in a covenant that draws us toward relationship that promotes human flourishing. The table is open to everyone, even and especially those who have been excluded through poverty, oppression, and marginalization; it includes particularly people who have been moral outcasts. As we partake of the Eucharist, we enter communion with all others and are called to become servants to one another, especially to people in need. We are invited to seek

61. Ibid., 238.
62. Ibid., 259.

reconciliation with everyone at the table and with anyone who is unable to join us. In the liturgy of this sacrament, we mourn the death of Jesus Christ as a convicted criminal, and we find hope in the coming of God's reign in fullness. We long for justice, love, peace, forgiveness, and life. The eucharistic vision transforms our consciousness and ought to draw us into confrontation with our failures of criminal and social justice.

Our eucharistic life calls us to justice. In our circumstances in the United States today, Catholics and other Christians should respond to this call by joining the movement to end mass incarceration. We must work for restorative justice and rehabilitation. We must work for the downscaling of our prison populations and advocate for the use of prisons only when necessary for public safety. We must join with others to ensure that prisons are places where people can find the resources for internal reform and social reintegration and that we do not punish for the purpose of inflicting pain or for retribution. We must mitigate the effects of mass incarceration on social justice by advocating policies and practices that foster economic inclusion, incorporation in political life, repair of families, making communities safer, and rebuilding communities that have been broken by the cradle-to-prison pipeline. And we should pursue this reform agenda while participating in multiracial—and interreligious—coalitions that cultivate the transformation of consciousness about the kind of society we want to become. Such coalitions will be necessary for addressing the roots of mass incarceration in social injustice. As we engage in this movement, we must always remember that our commitment to justice flows forth from the eucharistic vision, the source and summit of our moral life as Christians.

ADDRESSING INJUSTICE WITHIN THE CHURCH

While we are called by our participation in the Eucharist toward the work of justice, Catholics in the United States, especially white Catholics, must also recognize and acknowledge the ways in which we as church, as *ekklesia*, have fallen and continue to fall short of a eucharistic understanding of justice, particularly with respect to matters of race and ethnicity. Some humility is necessary among Catholics as we work for justice in the world because we often fail to realize justice even within the church. Although we proclaim a table open to all people, the Catholic Church in the United States has not always proven to be welcoming and inclusive, particularly across boundaries of race. Womanist Catholic theologian Diana Hayes describes the quandary that many black Catholics face as they "must . . . constantly prove the legitimacy of their presence within the Roman Catholic Church as a distinct group with a history, culture, and traditions worthy not only of preservation but of sharing with the church as a whole."[63] Often African-American expressions of faith have been pushed to the edges of the church, and African-American Catholics have been viewed as strange hybrids that do not fit within the mold of "mainstream" Catholicism. Hayes feels compelled to proclaim "to the church and the world at large that to be black and Catholic is not a paradox; it is not a conflict; it is not a contradiction. To be black and Catholic is correct; it is authentic; it is who we are and have always been."[64] Her proclamation indicates the sense of exclusion that many black Catholics, as well as members of other nondominant racial and ethnic groups, have felt from the church. Despite the inclusiveness of the eucharistic vision, our liturgical and sacramental practices have too often internalized the marginalization, disempowerment, and endangerment of certain members of our society within our faith communities.

The effects of this exclusion have extended to formal Catholic reflections on racism in U.S. society and culture. Moral theologian Bryan Massingale has analyzed "Brothers and Sisters to Us," the most recent statement written collectively by the U.S. bishops specifically about race, published in 1979, and he finds several ways in which this document fails to address racism in the United States and in the church.[65] While he finds the USCCB's analysis of racism to be "more impressionist and anecdotal" because of a lack of grounding in social sciences, Massingale also critiques the bishops for offering little theological or ethical reflection on racism and for providing little direction for implementing their teachings.[66] His most significant observation is that the document is marked by "pervasive paternalism" as the bishops "neglected . . . listening to the voices of the victims [of racism] and examining the situation from their perspective."[67] It is a document written by, to, and for white Catholics, evidenced most clearly, Massingale notes, by its title. He asks, "Who's the 'us'?"[68] The result of this paternalism is that the document presents an excessively optimistic picture of the demise of racism because the bishops downplay racism's structural dimensions. Massingale writes, "The major shortcoming of the Catholic approach to racial justice is that it is insufficiently attentive—if not blind—to the nexus of race and cultural power and social

---

63. Diana L. Hayes, *Standing in the Shoes My Mother Made: A Womanist Theology* (Minneapolis: Fortress Press, 2011), 109.

64. Ibid., 30.

65. 1979!

66. Bryan Massingale, *Racial Justice and the Catholic Church* (Maryknoll, NY: Orbis, 2010), 74. For full text of "Brothers and Sisters to Us," see *Origins* 9 (1979): 381–89.

67. Massingale, *Racial Justice*, 75.

68. Ibid., 75.

privilege, and the need to sever this linkage."[69] Despite the bishops' acknowledgment that racism is a "radical evil," they fail to rouse any passion to work for racial justice. "It is difficult *not* to conclude that Catholic engagement with racism is a matter of low institutional commitment, priority, and importance."[70]

If Catholics are to participate in a multiracial movement for criminal and social justice, we must also recognize and acknowledge racial dynamics within the church and work toward justice internally as well as in the wider world. Several strategies described by Diana Hayes could further these efforts. She calls white Catholics to drop "the question of authenticity" often directed to black Catholics, who are often seen as "newcomers or children" in the church.[71] The church must also attend to the diversity of Catholicism throughout the world and from its earliest days, extending to our own place and time. Hayes recommends greater attention to young African Americans who may feel that they have no place in the Catholic Church, often because they have been discouraged by other Catholics from participating fully and from assuming leadership roles in their communities. Church leaders should receive more extensive training about working with predominately black Catholic communities, with congregations in majority black (and often poor and urban) neighborhoods, and with African-American individuals in congregations typically dominated by whites. Such training should be incorporated in the core curriculum of seminaries, just as courses on Spanish and Hispanic culture are often already required for future lay, religious, and ordained ministers of the church.

While these concrete strategies are necessary for undoing "the church's complicity in and bondage to a racialized culture," the work toward justice within the church ought to be grounded in the same reality that grounds our work for justice in the world—the Eucharist.[72] Hayes remarks,

> Everything that we are, all that we stand for as a church arises from our understanding of and celebration of the Eucharistic liturgy. It is the symbol par excellence of the Roman Catholic Church . . . . If we can't get that right, if we do not understand the significance of liturgical enculturation, if the Eucharistic celebration is not a reflection of all of us—old and young, black, white, and every color

69. Ibid., 76.
70. Ibid., 77.
71. Hayes, *Standing*, 110.
72. Massingale, *Racial Justice*, 77.

and language under the sun, as various in its celebration as the sands of the seashore and the stars in the sky—then all else that flows from there will be of little value.[73]

The work for justice within and beyond the church is rooted first and foremost in our public service of worshiping God in the Eucharist. In our worship, then, we should strive always to emulate Christ's "shockingly inclusive table fellowship."[74] Partaking of this fellowship, we are drawn into opposition with the persistence of injustice in light of the awakening of our eschatological imaginations, which disclose the ultimate promises of justice in the fullness of God's reign. With respect to racism, the Eucharist calls us to solidarity with those who have been excluded both from our sacramental table and from the dignity, unity, and equality of all people. Womanist Catholic theologian Shawn Copeland writes,

> Eucharist is countersign to the devaluation and violence directed toward the exploited, despised black body. . . . Eucharistic imagination teaches us to imagine, to hope for, and to create new possibilities. Because that solidarity enfolds us, rather than dismiss "others," we act in love; rather than refuse "others," we respond in acts of self-sacrifice, committing ourselves to the long labor of creation, of the enfleshment of freedom.[75]

In the Eucharist, we are called as the church to enter a world-picture that upholds the dignity of all human persons and to serve those whose dignity has been denied. As we make this vision of the world and its possibilities our own, we must work for justice both in the world and within the *ekklesia*.

The sacrament of Penance may help Catholics discern our culpability for marginalizing members of our communities. The social injustices that are intertwined with our criminal justice crisis are the product of social sin, and we must seek redemption for our participation in oppression. The reconciling work of the church must extend beyond its focus on personal sin and individual wrongdoing to examine our complicity in social injustice. The combined communal and private rite of Penance and Reconciliation can be used to foster our consciousness about our crises of criminal and social justice and our

73. Hayes, *Standing*, 36–37.

74. Massingale, *Racial Justice*, 124.

75. M. Shawn Copeland, *Enfleshing Freedom: Body, Race, and Being* (Minneapolis: Fortress Press, 2010), 127–28.

responsibility for them. We can come to recognize the ways in which we all fall short so that we can better seek forgiveness and respond to the call of reconversion toward the eucharistic vision for ourselves as individuals and for our society as a whole. Our reconversion requires that we turn away from our past lives so these penitential practices can become a setting for discerning prophetic methods for working toward justice in a new movement for change.

CATHOLIC RESOURCES FOR A JUSTICE MOVEMENT

Catholics already have some resources that can empower them to join this movement, although many of these resources could be strengthened. Through the USCCB, Catholics in the United States have access to a national network that could become a center for organizing their involvement in a justice movement. Unfortunately, this network and the leadership of the bishops are too often narrowly focused on a small number of issues. The bishops ought to diversify their efforts for justice and treat mass incarceration—which affects individuals, families, communities, and our society as a whole—like the evil that it is. In this work, Catholics in the United States must also be willing to move beyond the guidance of international Catholic statements on criminal justice issues, such as Pope John Paul II's 2000 Jubilee letter, because our circumstances are unique in the international community. Our crises of criminal and social justice are distinctive to the Untied States, and so we must respond using distinctively national resources.

Other organizing efforts led by the USCCB provide templates for what could be done regarding our criminal and social justice crises. The USCCB has an extensive office focused on human life issues from abortion through euthanasia.[76] This office organizes "Respect Life Sunday" on the first Sunday of every October, kicking off a month of activities around human life issues. Each year this office compiles a program packet containing pamphlets and bulletin inserts, a liturgy guide, posters and other awareness raising materials, and prayer resources. The office also produces policy papers and guidance for how Catholics can contact their elected representatives about their particular concerns. Through the USCCB's Respect Life Program, Catholics in the United States can learn easily what the church teaches about these issues and find ways to join a movement on individual, organizational, and congregational levels to bring about the changes advocated by the bishops.

---

76. "Respect Life Program," U.S. Conference of Catholic Bishops, http://www.usccb.org/about/pro-life-activities/respect-life-program/.

The USCCB also has several offices concerned with immigration issues, including offices that work against human trafficking and for refugee resettlement and migration policy.[77] These offices use many organizing practices similar to those of the Respect Life Program, but they also provide services directly to immigrants, refugees, and victims of human trafficking. The Office of Migration Policy and Public Affairs works with grassroots Catholic networks to advocate for passage of comprehensive immigration reform. Its Justice for Immigrants Campaign began in 2005 and spearheads efforts to communicate Catholic stances on immigration issues to the Administration and Congress. This office also works to educate Catholics throughout the United States about immigration. In addition to advocacy work, the USCCB facilitates direct services for immigrants and refugees, for example, through their Office for Resettlement Services and their Anti-Trafficking Program. The Office for Resettlement Services provides support to refugees including food, clothing, shelter, education, and orientation to U.S. society and culture. It also finds foster care for unaccompanied minors who are refugees or undocumented migrants. This office resettles about 30 percent of refugees who arrive in our country each year. The Anti-Trafficking Program offers intensive case management for victims of human trafficking. It conducts a training program to help identify victims and bring them to safety, and this program is involved in research with Georgetown University about how to assist victims most effectively. The work of the USCCB around immigration issues provides a template for how to join advocacy for policy changes with direct services to people most directly affected by a particular social injustice.

Finally, the Fortnight for Freedom Campaign offers a third model for what the USCCB could do with respect to mass incarceration.[78] The bishops called for special events during the last two weeks of June 2012, culminating in a march in Washington, DC on July 4, on the issue of religious freedom. Prompted by the mandate from the Department of Health and Human Services (HHS) to provide full insurance coverage for contraceptives, this campaign included consciousness-raising activities such as text-message alerts, study guides for groups and individuals, and other educational resources. The USCCB composed with other religious groups a statement on religious freedom, "Free Exercise of Religion: Putting Beliefs into Practice."[79] They also gave guidance on how to contact elected representatives about the HHS

77. "Immigration," U.S. Conference of Catholic Bishops, http://www.usccb.org/issues-and-action/human-life-and-dignity/immigration/.

78. "Fortnight for Freedom," U.S. Conference of Catholic Bishops, http://www.usccb.org/issues-and-action/religious-liberty/fortnight-for-freedom/.

mandate, including the body of a message to be sent to Congress and the Administration that could be personally revised by each constituent. The Fortnight for Freedom provides an example of intensive organizing by the USCCB around a particular issue.

These examples suggest some possibilities for action by the USCCB in a movement to address our criminal and social justice crises. The USCCB has extensive resources for policy development and advocacy, including a prominent public platform for disseminating information about an issue. The bishops have the capacity to provide educational materials to Catholics throughout the United States. They can circulate these materials through a sustained effort, such as that of the Respect Life Program, and they can do so in more intensive bursts, such as that of the Fortnight for Freedom. Moreover, the USCCB has the networks necessary to connect individuals, organizations, and congregations to grassroots efforts for justice and to unite these efforts nationally. The bishops can also team with researchers from Catholic colleges and universities around the United States to generate more knowledge about effective responses to mass incarceration and the individuals, families, and communities most directly affected by it. All of these resources would be valuable assets in a movement for justice. In addition, the USCCB could draw upon its capacity to provide services to assist people affected by our criminal and social justice crises. Direct service can deepen commitment to work for change as the injustices we confront can become more apparent in the lives of people in need of assistance and support. The bishops also have the power to tie these advocacy, educational, and service efforts together in the liturgical life of the church. Each of the above examples draws upon prayer, liturgy, and the sacramental life of the church to remind Catholics that this work is a central aspect of the public service of the church in consecrating the world.

If the USCCB were to employ their myriad resources to join a movement to end our justice crises, they would need to expand significantly their current office for criminal justice in their Department of Justice, Peace, and Human Development. The website of this office reflects the focus of the bishops on crime and individual wrongdoing in *Responsibility, Rehabilitation, and Restoration* and their failure to recognize fully the ways in which criminal and social justice are intertwined. It presents a quotation from Pope John Paul II's Jubilee letter as central to the work of this office:

79. "Free Exercise of Religion: Putting Beliefs into Practice," U.S. Conference of Catholic Bishops, http://www.usccb.org/issues-and-action/religious-liberty/fortnight-for-freedom/upload/Free-Exercise-of-Religion-Putting-Beliefs-into-Practice.pdf.

> We are still a long way from the time when our conscience can be certain of having done everything possible to prevent crime and to control it effectively so that it no longer does harm and, at the same time, to offer to those who commit crimes a way of redeeming themselves and making a positive return to society.[80]

The bishops need to instruct this office to deepen its understanding of the roots and effects of mass incarceration and to seek answers beyond crime prevention and control. They also need to recognize that the death penalty is but one aspect of the problems of with these systems (albeit a very important aspect that cannot be ignored). The office should be provided the means necessary to conduct efforts similar to those of the Respect Life Program, the offices concerned with immigration issues, and the Fortnight for Freedom.

Movements for justice also need grassroots involvement; top-down efforts by bishops will not be sufficient. Catholic individuals and congregations also have several ways by which they could join a movement for justice. Healing Communities, organized by the Annie E. Casey Foundation, offer one opportunity for Catholic parishes to engage in criminal and social justice issues. This framework can help congregations identify their strengths in developing their capacity to assist people in prison, ex-prisoners, their families, and communities affected by mass incarceration. It can also enable different faith communities drawing upon the concept of Healing Communities to connect with each other across boundaries of race, ethnicity, class, geography, and religious identity. Experiences of building relationships with people directly affected by our criminal justice systems can inspire further work for justice. The AECF notes, "Congregations are more likely to mobilize around social issues when introduced to them through the lived experiences of those they work with, as opposed to adopting an advocacy position based on the content of the issue itself."[81] Witnessing the effects of our criminal and social justice crises in the lives of individuals, families, and communities can foster a drive for justice in congregations, leading their members to join a movement for change.

In addition to action within the church hierarchy and grassroots activity, Catholics have created numerous organizations such as charities, hospitals, parochial schools, and colleges and universities that could take important roles in this movement. Organizations such as Catholic Charities provide important services to people on the margins of our society while also engaging in

---

80. "Criminal Justice/Restorative Justice," U.S. Conference of Catholic Bishops, http://www.usccb.org/issues-and-action/human-life-and-dignity/criminal-justice-restorative-justice/index.cfm.

81. "Healing Communities," AECF, 16.

advocacy work to change policies that contribute to marginalization. Criminal justice could become one focus of their work, along with complementing the work of other organizations in projects like the Harlem Children's Zone and Promise Neighborhoods. Hospitals can offer clinical services in vulnerable neighborhoods, such as those services recommended by the Children's Defense Fund that can help break down the cradle-to-prison pipeline. Parochial schools, especially those in or near neighborhoods plagued by the concentration of mass incarceration, could also become hubs within Promise Neighborhoods. Catholic colleges and universities can draw on their resources to offer educational programs in prisons and for ex-prisoners. They can also provide assistance to students now on new cradle-through-college pipelines. University Beyond Bars and the Inside-Out Prison Exchange Program offer models for how Catholic colleges and universities can begin some of this work. Loyola University in New Orleans offers another model.[82] The Loyola Institute for Ministry has operated an extension program that enables people around the world to earn a graduate-level degree in their own localities. In 2010, this program began offering courses in the Louisiana State Penitentiary in Angola. These activities in various Catholic organizations can also help Catholics on individual, organizational, and congregational levels understand the lived experiences of people harmed by mass incarceration and lead them to engage in a multiracial, interreligious movement for justice.

CONCLUSION

The work for justice, for Catholics and many other Christians, must ultimately be grounded in the liturgical and sacramental life of the church. Our consciousness is transformed as we participate in the sacraments, and the world-picture presented to us especially in the Eucharist calls us to end our criminal and social justice crises. A movement for justice in the United States demands that everyone acknowledge the dignity of every other human person regardless of racial, ethnic, and class boundaries. The inclusiveness of Christ's table reminds us of this dignity even in people who are despised and degraded. A movement for justice compels us to oppose anything that marginalizes, disempowers, or endangers anyone. The memory of Christ's triumph over the principalities and powers of this world, which is rekindled in the eucharistic liturgy, gives us hope that through the grace of God we too will be able to bring an end to the marginalization, disempowerment, and endangerment of

---

82. "Loyola Institute for Ministry Extension Program," Loyola Institute for Ministry, http://lim.loyno.edu/onsite.

many members of our society. A movement for justice demands that we ensure everyone has access to the conditions necessary to flourish as human persons. The anticipation that we experience in the Eucharist of God's reign of love, peace, forgiveness, and life provides a vision of what this world would look like if we achieved these conditions. And a movement for justice requires us all to acknowledge our complicity in mass incarceration and its related social injustices. The requirement that we discern our consciences before partaking of the Eucharist and that we all seek our constant conversion from personal and social sin in Penance and Reconciliation offers a path for recognizing our responsibility and beginning anew. In the public service of our liturgy and the consecration of the sacraments, we can find the heart of Catholic tradition that draws us to justice.

Epilogue

To untangle our criminal and social justice crises, we must begin by learning to care about people in prison. Many of us are able to avoid caring about them because prisons lie outside of our immediate realms of experience. Without direct experience of prisons and prisoners, it is easier to maintain the perspective that incarcerated people are dangerous, dirty, and despicable, mere animals in cages. Although we live in the first genuine prison society, we can live most of our lives without awareness of the harsh realities surrounding mass incarceration and the ways in which many people in prison have been degraded and demeaned throughout their lives. Insulated by racial, ethnic, and class privilege, many Americans know little about the New Jim Crow. To overcome our indifference toward people in prison and to begin to address the problem of mass incarceration, we must come to care across racial, ethnic, and class divisions and to recognize that people in prison are indeed human persons. We must also begin to envision a new kind of society that is not so willing to throw people away, especially people who have already been pushed to the edges of our communities.

As Catholics seek ways to contribute to resolving these crises, we ought to draw on the heart of our tradition: liturgy and sacraments. Most Catholics in the United States may not ever have loved a person in prison, an experience that can pique one's conscience about the problems of mass incarceration. Most will not read the U.S. Conference of Catholic Bishops' *Responsibility, Rehabilitation, and Restoration.* Realistically speaking, most will not be moved by an intellectual appeal to liturgical and sacramental ethics. But Catholics will be shaped by their participation in liturgy and sacraments. The experience of God's grace disclosed in the Eucharist is the most important experience in our lives as individual Christians and as the gathered church. As we partake of the Eucharist, we are called to discern our consciences about the ways in which we continue to participate in broken relationships and to seek reconciliation through the sacrament of Penance. If Catholics are to come to stand for an end to our criminal and social justice crises, they will do so because of the vision of justice in God's reign conveyed by liturgy and sacraments. We must begin our work for justice by seeing it as integrated with the liturgical and sacramental heart of Catholicism.

Our liturgical and sacramental practices summon us to care for all people, regardless of the social, cultural, economic, and political boundaries that currently divide us from one another. The public service of the church embodied in liturgy draws us more deeply into the world in anticipation of God's life, freedom, justice, love, and peace. The grace of God disclosed in the sacraments consecrates our lives in the world. Our consciousness of the injustices of this world is transformed as we enter the world-picture of God's reign. In our celebration of the Eucharist, we are invited into a covenant in which all people are ultimately included and the needs of everyone—especially the degraded and demeaned—are fulfilled. We anticipate the triumph of God's justice even as we remember the death of Jesus Christ as a convicted criminal. As we participate in Penance and Reconciliation, we repent of our sins. We must be mindful not only of our personal sins, but also our complicity in social sin. Within our communities, we seek ways to repair broken relationships and to be redeemed in the hope that through forgiveness, we can walk together again. The repentance and communion tied together in Reconciliation and the Eucharist draw us toward relationship, inclusion, forgiveness, and hope. Based upon this vision, our care for others must extend even into the prison cell, as well as across the boundaries upon which mass incarceration depends.

As our consciousness is transformed in these ways by participation in liturgy and sacraments, we must also envision a new kind of society that can replace the first genuine prison society. If we come to care about all persons through our experience of the eucharistic table, then we cannot be content any longer with a society that is willing to throw people away. We must endeavor to create a new society that takes seriously the inviolable and inalienable dignity of every human person. We must ensure that our society serves the good of all people. We must commit ourselves to the common good—a good that ultimately excludes no one. And we must be willing to dismantle any structures, including prisons, that impede the realization of this vision.

Expressing our care for others and creating our new society will require action on multiple levels, beginning with criminal justice reform. We need not depend so much on prisons to promote public safety. We have much more effective resources in rehabilitation and restorative justice for fostering internal reform and social reintegration of people who commit crime. Furthermore, these resources can much more readily guarantee that even people who commit crime are treated as full human persons who are responsible for their wrongdoing, but also who cannot be treated as means to an end or punished for the sake of punishment alone. But we must not stop with responses to crime and individual wrongdoing. We must also attend to the social injustices that our crisis of criminal justice helps sustain. Our efforts must foster social, cultural, economic, and political inclusion for ex-prisoners, cultivate conditions for families to thrive, and advance efforts to make safer and stronger communities. Moreover, we must address the various factors rooted in social injustice that led to the creation of the first genuine prison society in the first place. Doing so will require a multiracial and interreligious coalition of partners joined in a movement for justice. As Catholics join this movement, we may find sustenance for our work in our liturgical and sacramental lives.

Bibliography

Acorn, Annalise. *Compulsory Compassion: A Critique of Restorative Justice.* Seattle: University of Washington Press, 2005.

Alexander, Michelle. *The New Jim Crow: Mass Incarceration in the Age of Colorblindness.* New York: New Press, 2012.

"Alternatives to Violence Project—USA." http://www.avpusa.org/.

American Leadership Forum Class XXV. "Dismantling the Cradle-to-Prison Pipeline in Houston and Texas: A Study of Solutions." http://rehak.com/alf/90084%20ALF%20Report%2014.pdf.

Anderson, E. Byron. "A Body in the Spirit for the World: Eucharist, Epiclesis, and Ethics." *Worship* 85, no. 2 (2011): 98–116.

Anderson, Elijah. *Code of the Street: Decency, Violence, and the Moral Life of the Inner City.* New York: Norton, 1999.

Andrews, Donald A. "Enhancing Adherence to Risk-Need-Responsivity: Making Quality a Matter of Policy." *Criminology and Public Policy* 5, no. 3 (August 2006): 595–602.

———, and James Bonta. *The Psychology of Criminal Conduct.* 2nd edition. Cincinnati: Anderson, 1998.

———, and James Bonta. *The Psychology of Criminal Conduct.* 3rd edition. Cincinnati, OH: Anderson, 2003.

———, James Bonta, and R. D. Hoge. "Classification for Effective Rehabilitation: Rediscovering Psychology." *Criminal Justice and Behavior* 17 (1990): 19–52.

———, James Bonta, and J. Stephen Wormith. "The Recent Past and Near Future of Risk and/or Need Assessment." *Crime and Delinquency* 52 (2006): 7–27.

———, and Craig Dowden. "Managing Correctional Treatment for Reduced Recidivism: A Meta-Analytic Review of Programme Integrity." *Legal and Criminological Psychology* 10 (2005): 173–87.

The Annie E. Casey Foundation. "2008 KIDS COUNT Message FACT SHEET: A Road Map for Juvenile Justice." The Annie E. Casey Foundation. Posted 2009. http://www.aecf.org/ KnowledgeCenter/Publications.aspx?pubguid={29CFCA70-348B-416B-8546-63C297710C5D}.

———. "Healing Communities: A Framework for Congregations in Their Ministry to Families Affected by Incarceration." Accessed November 8, 2012. http://www.healingcommunitiesusa.org/Documents/ aecfHealingCommunitiesrptfinal.pdf.

———. "Juvenile Detention Alternatives Initiative." Accessed January 14, 2013. http://www.aecf.org/MajorInitiatives/JuvenileDetentionAlternatives Initiative.aspx.

———. "Reentry: Helping Former Prisoners Return to Communities." Accessed January 13, 2013. http://www.aecf.org/upload/publicationfiles/ ir2980d32.pdf.

Apel, Robert, and Daniel S. Nagin. "General Deterrence: A Review of Recent Evidence." In *Crime and Public Policy*, edited by James Q. Wilson and Joan Petersilia, 411–36. New York: Oxford University Press, 2011.

Aquinas, Thomas. *Summa Theologica*. Trans. Fathers of the English Dominican Province. Notre Dame: Christian Classics, 1981. www.newadvent.org/ summa.

Archer, Deborah N., and Kele S. Williams. "Making America 'The Land of Second Chances': Restoring Socioeconomic Rights for Ex-Offenders." *New York University Review of Law & Social Change* 30 (2006): 527–84.

"Assisting Families of Inmates, Inc.," accessed January 14, 2013, http://www.afoi.org/.

Balasuriya, Tissa. *The Eucharist and Human Liberation*. Maryknoll, NY: Orbis, 1979.

Bazemore, Gordon. "Whom and *How* Do We Reintegrate?: Finding Community in Restorative Justice." *Criminology and Public Policy* 4, no. 1 (2005): 131–48.

———, and Mara Schiff. *Juvenile Justice Reform and Restorative Justice: Building Theory and Policy from Practice*. Portland, OR: Willan, 2005.

———, and Lode Walgrave. "Restorative Juvenile Justice: In Search of Fundamentals and an Outline for Systemic Reform." In *Restorative Juvenile Justice: Repairing the Harm of Youth Crime*, edited by Gordon Bazemore and Lode Walgrave, 45–74. Monsey, NY: Criminal Justice Press, 1999.

Behan, Cormac, and Ian O'Donnell. "Prisoners, Politics, and the Polls: Enfranchisement and the Burden of Responsibility." *British Journal of Criminology* 48, no. 3 (2008): 319–36.

Bellah, Robert N., Richard Madsen, William M. Sullivan, Ann Swidler, and Steven M. Tipton. *Habits of the Heart: Individualism and Commitment in American Life*. Berkeley: University of California Press, 1985.

Berkman, John. "Being Reconciled: Penitence, Punishment, and Worship." In *The Blackwell Companion to Christian Ethics*, edited by Stanley Hauerwas and Samuel Wells, 95–109. Malden, MA: Blackwell, 2006.

Berman, Greg, and Aubrey Fox. *Trial and Error in Criminal Justice Reform: Learning from Failure.* Washington, DC: Urban Institute Press, 2010.

Besser, Terry, and Margaret Hanson. "The Development of Last Resort: The Impact of New Prisons on Small Town Economies." *Journal of the Community Development Society* 35 (2004): 1–16.

Bieler, Andrea, and Luise Schottroff. *The Eucharist: Bodies, Bread, and Resurrection.* Minneapolis: Fortress Press, 2007.

Blankenship, Susan, and Ernest Yanarella. "Prison Recruitment as a Policy Tool of Local Economic Development: A Critical Evaluation." *Contemporary Justice Review* 7 (2004): 183–98.

Blumstein, Alfred, and Allen J. Beck. "Population Growth in U.S. Prisons, 1980-1996." In *Prisons*, edited by Michael Tonry and Joan Petersilia, 17–62. Chicago: University of Chicago Press, 1999.

———, Michael Tonry, and Asheley Van Ness. "Cross-national Measures of Punitiveness." In *Crime and Punishment in Western Countries, 1980-1999*, edited by Michael Tonry and David P. Farrington, 347–76. Chicago: University of Chicago Press, 2005.

Bonta, James, Rebecca Jesseman, Tanya Rugge, and Robert Cormier. "Restorative Justice and Recidivism: Promises Made, Promises Kept?" In *Handbook of Restorative Justice: A Global Perspective*, edited by Dennis Sullivan and Larry Tifft, 108–20. New York: Routledge, 2006.

Boyle, Gregory. *Tattoos on the Heart: The Power of Boundless Compassion.* New York: Free Press, 2010.

Braga, Anthony A. "Pulling Levers Focused Deterrence Strategies and the Prevention of Gun Homicide." *Journal of Criminal Justice* 36, no. 4 (2008): 332–43.

———, David M. Kennedy, Elin J. Waring, and Anne M. Piehl. "Problem-Oriented Policing, Deterrence, and Youth Violence: An Evaluation of Boston's Operation Ceasefire." *Journal of Research in Crime and Delinquency* 38, no. 3 (2001): 195–225.

———, and Glenn L. Pierce. "Disrupting Illegal Firearms Markets in Boston: The Effects of Operation Ceasefire on the Supply of New Handguns to Criminals." *Criminology & Public Policy* 4 (2005): 717–48.

———, Glenn L. Pierce, Jack McDevitt, Brenda J. Bond, and Shea Cronin. "The Strategic Prevention of Gun Violence Among Gang-Involved Offenders." *Justice Quarterly* 25, no. 1 (2008): 132–62.

———, and David L. Weisburd. "The Effects of 'Pulling Levers' Focused Deterrence Strategies on Crime." *Campbell Systematic Reviews* 6 (2012): 90. Accessed January 14, 2013. doi: 10.4073/csr.2012.6.

Braithwaite, John. *Restorative Justice and Responsive Regulation.* New York: Oxford University Press, 2002.

Braman, Donald. "Families and Incarceration." In *Invisible Punishment: The Collateral Consequences of Mass Imprisonment*, edited by Marc Mauer and Meda Chesney-Lind, 117–35. New York: New Press, 2002.

———, and Jennifer Wood. "From One Generation to the Next: How Criminal Sanctions Are Reshaping Family Life in Urban America." In *Prisoners Once Removed: The Impact of Incarceration and Reentry on Children, Families, and Communities*, edited by Jeremy Travis and Michelle Waul, 157–88. Washington, DC: Urban Institute Press, 2003.

Bureau of Justice Statistics. "Defense Counsel in Criminal Cases." U.S. Department of Justice. Posted November 2000. bjs.ojp.usdoj.gov/content/pub/pdf/dccc.pdf.

———. "Key Facts at a Glance: Correctional Populations." U.S. Department of Justice. Posted July 2010. http://bjs.ojp.usdoj.gov/content/glance/tables/corr2tab.cfm.

———. "Recidivism." U.S. Department of Justice. Posted June 16, 2010. http://bjs.ojp.usdoj.gov/index.cfm?ty=tp&tid=17.

Burnett, Ros, and Shadd Maruna. "The Kindness of Prisoners: Strength-Based Resettlement in Theory and in Action." *Criminology and Criminal Justice* 6 (2006): 83–106.

The Campaign to Promote Equitable Telephone Charges. "The Campaign to Promote Equitable Telephone Charges." Accessed December 4, 2012. http://www.etccampaign.com/.

Cantalamessa, Raniero. *The Eucharist: Our Sanctification.* Collegeville, MN: Liturgical, 1993.

———. *"This Is My Body": Eucharistic Reflections Inspired by* Adoro Te Devote *and* Ave Verum. Boston: Pauline, 2005.

Cassidy, Laurie M., and Alex Mikulich, eds. *Interrupting White Privilege: Catholic Theologians Break the Silence.* Maryknoll, NY: Orbis, 2007.

Catholic Bishops of the United States. "Rebuilding Human Lives." *Origins* 3 (1973): 344–50.

Catechism of the Catholic Church. Vatican City: Libreria Editrice Vaticana, 1994.

Cavanaugh, William T. *Torture and Eucharist: Theology, Politics, and the Body of Christ.* Oxford: Blackwell, 1998.

Center for the Study of Social Policy. "Results-Based Public Policy Strategies for Promoting Workforce Strategies for Reintegrating Ex-Offenders." Accessed August 21, 2012. http://www.cssp.org/policy/papers/Promoting-Workforce-Strategies-for-Reintegrating-Ex-Offenders.pdf.

Children's Defense Fund. "Cradle-to-Prison Pipeline." Accessed January 2, 2013. http://www.childrensdefense.org/programs-campaigns/cradle-to-prison-pipeline/.

———. "America's Cradle to Prison Pipeline." Posted October 2007. http://www.childrensdefense.org/child-research-data-publications/data/cradle-prison-pipeline-report-2007-full-highres.html.

Clear, Todd R. "The Effects of Higher Imprisonment Rates on Communities." *Crime and Justice* 37, no. 1 (2008): 97–132.

———. *Imprisoning Communities: How Mass Imprisonment Makes Disadvantaged Neighborhoods Worse.* New York: Oxford University Press, 2007.

———. "The Problem with 'Addition by Subtraction': The Prison-Crime Relationship in Low-Income Communities." In *Invisible Punishment: The Collateral Consequences of Mass Imprisonment*, edited by Marc Mauer and Meda Chesney-Lind, 181–93. New York: New Press, 2002.

———, Dina R. Rose, Elin Waring, and Kristen Scully. "Coercive Mobility and Crime: A Preliminary Investigation of Concentrated Incarceration and Social Disorganization." *Justice Quarterly* 20, no. 1 (2003): 33–64.

Coates, Robert B., and John Gehm. "An Empirical Assessment." In *Mediation and Criminal Justice: Victims, Offenders, and Community*, edited by Martin Wright and Burt Galaway, 251–63. London: Sage, 1989.

———, and John Gehm. *Victim Meets Offender: An Evaluation of Victim-Offender Reconciliation Programs.* Valparaiso, IN: PACT Institute of Justice, 1985.

Copeland, M. Shawn. *Enfleshing Freedom: Body, Race, and Being.* Minneapolis: Fortress Press, 2010.

Corsaro, Nicholas, and Edmund McGarrell. *An Evaluation of the Nashville Drug Market Initiative (DMI) Pulling Levers Strategy.* East Lansing: Michigan State University, School of Criminal Justice, 2010.

————. "Testing a Promising Homicide Reduction Strategy: Re-assessing the Impact of the Indianapolis 'Pulling Levers' Intervention." *Journal of Experimental Criminology* 5 (2009): 63–82.

Cristo Rey Network. "Cristo Rey Network." www.cristoreynetwork.org.

Cross, James T. "Communal Penance and Public Life: On the Church's Becoming a Sign of Conversion from Social Sin." In *Faith in Public Life*, edited by William J. Collinge, 284–97. Maryknoll, NY: College Theology Society, 2007.

Cullen, Francis. "Rehabilitation and Treatment Programs." In *Crime: Public Policies for Crime Control*, edited by James Q. Wilson and Joan Petersilia, 253–90. Oakland, CA: Institute for Contemporary Studies, 2002.

————, and Paul Gendreau. "Assessing Correctional Rehabilitation: Policy, Practice, and Prospects." *Criminal Justice* 3 (2000): 109–75.

Dalton, Erin. "Targeted Crime Reduction Efforts in Ten Communities: Lessons for the Project Safe Neighborhoods Initiative." *U.S. Attorney's Bulletin* 50 (2002): 16–25.

Davies, Scott, and Julian Tanner. "The Long Arm of the Law: Effects of Labeling on Employment." *Sociological Quarterly* 44 (2003): 385–405.

Davis, Angela. *The Prison-Industrial Complex* (Oakland, CA: AK Press, 2001).

Davis, Mike. "Hell Factory in the Field: A Prison Industrial Complex." *The Nation*, February 20, 1995.

Dickens, Charles. *American Notes*. Introduction by Christopher Lasch. Gloucester, MA: Peter Smith, 1842/1968.

Doob, Anthony N., and Cheryl Marie Webster. "Sentence Severity and Crime: Accepting the Null Hypothesis." In *Crime and Justice: A Review of Research*, vol. 30, edited by Michael Tonry, 143–95. Chicago: University of Chicago Press, 2003.

Durlauf, Steven, and Daniel Nagin. "Imprisonment and Crime: Can Both Be Reduced?" *Criminology & Public Policy* 10, no. 1 (2011): 13–54.

Edin, Kathryn, Timothy J. Nelson, and Rechelle Paranal. "Fatherhood and Incarceration as Potential Turning Points in the Criminal Careers of Unskilled Men." In *Imprisoning America: The Social Effects of Mass Incarceration*, edited by Mary Pattillo, David Weiman, and Bruce Western, 46–75. New York: Russell Sage Foundation, 2004.

Elliott, Delbert S. "Serious Violent Offenders: Onset, Development Course, and Termination—the American Society of Criminology 1993 Presidential Address." *Criminology* 32, no. 1 (1994): 1–21.

Equal Employment Opportunity Commission. "Consideration of Arrest and Conviction Records in Employment Decisions Under Title VII of the Civil Rights Act of 1964." Accessed August 26, 2012. http://www.eeoc.gov/laws/guidance/arrest_conviction.cfm#VIII.

Everett, William. "Liturgy and Ethics: A Response to Saliers and Ramsey." *Journal of Religious Ethics* 7, no. 2 (1979): 203–14.

Families Against Mandatory Minimums. "Families Against Mandatory Minimums." Accessed January 14, 2013. www.famm.org.

Farley, Margaret. "Beyond the Formal Principle: A Reply to Ramsey and Saliers." *Journal of Religious Ethics* 7, no. 2 (1979): 191–202.

Farrington, David P., Patrick Langan, and Michael Tonry, eds. *Cross-National Studies in Crime and Justice*. Washington, DC: Bureau of Justice Statistics, 2004.

Federal Bonding Program. "The Federal Bonding Program: A U.S. Department of Labor Initiative." Accessed January 14, 2013. http://www.bonds4jobs.com/.

Flannery, Austin, ed. *Vatican Council II: The Conciliar and Post Conciliar Documents*. Vol. 1.Northport, NY: Costello, 1998.

Forst, Brian. "Prosecution." In *Crime: Public Policies for Crime Control*, edited by James Q. Wilson and Joa Petersilia, 509–36. Oakland, CA: ICS Press, 2002.

Freeman, Richard B. "Crime and the Employment of Disadvantaged Youth." In *Urban Labor Markets and Job Opportunity*, edited by George Peterson and Wayne Vroman. Washington, DC: Urban Institute Press, 1992.

Fremon, Celeste. *G-Dog and the Homeboys: Father Greg Boyle and the Gangs of East Los Angeles*. Revised edition. Albuquerque: University of New Mexico Press, 2008.

Galaway, Burt. "The New Zealand Experience Implementing the Reparation Sentence." In *Restorative Justice on Trial: Pitfalls and Potentials of Victim-Offender Mediation—International Perspectives*, edited by Heinz Messmer and Hans-Uwe Otto, 55–80. Dordrecht: Kluwer, 1992.

Garland, David. "Introduction: The Meaning of Mass Imprisonment." In *Mass Imprisonment: Social Causes and Consequences*, edited by David Garland, 1–3. Thousand Oaks, CA: Sage, 2001.

———. *Punishment and Modern Society: A Study in Social Theory*. Chicago: University of Chicago Press, 1990.

Gendreau, Paul, and Donald A. Andres. "Tertiary Prevention: What a Meta-Analysis of the Offender Treatment Literature Tells Us About 'What Works.'" *Canadian Journal of Criminology* 32 (1990): 173–84.

"Girl Scouts Beyond Bars," Girl Scouts, http://www.girlscouts.org/who_ we_are/our_partners/government_grants/community/gsbb.asp.

Glaze, Lauren E., and Laura M. Maruschak. "Parents in Prison and Their Minor Children."Bureau of Justice Statistics. U.S. Department of Justice. Posted August 2008. http://bjs.ojp.usdoj.gov/content/pub/pdf/pptmc.pdf.

Gorringe, Timothy. *God's Just Vengeance: Crime, Violence, and the Rhetoric of Salvation.* Cambridge: Cambridge University Press, 1996.

Gottfredson, Don M. "Effects of Judges Sentencing Decisions on Criminal Careers." In *NIJ Research in Brief.* Washington, DC: U.S. Department of Justice, 1999.

Greene, Judith A. "Entrepreneurial Corrections: Incarceration as a Business Opportunity." In *Invisible Punishment: The Collateral Consequences of Mass Imprisonment,* edited by Marc Mauer and Meda-Chesney Lind, 95–113. New York: New Press, 2002.

———, and Marc Mauer. *Downscaling Prisons: Lessons from Four States.* Washington, DC: The Sentencing Project, 2010.

Griffith, Lee. *The Fall of the Prison: Biblical Perspectives on Prison Abolition.* Grand Rapids: Eerdmans, 1993.

Guroian, Vigen. "Liturgy and the Lost Eschatological Vision of Christian Ethics." *Annual of the Society of Christian Ethics* 20 (2000): 227–38.

Hagan, John, and Ronit Dinovitzer. "Collateral Consequences of Imprisonment for Children, Communities, and Prisoners." In *Prisons,* edited by Michael Tonry and Joan Petersilia, 121–62. Chicago: University of Chicago Press, 1999.

Hairston, Creasie F. "Prisoners and Families: Parenting Issues during Incarceration." Paper presented at the Urban Institute's From Prison to Home conference, Washington, DC, January 30–31, 2002.

———. "Prisoners and Their Families: Parenting Issues during Incarceration." In *Prisoners Once Removed: The Impact of Incarceration and Reentry on Children, Families, and Communities,* edited by Jeremy Travis and Michelle Waul, 259–82. Washington, DC: Urban Institute Press, 2003.

Haley, John. "Victim-Offender Mediations: Japanese and American Comparison." In *Restorative Justice on Trial: Pitfalls and Potentials of Victim-Offender Mediation—International Perspectives,* edited by Heinz Messmer and Hans-Uwe Otto, 105–30. Dordrecht: Kluwer, 1992.

Hamm, Theodore. "Our Prison Complex." *The Nation,* October 11, 1999.

Harcourt, Bernard E. *Illusion of Order: The False Promise of Broken Windows Policing.* Cambridge, MA: Harvard University Press, 2001.

Harlem Children's Zone. "Harlem Children's Zone." Accessed December 18, 2012. www.hcz.org.

———. "The HCZ Project." Accessed December 18, 2012. http://hcz.org/index.php/about-us/the-hcz-project.

Harrison, Byron, and Robert C. Schehr. "Offenders and Post-Release Jobs: Variables Influencing Success and Failure." *Journal of Offender Rehabilitation* 39 (2004): 35–68.

Harris, M. Kay. "In Search of Common Ground: The Importance of Theoretical Orientations in Criminology and Criminal Justice." *Criminology and Public Policy* 4 (2005): 311–28.

———. "Reflections of a Skeptical Dreamer: Some Dilemmas in Restorative Justice Theory and Practice." *Contemporary Justice Review* 1 (1998): 57–69.

Hauerwas, Stanley, and Samuel Wells. "Christian Ethics as Informed Prayer." In *The Blackwell Companion to Christian Ethics*, edited by Stanley Hauerwas and Samuel Wells, 6. Malden, MA: Blackwell, 2004.

Hayes, Diana L. *Standing in the Shoes My Mother Made: A Womanist Theology.* Minneapolis: Fortress Press, 2011.

Hellwig, Monika K. *The Eucharist and the Hunger of the World.* 2nd edition. Kansas City, MO: Sheed & Ward, 1992.

———. *The Meaning of the Sacraments.* Dayton, OH: Pflaum, 1972.

———. *Sign of Reconciliation and Conversion: The Sacrament of Penance for Our Times.* Wilmington, DE: Michael Glazier, 1984.

Hidber, Bruno. "From Anguish to Refound Freedom: Penance in the Tension between Sacraments and Ethics." *Worship* 68, no. 2 (1994): 98–117.

Himes, Kenneth R. "Eucharist and Justice: Assessing the Legacy of Virgil Michel." *Worship* 62, no. 3 (1988): 201–24.

Hogan, John P. "The Eucharist and Social Justice." In *Romero's Legacy: The Call to Peace and Justice*, edited by Pilar Hogan Closkey and John P. Hogan, 25–34. Lanham, MD: Sheed & Ward, 2007.

Holzer, Harry J., Steven Raphael, and Michael A. Stoll. "Will Employers Hire Former Offenders?: Employer Preferences, Background Checks, and Their Determinants." In *Imprisoning America: The Social Effects of Mass Incarceration*, edited by Mary Pattillo, David Weiman, and Bruce Western, 205–43. New York: Russell Sage Foundation, 2004.

Hooks, Gregory, Clayton Mosher, Shaun Genter, Thomas Rotolo, and Linda Lobao. "Revisiting the Impact of Prison Building on Job Growth: Education, Incarceration, and County-Level Employment." *Social Science Quarterly* 91, no. 1 (2010): 228–44.

Hughes, H. Kathleen. "Liturgy and Justice: An Intrinsic Relationship." In *Living No Longer for Ourselves: Liturgy and Justice in the Nineties*, edited by Kathleen Hughes and Mark R. Francis, 36–51. Collegeville, MN: Liturgical, 1991.

Hughes, Timothy A., Doris James Wilson, and Allen J. Beck. *Reentry Trends in the United States: Inmates Returning to the Community After Spending Time in Prison.* Washington, DC: Bureau of Justice Statistics, 2006.

Huling, Tracy. "Building a Prison Economy in Rural America." In *Invisible Punishment: The Collateral Consequences of Mass Imprisonment*, edited by Marc Mauer and Meda Chesney-Lind, 197–214. New York: New Press, 2002.

Hull, Elizabeth A. *The Disenfranchisement of Ex-Felons.* Philadelphia: Temple University Press, 2006.

"The Inside-Out Prison Exchange Program," accessed January 4, 2012, www.insideoutcenter.org.

Irwin, John. *The Warehouse Prison: Disposal of the New Dangerous Class.* Los Angeles: Roxbury, 2005.

Jacobson, Michael. *Downsizing Prisons: How to Reduce Crime and End Mass Incarceration.* New York: New York University Press, 2005.

John Paul II. *Jubilee in Prisons.* Vatican Web site. June 24, 2000. http://www.vatican.va/holy_father/john_paul_ii/messages/documents/hf_jp-ii_mes_20000630_jubilprisoners_en.html.

———. *Evangelium Vitae.* Vatican Web site. March 25, 1995. http://www.vatican.va/holy_father/john_paul_ii/encyclicals/documents/hf_jp-ii_enc_25031995_evangelium-vitae_en.html.

———. *Sollicitudo Rei Socialis.* Vatican Web site. December 30, 1987. http://www.vatican.va/holy_father/john_paul_ii/encyclicals/documents/hf_jp-ii_enc_30121987_sollicitudo-rei-socialis_en.html.

Johnson, Byron. *More God, Less Crime: Why Faith Matters and How It Could Matter More.* Philadelphia: Templeton, 2012.

Johnson, Elizabeth I., and Jane Waldfogel. "Children of Incarcerated Parents: Multiple Risks and Children's Living Arrangements." In *Imprisoning America: The Social Effects of Mass Incarceration*, edited by Mary Pattillo, David Weiman, and Bruce Western, 97–131. New York: Russell Sage Foundation, 2004.

Johnson, Rucker C., and Steven Raphael. *The Effects of Male Incarceration on Dynamics of AIDS Infection Rates Among African-American Women and Men.* Berkeley, CA: Goldman School of Public Policy, University of California, 2005.

Justice Center: The Council of State Governments. "Children of Incarcerated Parents: An Action Plan for Federal Policymakers." Accessed January 10, 2013. http://www.reentrypolicy.org/jc_publications/federa_action_plan_/Children_Incarcerated_Parents_v8.pdf.

"Kairos Prison Ministry International, Inc." Accessed January 12, 2013. http://www.kairosprisonministry.org/.

Keifer, Ralph A. "Liturgy and Ethics: Some Unresolved Dilemmas." In *Living No Longer for Ourselves: Liturgy and Justice in the Nineties*, edited by Kathleen Hughes and Mark R. Francis, 68–83. Collegeville, MN: Liturgical, 1991.

Kelling, George E., and Catherine M. Coles. *Fixing Broken Windows: Restoring Order and Reducing Crime in Our Communities.* New York: Touchstone, 1996.

Kennedy, David M. *Don't Shoot: One Man, A Street Fellowship, and the End of Violence in Inner-City America.* New York: Bloomsbury, 2011.

———, Anne M. Piehl, and Anthony A. Braga. "Youth Violence in Boston: Gun Markets, Serious Youth Offenders, and a Use-Reduction Strategy." *Law and Contemporary Problems* 59 (1996): 147–96.

King, Ryan S., Marc Mauer, and Tracy Huling. "An Analysis of Economics of Prison Siting in Rural Communities." *Criminal Public Policy* 3 (2004): 453–80.

———, Marc Mauer, and Malcolm C. Young. "Incarceration and Crime: A Complex Relationship." The Sentencing Project. Posted January 2005. http://www.sentencingproject.org/doc/publications/inc_iandc_complex.pdf.

Koester, Anne Y., ed. *Liturgy and Justice: To Worship God in Spirit and Truth.* Collegeville, MN: Liturgical, 2002.

Koritansky, Peter Karl. *Thomas Aquinas and the Philosophy of Punishment.* Washington, DC: Catholic University of America Press, 2012.

Kurki, Leena. "Evaluating Restorative Justice Practices." In *Restorative Justice and Criminal Justice*, edited by Andrew von Hirsch, Julian Roberts, Anthony E. Bottoms, Kent Roach, and Mara Schiff, 293–314. Portland, OR: Hart, 2003.

Kyckelhahn, Tracey. "State Corrections Expenditures, FY1982-2010." Bureau of Justice Statistics. Accessed January 10, 2013. http://bjs.ojp.usdoj.gov/content/pub/pdf/ scefy8210.pdf.

Kwong, Jessica. "Inmate Cooks Give Back at Food Bank." *San Antonio Express.* February 4, 2012. Accessed January 10, 2013. http://www.mysanantonio.com/news/local_news/article/Inmate-cooks-give-back-at-food-bank-3009175.php.

Langan, Patrick, and David Levin. *Recidivism in Prisoners Released in 1994.* Washington, DC: Bureau of Justice Statistics, 2002.

Levad, Amy. *Restorative Justice: Theories and Practices of Moral Imagination*. El Paso, TX: LFB Scholarly Publishing, 2012.

———. "'I Was in Prison and You Visited Me': A Sacramental Approach to Rehabilitative and Restorative Justice." *Journal of the Society of Christian Ethics* 31, no. 3 (2011): 93–112.

Liedka, Raymond V., Anne Morrison Piehl, and Bert Useem. "The Crime-Control Effect of Incarceration: Does Scale Matter?" *Criminology and Public Policy* 5 (2006): 245–76.

Liptak, Adam. "U.S. Prison Population Dwarfs That of Other Nations." *New York Times*, April 23, 2008.

Logan, James Samuel. *Good Punishment? Christian Moral Practice and U.S. Imprisonment*. Grand Rapids: Eerdmans, 2008.

Lotke, Eric, and Peter Wagner. "Prisoners of the Census: Electoral and Financial Consequences of Counting Prisoners Where They Go, Not Where They Come From." *Pace Law Review* 24, no. 587 (2004): 587–607.

Loyola Institute for Ministry. "Loyola Institute for Ministry Extension Program." Accessed January 22, 2013. http://lim.loyno.edu/onsite.

Lucken, Karol, and Lucille M. Ponte. "A Just Measure of Forgiveness: Reforming Occupational Licensing Regulations for Ex-Offenders Using BFOQ Analysis." *Law and Policy* 30, no. 1 (2008): 46–72.

Lynch, James P., and William Alex Pridemore. "Crime in International Perspective." In *Crime and Public Policy*, edited by James Q. Wilson and Joan Petersilia, 5–52. New York: Oxford University Press, 2011.

———, and William J. Sabol. "Effects of Incarceration on Informal Social Control in Communities." In *Imprisoning America: The Social Effects of Mass Incarceration*, edited by Mary Pattillo, David Weiman, and Bruce Western, 135–64. New York: Russell Sage Foundation, 2004.

MacKenzie, Doris Layton. *What Works in Corrections: Reducing the Recidivism of Offenders and Delinquents*. Cambridge: Cambridge University Press, 2006.

Maguire, Kathleen, ed. *Sourcebook of Criminal Justice Statistics* (table 6.28.2009). Posted June 2009. http://www.albany.edu/sourcebook/pdf/t6282009.pdf.

Mahoney, Roger. "The Eucharist and Social Justice." *Worship* 57, no. 1 (1983): 52–61.

Mannion, M. Francis. "Liturgy and the Present Crisis of Culture." *Worship* 62, no. 2 (1988): 98–123.

Marshall, Christopher D. *Beyond Retribution: A New Testament Vision for Justice, Crime, and Punishment*. Grand Rapids: Eerdmans, 2001.

Marshall, Tony. "Restorative Justice on Trial in Britain." In *Restorative Justice on Trial: Pitfalls and Potentials of Victim-Offender Mediation—International Perspectives*, edited by Heinz Messmer and Hans-Uwe Otto, 15–28. Dordrecht: Kluwer, 1992.

Martinson, Robert. "What Works: Questions and Answers about Prison Reform." *Public Interest* 35 (1974): 22–54.

Martos, Joseph. *Doors to the Sacred: A Historical Introduction to Sacraments in the Catholic Church.* Revised Edition. Liguori, MO: Liguori/Triumph, 2001.

Maruna, Shadd, and Thomas P. LeBel. "Welcome Home?: Examining the Reentry Court Concept from a Strengths-Based Perspective." *Western Criminology Review* 4, no. 2 (2003): 91–107.

Marx, Paul. *Virgil Michel and the Liturgical Movement.* Collegeville, MN: Liturgical, 1957.

Massingale, Bryan. *Racial Justice and the Catholic Church.* Maryknoll, NY: Orbis, 2010.

Mauer, Marc. "The Causes and Consequences of Prison Growth in the United States." In *Mass Imprisonment: Social Causes and Consequences*, edited by David Garland, 4–14. Thousand Oaks, CA: Sage, 2001.

———. "The Hidden Problem of Time Served in Prison." *Social Research* 74, no. 2 (2007): 701–6.

———. "Mass Imprisonment and the Disappearing Voters." In *Invisible Punishment: The Collateral Consequences of Mass Imprisonment*, edited by Marc Mauer and Meda Chesney-Lind, 50–58. New York: New Press, 2002.

———. *Race to Incarcerate.* 2nd edition. New York: New Press, 2006.

Maxwell, Gabrielle M., and Allison Morris. "Research on Family Group Conferences with Young Offenders in New Zealand." In *Family Group Conferences: Perspectives on Policy and Practice*, edited by Joe Hudson, Allison Morris, and Gabrielle M. Maxwell, 88–110. Monsey, NY: Criminal Justice Press, 1996.

McBrien, Richard P. *Catholicism.* Study edition. San Francisco: HarperCollins, 1981.

McCold, Paul, and Benjamin Wachtel. "Community Is Not a Place: A New Look at Community Justice Initiatives." *Contemporary Justice Review* 1 (1998): 71–86.

———, and Benjamin Wachtel. *Restorative Policing Experiment: the Bethlehem Pennsylvania Police Family Group Conferencing Project.* Pipersville, PA: Community Service Foundation, 1998.

———, and Ted Wachtel. "Restorative Justice Theory Validation." Paper presented at the Fourth International Conference on Restorative Justice for Juveniles, Tübingen, Germany, 2000.

McCoy, Mary Pattillo. *Black Picket Fences: Privilege and Peril Among the Black Middle Class.* Chicago: University of Chicago Press, 1999.

McGarrell, Edmund F. *Restorative Justice Conferences as an Early Response to Young Offenders.* Washington, DC: Office of Juvenile Justice and Delinquency Prevention, U.S. Department of Justice, 2001. Accessed July 16, 2007. http://purl.access.gpo.gov/ GPO/LPS18711.

———, and Steven Chermak. "Problem Solving to Reduce Gang and Drug-Related Violence in Indianapolis." In *Policing Gangs and Youth Violence*, edited by Scott H. Decker, 77–101. Belmont, CA: Wadsworth, 2003.

———, Steven Chermak, Jeremy Wilson, and Nicholas Corsaro. "Reducing Homicide through a 'Lever-Pulling' Strategy." *Justice Quarterly* 23 (2006): 214–29.

———, Kathleen Olivares, Kay Crawford, and Natalie Kroovand. *Returning Justice to the Community: The Indianapolis Juvenile Restorative Justice Experiment.* Indianapolis: Hudson Institute, 2000.

Merkle, Judith A. "The Eucharist and Justice." *Liturgical Ministry* 17 (2008): 133–38.

Michel, Virgil. "Are We One in Christ?" *Ecclesiastical Review* 81 (1934): 395–401.

———. *The Christian in the World.* Collegeville, MN: Liturgical, 1939.

———. "The Liturgy the Basis of Social Regeneration." *Orate Fratres* 9 (1934–35): 536–45.

———. "The Scope of the Liturgical Movement." *Orate Fratres* 10 (1935–36): 485–90.

———. "With Our Readers." *Orate Fratres* 5 (1930–31): 430–31.

Miller, Jerome G. "Is Rehabilitation a Waste of Time?" *Washington Post*, April 23, 1989.

Moore, David B., and L. Forsythe. *A New Approach to Juvenile Justice: An Evaluation of Family Conferencing in Wagga Wagga.* Wagga Wagga, Australia: Charles Sturt University, 1995.

Moore, Kristin Anderson, David Murphey, Carol Emig, Kathleen Hamilton, Alena Hadley, and Katie Sidorowicz. *Results and Indicators for Children: An Analysis to Inform Discussions about Promise Neighborhoods.* Washington, DC: ChildTrends, 2009.

Mosher, Clayton, Gregory Hooks, and Peter B. Wood. "Don't Build It Here: The Hype Versus the Reality of Prisons and Local Employment." In *Prison Profiteers: Who Makes Money from Mass Incarceration*, edited by Tara Herivel and Paul Wright, 90–97. New York: New Press, 2007.

Murdoch, Iris. *The Sovereignty of Good.* New York: Routledge, 1970.

The Museum of the Moving Image. "The Livingroom Candidate." http://www.livingroomcandidate.org/.

National Association of State Budget Officers. *State Expenditure Report: Fiscal Year 2009.* Washington, DC: NASBO, 2010.

National Center for Education Statistics. "Literacy Behind Prison Walls." U.S. Department of Education. Posted October 1994. http://nces.ed.gov/pubs94/94102.pdf.

National Employment Law Project. "Ban the Box Major U.S. Cities and Counties Adopt Fair Hiring Policies to Remove Unfair Barriers to Employment of People with Criminal Records." Accessed January 13, 2013. http://www.nelp.org/page/-/SCLP/2011/CityandCountyHiringInitiatives.pdf?nocdn=1.

———. "Criminal Records and Employment." Accessed January 20, 2013. http://www.nelp.org/site/issues/category/criminal_records_and_employment/.

National Network for Safe Communities. "National Network for Safe Communities." Accessed January 17, 2013. http://www.nnscommunities.org/.

The National Resource Center on Children and Families of the Incarcerated. "The Family and Corrections Network." Accessed January 2, 2013. http://fcnetwork.org/.

Nurse, Anne M. "Returning to Strangers: Newly Paroled Young Fathers and Their Children." In *Imprisoning America: The Social Effects of Mass Incarceration*, edited by Mary Pattillo, David Weiman, and Bruce Western, 76–96. New York: Russell Sage Foundation, 2004.

Office of Juvenile Justice and Delinquency Prevention. "Statistical Briefing Book." U.S. Department of Justice. Office of Justice Programs. http://ojjdp.ncjrs.gov/ojstatbb/.

Page, Joshua. "Prison Officer Unions and the Perpetuation of the Penal Status Quo." *Criminology and Public Policy* 10, no. 3 (2011): 735–70.

———. *The Toughest Beat: Politics, Punishment, and the Prison Officers Union in California.* New York: Oxford University Press, 2011.

Papachristos, Andrew, Tracey Meares, and Jeffrey Fagan. "Attention Felons: Evaluating Project Safe Neighborhoods in Chicago." *Journal of Empirical Legal Studies* 4 (2007): 223–72.

Parenti, Christian. *Lockdown America: Police and Prisons in the Age of Crisis.* London, New York: Verso, 1999.

Parke, Ross D., and K. Alison Clarke-Stewart. "The Effects of Parental Incarceration on Children: Perspectives, Promises, and Policies." In *Prisoners Once Removed: The Impact of Incarceration and Reentry on Children, Families, and Communities,* edited by Jeremy Travis and Michelle Waul, 189–232. Washington, DC: Urban Institute Press, 2003.

Pate, Kim. "Victim-Offender Restitution Programs in Canada." In *Criminal Justice, Restitution, and Reconciliation,* edited by Burt Galaway and Joe Hudson, 135–44. Monsey, NY: Willow, 1990.

Pattillo-McCoy, Mary. *Black Picket Fences: Privilege and Peril Among the Black Middle Class.* Chicago: University of Chicago Press, 1999.

Pew Center on the States. "One in 100: Behind Bars in America." Posted February 2008. http://www.pewcenteronthestates.org/uploadedFiles/8015PCTS_Prison08_FINAL_2-1-1_FORWEB.pdf.

Piehl, Anne M., David M. Kennedy, and Anthony A. Braga. "Youth Violence and Problem Solving: An Evaluation of the Boston Gun Project." *American Law and Economics Review* 2, no. 1 (2000): 68–106.

Piquero, Alex R., and Alfred Blumstein. "Does Incapacitation Reduce Crime?" *Journal of Quantitative Criminology* 23, no. 4 (2007): 267–85.

Pontifical Council for Justice and Peace. *Compendium of the Social Doctrine of the Church.* Washington, DC: United States Conference of Catholic Bishops, 2004.

Porter, Thomas W., ed. *Conflict and Communion: Reconciliation and Restorative Justice at Christ's Table.* Nashville: Discipleship Resources, 2006.

Poschmann, Bernhard. *Penance and the Anointing of the Sick.* New York: Herder & Herder, 1964.

"Prisoner Visitation and Support." Accessed January 12, 2013. http://www.prisonervisitation.org/.

"Programs." North Texas Food Bank. Accessed January 10, 2013. http://www.ntfb.org/au_programs-texas-second-chance.cfm.

Purvis, Mayumi, Tony Ward, and Gwenda Willis. "The Good Lives Model in Practice: Offence Pathway and Case Management." *European Journal of Probation* 3, no. 2 (2011): 4–28.

Ramsey, Paul. "Liturgy and Ethics." *Journal of Religious Ethics* 7, no. 2 (1979): 139–71.

Raynor, Peter, and Gwen Robinson. *Rehabilitation, Crime, and Justice.* New York: Palgrave, 2005.

Redrawing the Lines. "Prisoners and the Census Count." Accessed January 14, 2013. http://www.redrawingthelines.org/prisonersthecensuscount.

Richie, Beth E. "The Social Impact of Mass Imprisonment on Women." In *Invisible Punishment: The Collateral Consequences of Mass Imprisonment*, edited by Marc Mauer and Meda Chesney-Lind, 136–49. New York: New Press, 2002.

Rose, Dina R., and Todd R. Clear. "Incarceration, Reentry, and Social Capital: Social Networks in the Balance." In *Prisoners Once Removed: The Impact of Incarceration and Reentry on Children, Families, and Communities*, edited by Jeremy Travis and Michelle Waul, 313–42. Washington, DC: Urban Institute Press, 2003.

———. "Incarceration, Social Capital, and Crime: Examining the Unintended Consequences of Incarceration." *Criminology* 36, no. 3 (1998): 441–79.

Rosenfeld, Richard, Robert Fornango, and Eric Baumer. "Did Ceasefire, Compstat, and Exile Reduce Homicide?" *Criminology & Public Policy* 4 (2005): 419–50.

Ross, Susan A. "Church and Sacraments." In *The Praxis of the Reign of God: An Introduction to the Theology of Edward Schillebeeckx*, edited by Mary Catherine Hilkert and Robert J. Schreiter, 133–48. New York: Fordham University Press, 2002.

———. *Extravagant Affections: A Feminist Sacramental Theology.* New York: Continuum, 1998.

———. "God's Embodiment and Women: Sacraments." In *Freeing Theology: The Essentials of Theology in Feminist Perspective*, edited by Catherine Mowry LaCugna, 185–209. San Francisco: HarperSanFrancisco, 1993.

———. "Liturgy and Ethics: Feminist Perspectives." *Annual of the Society of Christian Ethics* 20 (2000): 263–74.

———. "Salvation in and for the World: Church and Sacraments." In *The Praxis of Christian Experience: An Introduction to the Theology of Edward Schillebeeckx*, edited by Robert J. Schreiter and Mary Catherine Hilkert, 101–15. San Francisco: Harper & Row, 1989.

Rossi, Philip. "Narrative, Worship, and Ethics." *Journal of Religious Ethics* 7, no. 2 (1979): 239–48.

Rubinstein, Gwen, and Debbie Mukamal. "Welfare and Housing—Denial of Benefits to Drug Offenders." In *Invisible Punishment: The Collateral Consequences of Mass Imprisonment*, edited by Marc Mauer and Meda Chesney-Lind, 37–49. New York: New Press, 2002.

Saliers, Don E. "Liturgy and Ethics: Some New Beginnings." *Journal of Religious Ethics* 7, no. 2 (1979): 173–89.

Sampson, Robert J., Stephen W. Raudenbush, and Felton Earls. "Neighborhoods and Violent Crime: A Multilevel Study of Collective Efficacy." *Science* 277 (August 1997): 918–24.

Schillebeeckx, Edward. *The Eucharist*. New York: Burns & Oates, 1968.

Schmemann, Alexander. *The Eucharist: Sacrament of the Kingdom*. Crestwood, NY: St. Vladimir's Seminary Press, 1987.

———. *For the Life of the World: Sacraments and Orthodoxy*. Crestwood, NY: St. Vladimir's Seminary Press, 1963.

Schneider, Carl E. "The Rise of Prisons and the Origins of the Rehabilitative Ideal." *Michigan Law Review* 77 (1979): 707–46.

Scott, Margaret. *The Eucharist and Social Justice*. New York: Paulist, 2008.

Seasoltz, R. Kevin. "Justice and the Eucharist." *Worship* 58 (1984): 507–25.

———. *A Virtuous Church: Catholic Theology, Ethics, and Liturgy for the Twenty-First Century*. Maryknoll, NY: Orbis, 2012.

Segundo, Juan Luis. *The Sacraments Today*. Translated by John Drury. Maryknoll, NY: Orbis, 1974.

The Sentencing Project. "Felony Disenfranchisement Laws in the United States." Posted March 2011. http://www.sentencingproject.org/doc/publications/fd_bs_fdlawsinusMar11.pdf.

Shaw, Clifford R., and Henry D. McKay. *Juvenile Delinquency and Urban Areas*. Chicago: University of Chicago Press, 1942.

Sherman, Lawrence, and Heather Strang. *Restorative Justice: The Evidence*. London: The Smith Institute, 2007.

Skogan, Wesley, Susan Hartnett, Natalie Bump, and Jill Dubois. *Evaluation of CeaseFire-Chicago*. Evanston, IL: Northwestern University, Institute for Policy Research, 2008.

Skotnicki, Andrew. *Criminal Justice and the Catholic Church*. Lanham, MD: Rowman & Littlefield, 2008.

———. "Foundations Once Destroyed: The Catholic Church and Criminal Justice." *Theological Studies* 65 (2004): 792–816.

———. "How Is Justice Restored?" *Studies in Christian Ethics* 19, no. 2 (2006): 187–204.

——. *Religion and the Development of the American Penal System*. Lanham, MD: University Press of America, 2000.

Smith, Christian. *Soul Searching: The Religious and Spiritual Lives of American Teenagers*. New York: Oxford University Press, 2009.

Smith, Paula, Claire Goggin, and Paul Gendreau. *The Effects of Prison Sentences and Intermediate Sanctions on Recidivism: General Effects and Individual Differences*. Ottawa: Public Works and Government Services of Canada, 2002.

Snyder, T. Richard. *The Protestant Ethic and the Spirit of Punishment*. Grand Rapids: Eerdmans, 2001.

Solomon, Amy L., Kelley D. Johnson, Jeremy Travis, and Elizabeth C. McBride. *From Prison to Work: The Employment Dimensions of Prisoner Reentry*. Washington, DC: Urban Institute Press, 2004.

Soltis, Kathryn Getek. "Just Punishment? A Virtue Ethics Approach to Prison Reform in the United States." Ph.D. diss., Boston College, 2010.

Spelman, William. "The Limited Importance of Prison Expansion." In *The Crime Drop in America*, edited by Alfred Blumstein and Joel Walman, 97–129. New York: Cambridge University Press, 2000.

——. "What Recent Studies Do (and Don't) Tell Us about Imprisonment and Crime." In *Crime and Justice: A Review of Research*, vol. 27, edited by Michael Tonry, 419–94. Chicago: University of Chicago Press, 2000.

Steck, Christopher. "Graced Encounters: Liturgy and Ethics from a Balthasarian Perspective." *Horizons* 30, no. 2 (2003): 255–79.

Stewart, Gary. "Black Codes and Broken Windows: The Legacy of Racial Hegemony in Anti-Gang Civil Injunction." *The Yale Law Journal* 107 (1998): 2249–79.

Strang, Heather. *Victim Participation in a Restorative Justice Process*. Oxford: Oxford University Press, 2001.

——, and Lawrence W. Sherman. *The Victim's Perspective: RISE Working Paper 2*. Canberra: Law Program, RSSS, Australian National University, 1997.

Stubbs, David L. "Liturgy and Ethics, or Liturgy is Ethics." *Reformed Review* 57, no. 3 (2004): 1–12.

Sweeney, Megan. *Reading Is My Window: Books and the Art of Reading in Women's Prisons*. Chapel Hill: University of North Carolina Press, 2010.

Taylor, Mark Lewis. *The Executed God: The Way of the Cross in Lockdown America*. Minneapolis: Fortress Press, 2001.

"Texas Second Chance Program." San Antonio Food Bank. Accessed January 10, 2013. http://www.safoodbank.org/index.php/programs/more-programs/tx-second.

"Texas Second Chance." Southeast Texas Food Bank. Accessed January 10, 2013. http://setxfoodbank.org/programs/texas-second-chance/.

Thakker, Joanne, and Tony Ward. "The Good Lives Model and the Treatment of Substance Abusers." *Behavior Change* 27 (2010): 154–75.

Thomas, James C., and Elizabeth Torrone. "Incarceration as Forced Migration: Effects on Select Community Health Outcomes." *American Journal of Public Health* 96, no. 10 (2005): 1–5.

Tita, George, K. Jack Riley, Greg Ridgeway, Clifford Grammich, Allan Abrahamse, and Peter Greenwood. *Reducing Gun Violence: Results from an Intervention in East Los Angeles.* Santa Monica, CA: RAND Corporation, 2004.

Tonry, Michael. "Learning from the Limits of Deterrence Research." *Crime and Justice* 37, no. 1 (2008): 279–311.

———. *Punishing Race: A Continuing American Dilemma.* New York: Oxford University Press, 2011.

———, and David P. Farrington, eds. *Crime and Punishment in Western Countries, 1980-1999.* Chicago: University of Chicago Press, 2005.

———, and Joan Petersilia. "American Prisons at the Beginning of the Twenty-First Century." In *Prisons*, edited by Michael Tonry and Joan Petersilia, 1–16. Chicago: University of Chicago Press, 1999.

Tough, Paul. *Whatever It Takes: Geoffrey Canada's Quest to Change Harlem and America.* New York: Houghton Mifflin, 2008.

Travis, Jeremy. *But They All Come Back: Facing the Challenges of Prisoner Reentry.* Washington, DC: Urban Institute Press, 2005.

———, and Michelle Waul. "Prisoners Once Removed: The Children and Family of Prisoners." In *Prisoners Once Removed: The Impact of Incarceration and Reentry on Children, Families, and Communities*, edited by Jeremy Travis and Michelle Waul, 1–29. Washington, DC: Urban Institute Press, 2003.

Trenzcek, Thomas. "A Review and Assessment of Victim-Offender Reconciliation Programming in West Germany." In *Criminal Justice, Restitution, and Reconciliation*, edited by Burt Galaway and Joe Hudson, 109–24. Monsey, NY: Willow, 1990.

Uggen, Christopher, and Michelle Inderbitzin. "The Price and the Promise of Citizenship: Extending the Vote to Nonincarcerated Felons." In *Contemporary Issues in Criminal Justice Policy: Policy Proposals from the American Society of Criminology Conference*, edited by Natasha A. Frost, Joshua D. Freilich, and Todd R. Clear, 61–68. Belmont, CA: Cengage/Wadsworth, 2010.

———, and Jeff Manza. *Locked Out: Felon Disenfranchisement and American Democracy.* New York: Oxford University Press, 2008.

———, and Jeff Manza. "Lost Voices: The Civic and Political Views of Disenfranchised Felons." In *Imprisoning America: The Social Effects of Mass Incarceration,* edited by Mary Pattillo, David Weiman, and Bruce Western, 165–204. New York: Russell Sage Foundation, 2004.

———, Sara Wakefield, and Bruce Western. "Work and Family Perspectives on Reentry." In *Prisoner Reentry and Crime in America,* edited by Jeremy Travis and Christy Visher, 209–43. New York: Cambridge University Press, 2005.

Umbreit, Mark S. "Mediating Victim–Offender Conflict: From Single-Site to Multi-Site Analysis in the U.S." In *Restorative Justice on Trial: Pitfalls and Potentials of Victim-Offender Mediation—International Perspectives,* edited by Heinz Messmer and Hans-Uwe Otto, 431–44. Dordrecht: Kluwer, 1992.

———. *Mediation of Criminal Conflict: An Assessment of Programs in Four Canadian Provinces.* St. Paul, MN: The Center for Restorative Justice and Mediation, University of Minnesota, 1995.

———. *Victim Meets Offender: The Impact of Restorative Justice and Mediation.* Monsey, NY: Criminal Justice Press, 1994.

———, and Robert B. Coates. "Cross-Site Analysis of Victim-Offender Mediation in Four States." *Crime and Delinquency* 39, no. 4 (1993): 565–85.

———, Robert B. Coates, and Betty Vos. "The Impact of Victim-Offender Mediation: Two Decades of Research." *Federal Probation* 65, no. 3 (2001): 29–35.

———, and Ann Warner Roberts. *Mediation of Criminal Conflict in England: An Assessment of Services in Coventry and Leeds.* St. Paul, MN: The Center for Restorative Justice and Mediation, University of Minnesota, 1996.

United States Catholic Conference. "A Community Response to Crime." *Origins* 7 (1978): 593–604.

"University Beyond Bars." Accessed January 4, 2012. www.universitybeyondbars.org.

U.S. Conference of Catholic Bishops. "Brothers and Sisters to Us." *Origins* 9 (1979): 381–89.

———. "Criminal Justice/Restorative Justice." Accessed January 31, 2013. http://www.usccb.org/issues-and-action/human-life-and-dignity/criminal-justice-restorative-justice/index.cfm.

———. "Fortnight for Freedom." Accessed January 31, 2013. http://www.usccb.org/issues-and-action/religious-liberty/fortnight-for-freedom/.

———. "Free Exercise of Religion: Putting Beliefs into Practice." Accessed January 31, 2013. http://www.usccb.org/issues-and-action/religious-liberty/fortnight-for-freedom/upload/ Free-Exercise-of-Religion-Putting-Beliefs-into-Practice.pdf.

———. "Immigration." Accessed January 31, 2013. http://www.usccb.org/issues-and-action/human-life-and-dignity/immigration/.

———. "Respect Life Program." Accessed January 31, 2013. http://www.usccb.org/about/pro-life-activities/respect-life-program/.

———. *Responsibility, Rehabilitation, and Restoration: A Catholic Perspective on Crime and Criminal Justice.* Washington, DC: United States Conference of Catholic Bishops, 2000. http://www.nccbuscc.org/sdwp/criminal.shtml.

U.S. Department of Education. "Secretary Duncan Announces Seventeen 2012 Promise Neighborhoods Winners in School Safety Address at Neval Thomas Elementary School." Accessed January 3, 2013. http://www.ed.gov/news/press-releases/secretary-duncan-announces-seventeen-2012-promise-neighborhoods-winners-school-s.

Vatican Council II. *Gaudium et Spes.* In *Vatican Council II: The Conciliar and Post Conciliar Documents.* Study Edition, edited by Austin Flannery. Northport, NY: Costello, 1975.

Venkatesh, Sudhir Alladi. "The Social Organization of Street Gang Activity in an Urban Ghetto."*American Journal of Sociology* 103, no. 1 (1997): 82–111.

Visher, Christy A. "Effective Reentry Programs." *Criminology and Public Policy* 5 (2006): 299–304.

Wacquant, Loïc. "Deadly Symbiosis: When Ghetto and Prison Meet and Mesh." In *Mass Imprisonment: Social Causes and Consequences*, edited by David Garland, 82–120. Thousand Oaks, CA: Sage, 2001.

Wadell, Paul. "What Do All Those Masses Do for Us?: Reflections on the Christian Moral Life and the Eucharist." In *Living No Longer for Ourselves: Liturgy and Justice in the Nineties*, edited by Kathleen Hughes and Mark R. Francis, 153–69. Collegeville, MN: Liturgical, 1991.

Wagner, Peter. "Breaking the Census: Redistricting in an Era of Mass Incarceration." *William Mitchell Law Review* 38, no. 4 (2012): 1241–60.

Wainwright, Geoffrey. "Eucharist and/as Ethics." *Worship* 62, no. 2 (1988): 123–38.

Walmsley, Roy. "World Prison Population List." 8th edition. International Centre for Prison Studies. King's College London. Posted January 2009. http://www.kcl.ac.uk/depsta/ law/research/icps/downloads/wppl-8th_41.pdf.

Ward, Tony. "The Good Lives Model of Offender Rehabilitation: Basic Assumptions, Etiological Commitments, and Practice Implications." In *Offender Supervision: New Directions in Theory, Research, and Practice*, edited by Fergus McNeill, Peter Raynor, and Chris Trotter, 41–64. Devon, UK: Willan, 2010.

——, and Mark Brown. "The Good Lives Model and Conceptual Issues in Offender Rehabilitation." *Psychology, Crime, and Law* 10 (2004): 243–57.

——, and Theresa A. Gannon. "Rehabilitation, Etiology, and Self-Regulation: The Good Lives Model of Sexual Offender Treatment." *Aggression and Violent Behavior* 11 (2006): 77–94.

——, Theresa M. Gannon, and Ruth E. Mann. "The Good Lives Model of Offender Rehabilitation: Clinical Implications." *Aggression and Violent Behavior* 12 (2007): 87–107.

——, and Robyn Langlands. "Repairing the Rupture: Restorative Justice and the Rehabilitation of Offenders." *Aggression and Violent Behavior* 14 (2009): 205–14.

——, and W. L. Marshall. "Good Lives, Aetiology, and the Rehabilitation of Sex Offenders: A Bridging Theory." *Journal of Sexual Aggression: Special Issue: Treatment and Treatability* 10 (2004): 153–69.

——, and Shadd Maruna. *Rehabilitation: Beyond the Risk Paradigm.* New York: Routledge, 2007.

——, and Claire Stewart. "Criminogenic Needs and Human Needs: A Theoretical Model." *Psychology, Crime, and Law* 9 (2003): 125–43.

Weisberg, Robert. "Restorative Justice and the Danger of 'Community.'" *Utah Law Review* 343 (2003): 343–74.

West, Heather C. "Prison Inmates at Midyear 2009—Statistical Tables." Bureau of Justice Statistics. U.S. Department of Justice. Posted June 2010. http://bjs.ojp.usdoj.gov/ content/pub/pdf/pim09st.pdf.

Western, Bruce. *Punishment and Inequality in America.* New York: Russell Sage Foundation, 2006.

——, and Katherine Beckett. "How Unregulated Is the US Labor Market: The Penal System as a Labor Market Institution." *American Journal of Sociology* 104 (1999): 1030–60.

——, Jeffrey R. Kling, and David F. Weiman. "The Labor Market Consequences of Incarceration." *Crime and Delinquency* 47 (2001): 410–27.

——, Leonard M. Lopoo, and Sara McLanahan. "Incarceration and the Bonds between Parents in Fragile Families." In *Imprisoning America: The Social*

Effects of Mass Incarceration, edited by Mary Pattillo, David Weiman, and Bruce Western, 21–45. New York: Russell Sage Foundation, 2004.

———, Becky Pettit, and Josh Guetzkow. "Black Economic Progress in the Era of Mass Imprisonment." In *Invisible Punishment: The Collateral Consequences of Mass Imprisonment*, edited by Marc Mauer and Meda Chesney-Lind, 165–80. New York: New Press, 2002.

Wilson, James Q., and George L. Kelling. "Broken Windows: The Police and Neighborhood Safety." *The Atlantic*. March 1982. http://www.theatlantic.com/magazine/ archive/1982/03/broken-windows/4465/.

Wilson, Robin J., and Pamela M. Yates. "Effective Interventions and the Good Lives Model." *Aggression and Violent Behavior* 14 (2009): 157–61.

Wilson, William Julius. *When Work Disappears: The World of the New Urban Poor.* New York: Alfred A. Knopf, 1997.

Wood, Graeme. "Prison Without Walls." *The Atlantic*, September 2010. www.theatlantic.com/magazine/archive/2010/09/prison-without-walls/8195.

Yates, Pamela M., and David S. Prescott. *Building a Better Life: A Good Lives and Self-Regulation Workbook.* Brandon, VT: Safer Society Press, 2011.

———, and Tony Ward. "Good Lives, Self-Regulation, and Risk Management: An Integrated Model of Sexual Offender Assessment and Treatment." *Sexual Abuse in Australia and New Zealand: An Interdisciplinary Journal* 1 (2008): 3–20.

Zimring, Franklin E., and Gordon Hawkins. *Incapacitation: Penal Confinement and the Restraint of Crime.* New York: Oxford University Press, 1995.

Index

Advancement Project, 160
Alexander, Michelle, 2, 8, 19, 41, 159, 181, 183–85
Alternatives to Violence Project, 141–42
Annie E. Casey Foundation, 163, 173, 193
Anselm, 46, 71
antiwar movement, 21
Aquinas, Thomas, 3, 4, 48, 49, 50–52, 53, 54–57, 71, 72, 78, 104, 132, 133; and legal justice, 53–56; and punishment, 49–53, 78
Assisting Families of Inmates (AFOI), 143
Augustine, 71

baby boomers, 20
"Ban the Box" campaigns, 156, 177, 180
Bazemore, Gordon, 113–14
Beck, Allen, 18
Bentham, Jeremy, 49
Berkman, John, 100, 106
Bieler, Andrea, 96
Blumstein, Alfred, 18
Bonta, James, 122, 124–25, 128–29
Boyle, Greg, 177–78
Braithwaite, John, 145
Braman, Donald, 33
"broken windows" policing. See policing: "broken windows"
Bush, George H. W., 26

Campaign to Promote Equitable Telephone Charges, 162
canonical penance. See also Penance and Reconciliation
Catechism of the Catholic Church, 6, 52, 64, 79, 92, 126

Catholic Charities, 177, 193
Catholic social teaching, 3, 15, 52, 56, 59, 62, 64
Cavanaugh, William, 88, 96–97, 111, 152
children of prisoners, 31, 33–36, 39, 143–44, 161–64, 170, 178. *See also* families of prisoners
Children's Defense Fund (CDF), 13, 171–74, 179, 194
citizen- and neighborhood-accountability boards. *See* restorative justice: types of
civil rights movement, 20–21, 23, 184
Clear, Todd, 37–38
Clinton, Bill, 26
Collaborative Project on Concentrated Incarceration, 38
collect phone calls, 35, 161, 178
collective efficacy, 24, 38, 39
College for the Incarcerated, 139–40
Colson, Charles, 46–47
common good, 3, 40–41, 43, 51–57, 62, 71, 72, 77, 145, 150, 153–54, 155, 164, 176–77, 198
community conferencing. *See* restorative justice: types of
community justice, 113
community policing. *See* policing
concentrated incarceration. *See* mass incarceration: and effects on communities
Constantine, 103, 117–18
Copeland, Shawn, 94, 189
Corrections Corporation of America (CCA), 42–43
cradle-to-prison pipeline, 67, 171–76, 179, 186, 194

crime, 2, 4, 7–8, 16–19, 20–21, 22, 25,
26, 27, 28–29, 31–32, 36, 43, 45, 48,
49–50, 51, 55, 57–58, 59–61, 63–64,
65, 66–67, 74, 77, 112, 113, 114,
117, 118, 119, 122, 125–26, 131,
132–33, 136, 145, 147, 149, 164–65,
166–70, 171, 173, 182–83, 192–93;
and drugs, 19, 27, 31–32, 41, 55,
158; as intergenerational, 36, 171; as
political issue, 26, 31–32, 43, 183;
fear of, 20–21, 26, 66, 67, 124, 167,
182; rates of (see crime rates); victims
of, 4, 8, 45, 57, 59, 60, 62–63, 65,
77, 109, 113–14, 116–17, 118–20,
123–24, 126, 149, 166–67; war on,
25, 26, 59, 67, 182–83
crime rates, 2, 16–19, 20, 24, 27, 28–29,
37–40, 60, 63, 66–67, 74, 77, 135,
137, 147, 149; among young black
men, 18–19, 25; and concentrated
incarceration, 37–40; compared to
incarceration rates, 2, 17–18, 28–29,
37–40, 63, 137; historical changes in,
17–18, 20; international
comparisons of, 16–17; of drug
offenses, 19, 24, 27, 29, 137; of
property offenses, 29, 137; of violent
offenses, 16–17, 24, 137;
socioeconomic status and, 24, 66–67
Cristo Rey Network, 179
Cross, James, 108

Davis, Angela, 46
Davis, Mike, 46
de Tocqueville, Alexis, 75
death penalty, 52, 193
Degrees of Freedom, 140
deindustrialization, 22–24, 26
Democratic party, 26, 32
Department of Justice, Peace, and
Human Development. See under
U.S. Conference of Catholic Bishops

determinate sentencing. See under
sentencing
deterrence, 5, 21–22, 28, 43, 49, 50–51,
58, 65, 72, 129, 145, 149
Dickens, Charles, 74–75
disenfranchisement, 32–33, 40, 158–60,
177
drugs, 1, 16, 17, 18–19, 24, 25, 26, 27,
28, 29, 31, 32, 34, 55, 63, 66, 126,
146, 158, 166, 168–70, 178, 182–83;
and overt drug markets (see overt
drug markets); rates of use (see
crimes rates: of drug offenses); war
on, 25, 182–83
Dukakis, Michael, 26

Equal Employment Opportunity
Commission, 156
eschatological imagination, 6, 96–97,
98, 109, 152, 180, 189. See also under
Eucharist
Eucharist, 6–7, 8–9, 64, 76, 80–81,
92–99, 100–01, 102–03, 104, 105,
109–10, 111, 112, 117, 135–36, 138,
144, 146, 150–54, 155, 176, 180,
185–86, 187, 188–90, 194–95, 197,
198 (see also liturgical and
sacramental ethics); and
eschatological imagination, 6,
96–97, 98, 109, 152, 180, 189; and
justice, 6–7, 8–9, 80, 93, 94, 95–96,
97–98, 109–10, 151–52, 153, 176,
180, 185–86, 188–90, 194–95, 197,
198; and moral formation, 6–7, 8–9,
92, 95–96, 97–98, 100–101, 109–10,
151–52, 185–86, 188–90; in the
New Testament, 94–96; moral
vision of, 6–7, 8–9, 80–81, 92–99,
138, 150–51, 153–54, 155, 176,
185–86, 188–90
Everett, William, 83

ex-prisoner(s), 30–33, 34, 139, 140, 155–60, 161, 176, 177, 178, 180, 193, 194, 199

Families Against Mandatory Minimums, 163
families of prisoners, 2, 15, 31, 33–36, 37, 38, 39, 40, 143–44, 161–64, 165, 169, 176, 178, 186, 192, 193. *See also* children of prisoners
Family and Corrections Network, 163
family-group conferencing. *See* restorative justice: types of
Farley, Margaret, 84–85
Federal Bonding Program, 155–56, 177, 180
first genuine prison society, 2, 4–5, 8, 16–20, 43, 67, 76, 146, 147, 149–50, 181, 183–84, 197–99
Foley, John, 179
food stamps, 31, 158, 162. *See also* welfare benefits
forgiveness, 7, 8, 92, 94, 99, 100, 101–2, 106, 108, 110, 111, 116, 135–36, 144, 190, 198
Fortnight for Freedom Campaign. *See under* U.S. Conference of Catholic Bishops
Foucault, Michel, 49

Garland, David, 14–15, 20, 48–49
Gaudium et Spes, 70, 105
gerrymandering. *See* prison-based gerrymandering
ghetto, 22–25, 37, 40–41, 66–67, 183
Girl Scouts Beyond Bars, 143–44
Giuliani, Rudy, 69
God's reign, 5–6, 7, 80, 86, 87–88, 89, 90, 92, 94, 95, 96, 97, 98, 109–10, 135, 138, 150, 151–52, 176, 185–86, 189, 195, 197, 198
Goldwater, Barry, 26

good lives model. *See under* rehabilitation
Gorringe, Timothy, 46
Griffith, Lee, 46

Harlem Children's Zone (HCZ), 173–76, 179, 181, 194
Harris, Kay, 118, 120, 127
Hart, H.L.A., 49
Hauerwas, Stanley, 85
Hayes, Diana, 94, 186–87, 188–89
Healing Communities, 163–64, 178–79, 193
Hellwig, Monika, 104, 106, 107–8
Himes, Kenneth, 83–84, 93, 153
Homeboy Industries, 177–78, 179
Horton, Willie, 26
Housing Opportunity Program Extension Act, 31–32
human dignity, 3, 7, 8, 9, 15–16, 27–28, 41, 45, 51–52, 54, 56–57, 58, 62, 63, 64, 77–78, 130, 134, 135, 146–47, 153–54, 171, 184–85, 189, 194, 198

image of God, 3, 7, 58, 70, 153, 164
incapacitation, 5, 21–22, 28–29, 43, 53, 58, 65, 68, 72, 129, 145–46, 149, 154
incarceration, 1, 8, 11–15, 16–20, 28–30, 32–41, 55, 61, 65, 66, 68, 73, 76, 112, 122, 129, 135–38, 145, 149, 155–64, 164–70, 170–76, 181 (*see also* mass incarceration); alternatives to, 8, 30, 60, 65, 68, 122, 135–37, 149, 173, 181 (*see also* rehabilitation, restorative justice); and communities, 2, 37–41, 160–61, 163–70, 170–76; concentration of, 37–40, 160–61; and disenfranchisement, 32–33, 158–60; and families, 2, 33–36, 161–64; financial costs of, 29–30, 181; and poverty, 12–13, 30–32, 155–58; rates

of (see incarceration rates); and
recidivism, 122, 129

incarceration rates, 11–15, 16–20,
28–29, 33, 60, 63, 166; among
juveniles, 13–14; compared to crime
rates, 16–20, 28–29, 60, 63; gender
differences in, 12; historical changes
in, 11–12, 14, 17–18, 20;
international comparisons of, 11–12,
16–17; racial and ethnic disparities
in, 12, 14–15, 18–19; socioeconomic
status and, 12–13

indeterminate sentencing. See
sentencing

individual wrongdoing, 2, 3, 4, 7, 58,
77, 80, 93, 96, 98–99, 100, 103,
105–7, 109–10, 112, 125, 134, 146,
149, 189, 192, 198. See also sin,
crime

injustice within the church. See under
liturgical and sacramental ethics

Inside-Out Prison Exchange Program,
139–40, 194

internal reform, 3, 7, 57, 65, 72–74,
76–77, 98, 106, 110, 111, 116, 121,
123, 125–26, 130, 134, 135–36, 138,
141, 144, 181, 186, 198

jail(s), 11–13, 14, 17, 20, 37, 38, 39–40,
41, 42, 43, 68, 128, 137, 145, 147,
156, 181–82

Jargowsky, Paul, 25

Jesus Christ, 5, 6, 9, 61, 64, 70, 79–80,
82, 86–87, 89, 92–93, 94–95, 96, 97,
100, 101, 106, 109, 138, 150, 151,
152, 153, 186, 198; as a convicted
criminal, 6, 70, 97, 109, 186, 198; as
sacrament, 79; table fellowship of, 6,
94–95, 138, 151, 153

Jim Crow, 19. See also New Jim Crow

John Paul II, Pope, 51–52; and death
penalty, 52; and Jubilee in Prisons, 57,
61–62, 190, 192

Johnson, Lyndon, 26

judgment, 7, 95, 98, 101–2, 106, 110,
111

justice. See Eucharist: and justice; legal
justice; liturgical and sacramental
ethics: injustice in church practices
and institutions; Penance and
Reconciliation: and justice;
restorative justice; social justice

Justice for Immigrants Campaign. See
U.S. Conference of Catholic Bishops

Juvenile Detention Alternatives
Initiative, 173

Kairos, 142

Kant, Immanuel, 49–50, 51, 53

Kelling, George L., 69

Kennedy, David, 24–25, 164–66

Koritansky, Peter Karl, 3, 47, 48, 49–53,
54, 55, 56–57, 70, 72, 78

Law Enforcement Assistance
Administration, 20

legal justice, 48, 53–55, 78

liturgical and sacramental ethics, 5–6, 7,
9, 78, 80, 81–85, 86–92, 109–10,
111, 116–17, 126, 130, 131–32, 134,
135–36, 138, 144, 152–53, 176–77,
197 (see also Eucharist; liturgy;
Penance and Reconciliation;
sacrament[s]); and injustice within
the church, 5, 83–84, 86, 89,
186–90; and moral formation, 6–7,
8–9, 90–92, 95–96, 97–98, 100–101,
109–10, 151–52, 185–86, 188–90;
and participation, 5, 79, 80–81,
84–85, 86, 87, 89–90, 95, 96, 98,
101, 125, 152, 186, 197, 198; and
pluralism, 5, 80, 82–83, 86, 88–89,
90, 152; and prison(s), 9, 78, 111,
135–36, 138, 144, 177, 197; and
privatization and politicization, 5,
80, 81–82, 86, 87–88, 90, 152; and
rehabilitation, 126, 130, 131–32,

134, 144; and restorative justice,
116–17, 126, 135, 136, 144; and
prison reform, 78, 111, 134, 136,
138–39, 144; and world-picture,
5–6, 91–92, 135, 150, 151, 152, 176,
185, 189, 198
liturgy, 5–6, 9, 78, 79–92, 93, 98, 99,
103, 109, 110, 150–51, 152, 154,
180, 186, 188, 192, 194–95, 197–98.
See also liturgical and sacramental
ethics
definition of, 5, 81, 86–87
Logan, James Samuel, 46
Loyola Institute for Ministry, 194
Lumen Gentium, 70
Lynch, James, 38

mandatory minimum sentencing. *See*
sentencing
Manza, Jeff, 21–22, 32, 158
Marshall, Christopher, 46
Martinson, Robert, 127, 129
Martos, Joseph, 103–4, 112
Maruna, Shadd, 127, 129, 131–32
mass imprisonment. *See* mass
incarceration
mass incarceration, 2, 3, 4, 5, 7, 8,
14–16, 17–18, 19, 20–28, 28–29,
33–41, 42–43, 47, 67, 76, 77–78,
109, 110, 118, 136, 149–50, 154,
155–64, 164–70, 170–76, 177, 179,
181–82, 183–86, 190–94, 195,
197–98 (*see also* incarceration,
incarceration rates); and
communities, 2, 37–41, 160–61,
163–64, 164–70, 170–76; and crime
rates, 2, 17–18, 28–29, 37–40, 64,
137; criteria for response to, 4–5, 7,
77–78, 109, 112, 149; definition of,
14–15; economic factors
contributing to, 2, 4, 22–25, 183;
and families, 2, 33–36, 161–64;
movement to end, 8–9, 67, 182–86,

188, 190–94, 194–95, 199; political
factors contributing to, 2, 4, 26–28,
183; and prison profiteering, 41–43,
181–82; social and cultural factors
contributing to, 2, 4, 20–22, 182–83
Massingale, Bryan, 94, 187–88
Mauer, Marc, 2, 12, 17, 41, 136, 137,
150, 181
McCold, Paul, 119
McConnell, Bob, 159–60
McKay, Henry, 23–24, 38
Medicaid, 162. *See also* welfare benefits
Murdoch, Iris, 90–91

National Academy of Sciences, 21
National Employment Law Project, 157
National Longitudinal Surveys of
Youth, 18–19
National Network for Safe
Communities, 24, 164–66
net widening, 68
New Jim Crow, 2, 8, 19, 159, 183–86,
197
Nietzsche, Friedrich, 49, 99–100
Nixon, Richard, 26

occupational licenses, 157, 180
Office of Juvenile Justice and
Delinquency Prevention (OJJDP),
13–14
Office of Migration Policy and Public
Affairs. *See under* U.S. Conference of
Catholic Bishops
Operation Ceasefire, 166–68
overt drug markets, 24, 168–70, 183

Parenti, Christian, 46
parole, 11, 27, 32, 74, 136, 137, 181
participation in sacrament and liturgy.
See under liturgical and sacramental
ethics
Paul, 95, 97, 98, 100–102, 106, 111
Pell Grants, 31, 139, 158
penal harm, 67–68

Penance. *See* Penance and
Reconciliation
Penance and Reconciliation, 6–7, 8, 9,
64, 76, 80, 92, 99–108, 109, 110,
111–12, 116–
17, 118, 125, 126, 129–30, 134, 135–36,
144, 146, 189–90, 195, 197, 198 (*see
also* liturgical and sacramental
ethics); canonical, 102, 103–4,
117–18; and community, 7, 101–2,
103, 104, 106, 110, 116, 117–18; and
forgiveness, 7, 100, 101, 102, 106,
110, 111, 116, 190, 198; and
incarceration, 135–36, 144; and
judgment, 7, 101, 102, 106, 110,
111; and justice, 7, 9, 107–8, 110,
189–90; moral vision of, 99–108; in
the New Testament, 100–101; and
rehabilitation, 8, 112, 126, 129–30,
134; and restorative justice, 8, 112,
116–17, 118, 125; tariff, 104–5; three
rites of, 105
penitentiary, 73, 75, 128, 130
Personal Responsibility and Work
Opportunity Reconciliation Act, 31,
158
pluralism. *See under* liturgical and
sacramental ethics
policing, 29, 63, 65, 69, 165–70, 178,
180–81; "broken windows," 65, 69,
165, 168, 169, 170, 178, 181;
community, 29, 65; pulling-levers,
166–70, 178, 180–81; zero-
tolerance, 165, 168, 169, 170, 178
poverty, 2, 7, 18–19, 23, 25, 26, 30–32,
34–35, 39, 65–67, 110, 151, 153,
155, 158, 160, 161, 164, 173, 180,
183. *See also* social justice
prison(s), 1–5, 8–9, 11–16, 16–20, 21,
25, 28–30, 31–35, 37, 39–40, 41–43,
46, 55–56, 59, 61–62, 67, 68–69,
72–76, 78, 100, 111, 121, 123, 125,
128–29, 136–38, 138–44, 145–46,

149–50, 154, 158–61, 161–64, 169,
171, 177–78, 180–82, 183, 186, 193,
197–99; alternatives to, 8, 30, 60, 65,
68, 122, 135–37, 149, 173, 181 (*see
also* rehabilitation, restorative
justice); as criminogenic, 29, 38;
downscaling, 8, 76, 136–38, 143–44,
149, 164, 181, 186; financial costs of,
29–30, 181; and liturgical and
sacramental ethics, 9, 78, 111,
135–36, 138, 144, 177, 197;
monastic and ecclesiastical, 4, 47,
72–73, 78, 81 (*see also* Skotnicki,
Andrew: and means of punishment);
privatization of, 41–43, 181–82;
reform of (*see* prison reform); as
social control, 19, 67–68
prison-based gerrymandering, 40,
160–61, 177
Prison Fellowship, 46–47
prison-industrial complex, 46
Prison Policy Initiative, 40, 160, 161
prison reform, 41, 47, 53, 55, 58–59, 65,
68, 76, 78, 111, 112, 134, 136–37,
138–44, 149; and community, 55,
141–42; and education, 55, 139–40;
and families, 55, 142–44; and
liturgical and sacramental ethics, 78,
111, 134, 136, 138–39, 144; and
vocational training, 55, 140–41
prison society. *See* first genuine prison
society
Prisoner Visitation and Support, 142
prisoner(s), 2, 12, 16, 30–33, 35, 38, 40,
41, 43, 55, 58–59, 61–62, 64, 70–74,
75–76, 129, 130, 137, 138–44,
154–55, 160, 161, 163–64, 178, 180,
181, 193, 197; children of (*see
children of prisoners); families of (*see
families of prisoners)
private prisons. *See* prison(s):
privatization of

privatization of worship. *See under* liturgical and sacramental ethics
probation, 11, 13, 32, 48, 63, 181
public defense, 13
public housing, 31, 158
public safety, 1, 4, 8, 65, 112, 137, 138, 144, 145, 149, 154, 157, 164–65, 169, 186, 198
punishment, 3, 4, 5, 7, 47, 48, 49–53, 53–55, 56–57, 58, 62, 63, 64–65, 68, 69–77, 77–78, 102, 106, 116, 121, 123, 126–27, 129, 134, 135, 138–39, 198; Andrew Skotnicki's theory of, 70–73; Aquinas' theory of, 3, 4, 49–53, 78; and legal justice, 48, 49, 50, 53–56; as medicinal, 3, 51, 54–55, 57, 77, 111, 126, 134; and mercy, 53, 56; norms in Catholic tradition, 56–57; retributive theory of, 49–50, 53, 54, 57, 134; utilitarian theory of, 3, 49, 50, 51, 53, 54, 57, 77
Quakers, 73, 74, 141
Quality Housing and Work Responsibility Act, 31

Ramsey, Paul, 84, 88–89
recidivism, 30, 34, 39, 74, 122–23, 128–32, 135, 144–45, 181. *See also* reoffending
Reconciliation. *See* Penance and Reconciliation
Rector, Ricky Ray, 26
reformatories, 75
rehabilitation, 1, 8, 21–22, 31, 49, 50–51, 53, 58–59, 62, 63, 65, 66, 67–68, 69, 73, 76, 112, 126–35, 137, 139, 144–47, 149, 154, 164, 181, 183, 186, 198; critiques of, 53, 127–28, 129–30, 133–34; evaluation of, 128–29, 130, 134–35; good lives model of, 8, 131–35, 137, 139, 144, 145; and liturgical and sacramental

ethics, 126, 130, 131–32, 134, 144; and Penance and Reconciliation, 8, 112, 126, 129–30, 134; risk-need-responsivity model of, 128–29, 131, 134
reintegration. *See* social reintegration
Republican party, 26
Respect Life Program. *See under* U.S. Conference of Catholic Bishops
retribution, 3, 5, 7, 43, 51, 53, 65, 70, 72, 116, 135, 138, 145, 149, 186. *See also* punishment: retributive theory of
reoffending, 4, 8, 50, 74, 112, 122, 125–26, 129, 130, 135, 136–37, 142, 149. *See also* recidivism
restorative justice, 8, 55, 65, 67, 112–26, 127, 129, 135, 137, 144–47, 149, 154, 164, 173, 181, 186, 198; and community, 117–21; and community justice, 113; critiques of, 117–25; definition of, 113–14; evaluation of, 122–25; features of, 114–16; and forgiveness, 116; and liturgical and sacramental ethics, 116–17, 126, 135, 136, 144; and Penance and Reconciliation, 8, 112, 116–17, 118, 125; and transformative justice, 113; types of, 113
Rockefeller Drug Laws, 27
Rose, Dina, 37–38
Ross, Susan, 86–87, 91, 94, 98

Sabol, William, 38
sacrament(s), 5–6, 7, 8, 9, 64, 70, 76, 78, 79–81, 82, 83, 84, 85, 86–92, 93, 94, 95, 96, 97, 99–100, 104, 105–6, 107, 109–10, 111, 112, 116, 125, 126, 129–30, 134, 135, 144, 146, 150–54, 176, 180, 185–86, 187, 189, 192, 194–95, 197–98 (*see also* liturgical and sacramental ethics); definition

of, 5, 81, 86–87; and God's reign,
5–6, 7, 80, 86, 87–88, 89, 90, 92, 94,
95, 96, 97, 109–10, 135, 150,
151–52, 176, 185–86, 189, 195, 197,
198; as morally formative, 5, 79–80,
84–85, 87, 89–90, 91, 92, 95, 104,
105, 107, 152, 185
sacramental and liturgical ethics. See
liturgical and sacramental ethics
sacramentality, 6, 79, 80, 86, 92
Saliers, Don, 5, 84, 85, 89–90, 150
Schmemann, Alexander, 88
Schneider, Carl E., 75
Schottroff, Luise, 96
Seasoltz, Kevin, 97, 152
Second Vatican Council, 64, 93, 99, 105
sentencing, 19, 27, 66, 125, 136–37,
163; determinate, 27; indeterminate,
27; mandatory minimum, 27, 63, 66,
136, 163; three-strikes, 27, 63, 66,
136; truth-in-sentencing, 27
sentencing commissions, 27
sentencing guidelines. See sentencing
Sentencing Project, The, 2, 12, 136, 150
Shaw, Clifford, 23, 38
sin, 7, 9, 54, 100, 102, 104, 105, 106,
107–8, 110, 116, 136, 189, 195, 198.
See also individual wrongdoing
Skotnicki, Andrew, 4, 47, 48, 67–77, 78,
81, 121–23, 125, 135, 165; and
criticism of U.S. Conference of
Catholic Bishops, 67–70; critique of,
74–77; and ecclesiology, 70; and
justification of punishment, 71; and
means of punishment, 4, 47, 70,
72–76, 135; and purpose of
punishment, 71–72
Snyder, T. Richard, 46
social control, 19, 22, 24, 37–38, 67–68
social disorganization, 23–24, 38, 40,
164, 183
social injustice. See social justice

social justice, 2–3, 4–5, 7, 8, 9, 15–16,
28, 29, 41, 43, 45, 47–48, 56, 58, 59,
60, 61, 63–64, 65, 66– 67, 76–77,
80–81, 84, 93, 96, 97–98, 99, 100,
106, 107–8, 109, 110, 112, 144,
146–47, 149, 150–55, 159, 161,
164–65, 170, 176–80, 182–86, 188,
189–90, 195, 198–99
social reintegration, 3, 7, 57, 72–74,
76–77, 98, 106, 110, 111, 112, 117,
118, 123, 125, 126, 130, 134–38,
140–42, 144, 149, 181, 186, 198
Soltis, Kathryn Getek, 4, 47, 48, 53–56,
57, 70, 72, 75, 76, 77–78, 133, 141,
145
Spear, Allan, 22

tariff penance, 104–105. See also
Penance and Reconciliation
Taylor, Mark Lewis, 46
Temporary Aid for Needy Families,
162. See also welfare benefits
Texas Second Chance, 140–41
three-strikes sentencing. See sentencing
transformative justice, 113
Travis, Jeremy, 36, 38
truth and reconciliation commissions.
See restorative justice: types of
truth-in-sentencing. See sentencing

Uggen, Christopher, 32, 158
University Beyond Bars, 139, 194
U.S. Conference of Catholic Bishops
(USCCB), 3–4, 47, 48, 57–67,
67–70, 72, 73, 76, 78, 93, 111, 112,
187–88, 190–93, 197; and "A
Community Response to Crime,"
59–61, 65; and "Brothers and Sisters
to Us," 187–88; Department of
Justice, Peace, and Human
Development, 192–93; Fortnight for
Freedom Campaign, 191–92, 193;
Justice for Immigrants Campaign,

191; Office of Migration Policy and
Public Affairs, 191; Respect Life
Program, 190–91, 192, 193; and
"Rebuilding Human Lives," 58–59,
60, 65; and *Responsibility,
Rehabilitation, and Restoration*, 47, 57,
61, 62–67, 67–70, 93, 113, 192, 197

Vatican Council II. *See* Second Vatican
Council
victim-offender mediation and dialogue.
See restorative justice: types of
victims. *See under* crime
Violent Crime Control and Law
Enforcement Act, 31, 158
virtue ethics, 55

Wachtel, Benjamin, 119
Wacquant, Loïc, 2, 16, 22
Walgrave, Lode, 113–14
Ward, Tony, 127, 129, 131–32
Waul, Michelle, 36
welfare benefits, 31, 40, 158. *See also*
food stamps; Medicaid; Temporary
Aid for Needy Families
Wells, Samuel, 85
Western, Bruce, 14, 29
Wilson, James Q., 69
Wilson, William Julius, 22, 37
world-picture. *See* liturgical and
sacramental ethics

CPSIA information can be obtained
at www.ICGtesting.com
Printed in the USA
BVHW08s1326170618
519215BV00010B/158/P